Here is what
Fifty

Ruth Baird Shaw's sermons exe... ... sound, biblical Methodism that still quietly resonates in thousands of churches across America. She is a lifelong Methodist who entered ordained ministry late in life and, remarkably, still preaches on the cusp of her 10th decade. I've never heard her preach in person but easily detect the power of her faith through the passion of her sermons in this book. Young people entering the ministry would greatly benefit from reading Ruth's sermons for the quality of both their prose and theology, harnessed in service to Christ.

Mark Tooley, President, Institute on Religion and Democracy, Washington, DC

Ruth Baird Shaw is a gifted servant of the Lord. She has a deep knowledge of God's words and a flair for eloquent narrative. Her sermons speak to the heart and challenge the mind. Do yourself a big favor, put Fifty-Two Sundays on your must-read list immediately.

David R. Stokes, Pastor, Broadcaster, Columnist and Best-Selling Author

Here are sermons that are a delight to read. They will enrich your heart and your soul. Ruth Baird Shaw's sermons are readable, real, biblical, related to life, and full of the wisdom that comes from intimate involvement in pastoral ministry. The biblical narratives are told well and supplemented wonderfully by the author's personal experiences and wide breadth of reading. You will be glad you read her sermons.

James V. Heidinger II, President and Publisher, emeritus, Good News, A Forum for Scriptural Christianity, Inc., within the United Methodist Church

Ruth Shaw is a beacon in a long line of outstanding evangelical Methodist women who have lived out their faith in every challenge and stage of life. Fortunately for the body of Christ, she became a United Methodist pastor, and fortunately for each of us, she published these sermons. She is an illustration of Solomon's words, "To everything there is a season, a time for every purpose under heaven." Her life reminds us it is never too late to embark on a new career or accomplish big things for God. Her sermons impart to the reader Biblical truth and timeless wisdom learned at the feet of Jesus and in the crucible of life.

Katy Kiser, author and United Methodist laywoman

In Psalm 119:162, the Psalmist celebrated the richness of God's Word when he said: "I rejoice in your laws as one who finds a great treasure." (LB) Walk with Ruth Baird Shaw through a delightful Fifty-Two Sundays and I assure you, your heart will be nourished and your mind edified as she illuminates that treasure with a true writer's gift and draws you readily into each sermon. I only wish I could have heard her deliver these gems in person."

Don Kroah, former pastor & host of The Don Kroah
Show on 105.1fm-WAVA in Washington, DC

I am not sure how many books of sermons exist by pastors who are great-grandmothers, but of them Ruth Baird Shaw's compilation would set the standard. With a heart full of grace Shaw weaves a full-orbed biblical theology, a sensitivity to tradition and an actually inviting biblical exegesis in a delightful and affable set of sermons which draw you in and challenge your heart. She touches on all the major real-life issues with the deft touch of a life suffused with the Word and godly wisdom. Arising out of years of daily ministrations of love Shaw speaks to our deepest needs: communion, holiness, truth and faithfulness. Her clear-headedness shines through in every sermon. She mixes scholarship with warmth and depth. Her Christology and soteriology are drawn from the whole Bible. Never preachy she is piercingly profound. Without pedantry she uncovers the illusions that keep us from a whole salvation. Here one finds the richness of a pastor's experience shared in a form that is useable in personal and family devotion or in any small group setting. If communicators of the Gospel would soak themselves in these sermons they would benefit from this practical theologian who, like most good grandmothers, can love you while applying strong correctives and leave you asking for more.

M. William Ury Ph.D.
Pastor and Theologian

God has a surprising, even audacious, way of calling servants willing to share the good news of Jesus to others. As I read these sermons of Rev. Ruth Baird Shaw, I was struck by her authentic and energetic expression of God's love and grace. May your heart be moved closer to God as was mine by these messages.

W. Martin Nicholas, Senior Pastor
Sugar Land First United Methodist Church, Sugar Land,
Texas

Come to Me, all you who labor and are heavy laden, and I will give you rest. Take My yoke upon you and learn from Me, for I am gentle and lowly in heart, and you will find rest for your soul. For My yoke is easy and My burden is light."

~Matthew 11:28-30~

Fifty-Two SUNDAYS

"Sermons That Speak to Your Heart and Challenge Your Mind"

Ruth Baird Shaw

Front cover
Artwork by
Benjamin Lewis
Copyright 2013

ISBN 978-1-304-17572-4

9 781304 175724

Acknowledgments

My appreciation goes to my daughter, Carol Shaw Johnston, for her talented and indispensable help and encouragement in the publication of *Life with Wings*, *The Chronicles of Ruth*, and especially for her editorial work on *Fifty-Two Sundays!*

My appreciation goes to my daughter, Joan Shaw Turrentine, for typing many of the homilies in *Fifty-Two Sundays* and for putting the best of my blog posts into book form earlier which was indispensable help in the publication of *The Chronicles of Ruth*.

My appreciation goes to daughters, Deborah Shaw Lewis, Sheila Matthews Shaw and Beth Shaw Roszel for their valuable help and computer expertise in the three successive publications of my first book, *Recipes, Rhymes and Reflections*.

My appreciation goes also to my daughter, Janice Shaw Crouse, who, in spite of our distance apart and her heavy writing and speaking schedule, is always available to help, encourage and applaud all my writing efforts.

Dedication

Fifty-Two Sundays is a collection of sermons prepared during my pastoral ministry. This work is dedicated to the people in the churches I served as pastor: Rico United Methodist in Palmetto, Georgia; Grantville First United Methodist in Grantville, Georgia; East Point Avenue United Methodist Church in East Point, Georgia, which I served as pastor for four years after reaching mandatory retirement age; Trinity United Methodist Church in Rome, Georgia on staff as "Minister of Congregational Care" for four years after moving to Rome in 1997; Lyerly United Methodist Church in the Rome District, serving as interim pastor for seven months after their pastor became critically ill; Oostanaula Church on Bells Ferry Road in 2001; and the Livingston Church in 2006, where I served as Retired Supply for one conference year.

Fifty-Two Sundays is also dedicated to my seven children - Janice, Joan, Terrell, Carol, Deborah, Beth and David - my daughters-in-law, Sheila and Vicki - and my sons-in-law, Gilbert, Jim, Ron, Gregg and Chuck. It is dedicated also to my grandchildren and great-grandchildren - each one precious to me in his or her own way.

Fifty-Two Sundays is lovingly dedicated to future descendants of Charles Columbus Shaw and Sarah Ruth Baird Shaw.

Fifty-Two Sundays is in loving memory of my husband, Charles Columbus Shaw, my parents, Benjamin Wilson Baird and Ieula Ann Dick Baird, and my eight siblings: Wilson Grice Baird, William Bogan Baird, Louise Baird McCullough Lee Campbell, Vera Mae Baird Loyd, Mary Elizabeth Baird Shepherd, Charles (Charlie) Morrison Baird, John Thomas Baird, and Jackson Irvin Baird. This book is also in honor of the children, grandchildren and future descendants of our beloved parents, Wilson and Ieula Baird.

Preface

My husband, the Rev Charles C. Shaw, reluctantly retired as a pastor in the North Georgia Conference of the United Methodist Church after 37 years as a pastor and after his second heart attack left him with heart damage. One Sunday morning, about a year after his retirement, as we were getting ready to attend a nearby church, the Atlanta-College Park District Superintendent called and asked Charles if he felt up to conducting the service and preaching that Sunday morning at Rico United Methodist, a church about twenty-five miles away. Their pastor could not continue there. About 30 minutes later, we were walking out the door of our home in East Point for the drive to the beautiful Rico church in Palmetto, where fewer than a dozen people were present - not knowing whether or not they would have a pastor with them that Sunday.

That one Sunday became many Sundays. The church grew with Charles as their loving pastor and gifted preacher. He served as pastor of Rico United Methodist Church for over a year, preaching every Sunday but two when he asked me to fill in for him. My husband preached his last sermon at Rico United Methodist Church on the first Sunday of Advent 1986 and had a fatal heart attack three days later on Wednesday December 3, 1986.

Two weeks after my husband's death, the District Superintendent called and told me that the people of Rico Church had asked the Bishop to appoint me as their pastor until the end of the conference year. The Bishop and cabinet agreed. Would I accept the appointment?

After much prayer and many tears, on the fourth Sunday of Advent in 1986, I stood to preach my first sermon as a pastor in the same pulpit where my husband had stood to preach his last sermon three weeks earlier. It was Christmas! We all needed to hear the Good News of Christmas.

This book is in celebration of the ministry into which the Lord graciously called me and the door He opened wide and invited me to enter! This book is also in celebration of the sermons prayerfully prepared after I answered God's amazing call and appointment to preach the Gospel from age of sixty-three forward.

I was baptized as an infant in the Methodist Church. During most of my adult life, my place in the church was to teach adult Sunday school classes and women's mission studies. I also studied and taught Methodist church history.

Blessedly, those earlier experiences provided many scripture passages, stories and illustrations that I was able to effectively reach for as I began my pastoral ministry.

Sermons, by definition, are oral. Many of the written forms of the sermons in *Fifty-Two Sundays* were prayerfully and joyfully prepared during the nearly four years I spent as pastor of Rico United Methodist Church while also a student at Candler School of Theology, Emory University.

Table of Contents

How Jacob Became Israel

Genesis 32: 22-31

And he said, "Your name shall no longer be called Jacob, but Israel, for you have struggled with God and with men and have prevailed."
~Genesis 32:28 (NKJV)~

A few years ago, I was visiting with an older couple. They had two grown children and several grandchildren. In the course of the conversation the man, a Mr. Edwards, told me, "I've finally conquered my 'want-er.'" I was not sure what he meant by "want-er."

He explained that he had grown up during the Great Depression. All his life he had worked hard and had struggled for money and the things money could buy. He had managed to buy a nice house, good furnishings, and a new car and truck. He and his wife lived on several acres of land. He said that no matter how much he accumulated there was always something else he needed or wanted. But now, even though he did not have all the things he had previously wanted, he no longer wanted anything more! He had conquered his want-er!

I thought of Mr. Edwards as I studied the life of Jacob. Jacob was a want-er! We are introduced to Jacob in Genesis 25:26, the day he was born as the second-born of twins. The Bible tells us Jacob came forth out of Rebekah's womb grabbing hold of his twin brother's heel.

In those days, you remember, the laws of primogeniture brought a great deal of advantage to the first-born son. So we are given a picture of the pre-born Jacob grabbing hold of his twin brother's heel as if he was trying to pull Esau back in, so he could get out first. [1]

---

[1]Dr. Gail O'Day, Class lecture at Candler School of Theology

This first picture of Jacob as a grabber is not a lovely picture. I love babies! Being a mother, grandmother and now a great-grandmother, I am a soft touch when it comes to babies. I can honestly say, "I have never seen a baby I did not like." If I am out in a mall and see even a stranger with a baby, I always turn with a smile to see the baby! To me, babies are more beautiful than even lovely flowers or landscapes. But even as a newborn baby, Jacob does not appear likeable.

We see Jacob as a grasper from birth and do not get out of chapter 25 where we first meet him until we find him taking advantage of his weak, hungry and apparently thoughtless twin brother Esau by buying his brother's birthright for a bowl of lentil soup.[2] Esau came in from the field, tired and hungry. Jacob had prepared some lentil soup. The Bible tells us Esau asked his brother for some of the soup. Jacob told Esau he would sell the soup in return for the birthright. Esau reasoned that he was about to die of hunger so the birthright would not help him. Thus, for "immediate gratification" Esau exchanged his birthright to Jacob for a bowl of soup.

The story of Jacob with his brother Esau becomes even more sordid. In those days, not only the birthright but a Father's blessing was of immense value - supernatural value. It was not enough that the wily Jacob had bought his brother's birthright; he just had to have the blessing, too. He wanted it all! So with the help of Rebekah, his mother, he deceived his blind father, Isaac, and stole his brother's blessing.

The importance placed on a father's blessing is recorded down through the annals of history in the desperate cry of Esau to his father Isaac, "Hast thou but one blessing, my father? Bless me, even me also, oh my father." (Genesis 27:38) There was no blessing left for Esau. Jacob wanted it all. Jacob had taken it all.

Esau threatened to kill Jacob. In fear for Jacob's life, Rebekah packed him off to her brother, Laban.[3] Jacob almost met his match for trickery in Uncle Laban who became his father-in-law. Jacob fell

---

[2]Genesis 25:29-34
[3]Genesis 29:16-1

in love with the beautiful Rachael, Laban's daughter. Laban made Jacob work seven years for Rachael, which, the Bible tells us, Jacob gladly did because of his great love for her.

But Laban tricked Jacob, and in the marriage customs of that time and place, he substituted his older daughter, Leah, in the marriage bed. So we find Jacob working another seven years for Rachael.

Most of us have heard about the Old Testament patriarchs, Abraham, Isaac and Jacob. We probably remember more about Abraham - how Abraham went from his home in Ur of the Chaldees in answer to the call of God. We are told in Chapter 15 of Genesis, how Abraham got into covenant with God and how God promised that his descendants would be as numerous as the stars and would be a blessing to the whole world.

Even though Sarah was well past menopause and Abram was ten years older, we read, "Abram believed God and it was accounted to him as righteousness." Abram believed the promise of God even when the years kept passing – and they kept getting older and older before their son Isaac was finally born to him and Sarah. (Genesis 19)

When we get down to today's lesson in Chapter 32 of Genesis, Abraham and Isaac are off the scene and the covenant is in the hands of grandson Jacob. But Jacob had his own agenda. Jacob, the grandson of Abraham, was reaping the benefits of the covenant, but he wanted to live life his way.

When we pick up today's scripture lesson, some twenty years have passed after Jacob's flight away from the angry threats of Esau. Jacob is coming home as a man who has prospered greatly and reappears as a person of success, with his two wives, Leah and Rachael, two handmaidens and eleven sons.

In Jacob's preparation for the reunion with Esau, we see something of the same old calculating Jacob. He divides his camp and sends presents on ahead to hopefully appease his improvident brother who had so easily been talked out of his birthright.

As I read the story, from several translations of the Bible, of Jacob's all night struggle, I thought, as a student of Methodist history, about the old time Methodist altar call where people were told to "pray through."

Jacob's prayer of desperation comes when he starts home to "face the music," and he realizes he has run out of slick tunes. While Jacob is on his way back home, he appeals to the God he met at Bethel on the way out - the God who has now summoned him home. Jacob finally confesses to God that he is not worthy of the blessing he stole from his brother. It is time to face the brother he has wronged. [4]

"Wronged" is too mild a word here for the reprehensible (we would say "criminal") act of deceiving a dying father and stealing from a weaker brother. It makes the prodigal son look like a saint. So the next picture we see is not one of God running out to embrace Jacob as we see in the unforgettable picture in Luke 15 of the Father running to embrace the prodigal son! Instead we see an "all night struggle" in the darkness of the brook Jabbok. The Scripture does not tell us the identity of the mysterious stranger who wrestles all night with Jacob, but after it is over, Jacob testifies that he has seen God face to face.

The God Jacob wrestled with at the brook Jabbok shows a different side of God. It is not the promise-filled aspect of the God he met at Bethel when Jacob saw the ladder reaching down from heaven and heard God's promise to him because of his grandfather Abraham.

As C. S. Lewis reminds us, "God whispers to us in our pleasures and shouts to us in our sorrows." We could say that God whispered his promises to Jacob at Bethel, but when we get down to the struggles that changed Jacob - changed him as a person - receiving a new name and a new nation - God shouted to Jacob.

---

[4]Walter Brueggemann, Interpretation Commentary, Vol.1. P. 268-269

We define ourselves by what we do. Jacob was defined and had defined himself as a trickster, but he was tired of being double-minded. The mysterious struggle was a two-way struggle. We are not told much about the wrestling - only that it lasted all night. At the breaking of the light of day, we read, "The sun rose upon Jacob as he passed Peniel." Jacob could finally say, "I have seen God face to face and yet my life is preserved." (Verse 30)

Jacob turned to God with the same determination and tenacity he had used on everyone else and he held on for dear life. He held on for a blessing. We are told Jacob prevailed and his life was preserved, but he carried for the rest of his life the mark of his struggle with God.

Jacob had dealt with the terrifying face of the One who is hidden in sovereignty but who loves us so much he "stoops to our weakness."[5] His old determination was still there but it seems to have been redirected. He came out of the struggle limping - but with a new name. "I know they call you a trickster," God said to Jacob, "let me tell you who you are: Your name is Israel! You are a prince!"

Dr. John Brown wrote, after the death of his wife whom he had dearly loved and patiently cared for during a long and severe illness: "I have been thinking of Jacob wrestling with the Angel, finding his weakness and strength at the same time and going through the rest of his life halting (limping) and rejoicing." Brown goes on to say, "I believe this is one great lesson of life - the being subdued by God. If this is done, all else is subdued and won."

On the night before Jacob was to meet his brother Esau - twenty years after deceiving his father Isaac into giving him the blessing - he struggled all night. Peace came at daybreak, the record tells us. Jacob was at peace with God and at peace with himself, and later he would finally be at peace with his brother Esau. Jacob was to learn that when God conquers us, we are victorious over self. Jacob had received the blessing from his father Isaac by deceit. He struggled

---

[5]Philippians 2: 5-8

all night and was subdued before he received the blessing of a new name from God.

Like Jacob, Mr. Edwards told me about his struggles all his life for "things." He had finally "conquered his want-er," he told me. Mr. Edwards had given up his "wants" for more and more "things." Like Jacob, it had been in a painful struggle with God. He had also been wounded in the struggle before he finally came out of his darkness into the sunlight.

> *"I found God in the struggle and the grief, and it is enough."*

Mr. Edwards's peace came about in the midst of agony over and finally acceptance of the terminal illness of his only son who had developed leukemia. Mr. Edwards, in the midst of his struggle and grief over the death of his son, had met God. He said, "I found God in the struggle and grief, and it is enough." In struggling and being subdued by God to the place of surrendering our illusions of our own strength and self-sufficiency, we know the strength of God's love, strength, forgiveness, and amazing grace! Amen.

Liberty in Law

Exodus 20: 1-17

*And God spoke all these words, saying: I am the Lord your God, who brought
you out of the land of Egypt, out of the house of slavery.*
~Exodus 20:1-2 (NRSV)~

One of the famous paintings of Norman Rockwell shows a woman
buying a turkey. The turkey is lying on the scales and the butcher is
standing in back of the counter with an apron tied around his waist
and a pencil behind his ear. Both the woman and the butcher have a
pleased expression on their faces as the butcher is pushing down on
the scales with his big thumb and the woman is pushing up on the
scales with her dainty forefinger and neither is aware of what the
other is doing. Both the woman and the butcher would be indignant
if anyone called them a thief. Neither of them would steal a car or
rob a bank, but apparently both of them saw nothing wrong with a
little deception that would make a few cents for the butcher or save
a few cents for the woman.[6]

This gives us a picture of our human tendency toward selfishness
and deceit. And here comes God with the Ten Commandments
reminding us that there are eternal laws in the universe by which we
must live if life is going to come out right.[7]

The Ten Commandments are a gift from God because the moral
laws of the universe were written in our bodies and our psyches
before they were put in our Book of Faith. Life will not support
stealing, will not support murder, and will not support adultery.
Life will not support working 24/7. God tells us to take one day a
week to stop and take time to rest and worship and remember we
are more than what we do.

This is just as true today as when Moses brought these important
instructions down from Mt. Sinai. In other words, God's

---

[6]Cecil Myers, *Thunder on the Mountain*, pp 119-20
[7]Maxie Dunnam. *Communicator's Commentary*, *Exodus*, Loyd Ogilvie, p.252.

commandments are our directions for life. They are our Manufacturer's instructions, straight from our Loving Father. God wants to protect us, just as we, who are parents, want to protect our children so they can live and enjoy life.

In a Zogby poll of college students, 97% said they believed their professors had given them a good education in ethics. But only a quarter of them said they had learned that there are clear and uniform standards of right and wrong.

A reporter from *Forbes Magazine* observed an ethics class at Harvard Business School where they discussed case studies but avoided coming to any moral conclusions. Students were graded on how well they could logically defend their positions, not on whether their positions were actually defensible.

I read recently a comment that students, rather than developing moral principles, merely, in the reporter's words, "develop skills enabling them to rationalize anything short of cannibalism."

How many of you think cannibalism is wrong? The fact that most of us believe cannibalism is wrong indicates that we all draw the line somewhere on issues of right and wrong. So, in our "postmodern age" when people say there are no absolutes and find it impossible to agree on standards of right and wrong, we are seeing scandals rocking the business world as well as our political world and college campuses.

What more and more of us are beginning to realize is that this kind of behavior is the logical result of the moral relativism that permeates our culture. It is so much a part of our daily news that we are all affected. A recent poll shows that over 50% of people who identify themselves as born again Christians do not believe in ultimate moral truth. But those of us who have been concerned by the economic and political scandals, college debaucheries and public school murders, are willing to take time to listen to biblical teaching on ethics.

No document has influenced the world as much as the Ten

Commandments! In our western civilization, Jews and Christians hold the Ten Commandments as principles upon which to build their lives and upon which to build a civilization. Indeed our civil laws of liberty and justice for all are rooted in this covenant law of God said to be on tablets of stone given to Moses at Mount Sinai.

Alabama Chief Justice Ray Moore made national news after the Alabama federal court of appeals said he must remove the monument of the Ten Commandments he had placed in the lobby of his state judicial building. Lawyers for the ACLU said if they allowed the Ten Commandments to stay there "every government building" could be topped with a cross, a menorah, a statue of Buddha, etc., depending upon the views of the officials.

With all due respect, our founding fathers were not Islamic or Buddhist or atheists. It was the Christian concept of freedom and justice for all that enabled us to become the "Great Land of Liberty" because Liberty in Law is a Judeo-Christian concept.

In the Judeo-Christian Bible, we are told that we are all made in the image of God. Thus all mortals are loved by God, including those accused of crime. Our due process tradition was not begun by the American Civil Liberties Union, the Islamists, the Buddhists or any other religion but by "The Book" they seem to be fighting to keep out of the hands of our school children.

I love the hymn "America the Beautiful." The second verse is "America, America, God mend thine every flaw. Confirm thy soul in self-control, *thy liberty in Law.*" The hymn writer knew and God knows that liberty is found in law and not in lawlessness.

A God of love gave us these laws. The Ten Commandments are the source of our laws and as such, early on, were framed and placed on the walls of courthouses and schools throughout our country.

So it is not some new or imported religion that Justice Moore and others wanted to start. The phrase "separation of church and state" simply means that The United States is not to have a "state church." England had and still has a state church. The Episcopal Church in

England was and is still the "Church of England." In fact, the Queen of England is the titular head of the church as well as the state.

The Egyptians never had a code of law: They considered their emperor to be LAW. George Washington was so loved and revered, we are told, that some wanted to make him king after our revolution. But Washington and our founding fathers decided we should not have a king. They wanted, not Rex Lex ("King is law") but Lex Rex ("Law is King"). We would also not have one Christian denomination to be "The Church of the United States" but have equality and freedom of religion. Some of our American founders were Deists, but most were Christians. None were of any other religion. But all religions have been welcomed into citizenship in the United States of America.

> *Our liberty in the United States was based on the Law of God as given to us in the Christian Bible.*

Some of you may remember a time when, after a revival meeting in the South, some people would remark, "John got religion last night," meaning, "John was converted to Christ." In other words, "religion" in the United States and the West was Christianity. Our liberty in the United States was based on the Law of God as given to us in the Christian Bible.

The heritage of the West is like none other the world has ever seen, in spite of its earlier acceptance of the worldwide system of slavery, class and race separation and some other flawed understandings.

Christianity gave us new concepts of law, government and human rights based on Biblical values that slowly brought about the New Testament teaching that God is not a respecter of persons which slowly but surely brought about laws promoting equality and opportunity for all.

Our artists and composers created masterpieces in the sciences, in literature, and art. We see the same story in medicine. For example,

Christians built the first hospitals. The Greek and Roman civilizations were great in many ways, but in the whole city of ancient Rome, there was not a single hospital. As Baron Von Hugal, a Christian theologian and writer, said, "Christianity taught the world to care."

Our founding fathers were wise enough not to want the state running the church, which would make problems for the church as well as the state. But it would have been unthinkable for our founding fathers to take all vestiges of the Christian faith from our schools or government offices. If we do not have laws, we become lawless. We are seeing lawlessness and terrorism now - even in some public schools and other public places.

"In God We Trust" is on our coins, and scripture verses are etched in stone at the Jefferson monument as well as many other historic places in Washington D.C. We have not always been good practitioners of our Christian faith, but our love and liberty that has welcomed other cultures to come into our country and enjoy our freedoms come from the Christian world view.

A few years ago, Ted Turner, in criticizing the negativity of the Ten Commandments came forth with his own "Ten Suggestions" and the Atlanta papers gave them a prominent space.

When we see our toddler hitting someone with his little hand and little strength, we might just suggest, "No, no honey." But when we see him running toward a hot stove, or running toward the road or some real or potential danger, we dash out and command that he stop.

I have used a computer to do a mountainous amount of typing for many years. I have found I have to follow certain instructions from the maker of the computer. If I ever decided I knew more than the maker of the computer, I would be in serious trouble. In fact, it is interesting that the computer is set up by commands, not suggestions.

We have to follow the instructions of the maker, and the more we follow, the better the computer works and the more awesome it is. In fact, it does not take long to realize one had better follow the commands or it will not work.

Some people seem to think God roams the world looking for people who may be having a good time so He can zap them. No! God's law is the gift of His love. It is in God's law that we are given freedom and liberty. God's rules for our life are not arbitrary because God knows that without rules we cannot successfully play the game of life!

My grandson, Dow, visited me one day when he was about 7 years old. When Dow came in, he said, "Well, Grandmother, what are we going to do today?"

I asked, "What would you like to do?"

He replied, "Let's Play *Clue*."

I said, "All right, if you will teach me the rules." I learned how to play the game of *Clue,* and we had a good time.

We have rules for games, rules for the road, and traffic laws. Otherwise there would be chaos. There is chaos if we do not obey the rules. Even to play a game of checkers we must have rules, directions, or laws. We do not just move the pieces here and there without rules. We do not break the laws of God; we only break ourselves if we ignore them.

My daughter, Carol, had an Easter egg hunt for her eight-year-old son and other children in her neighborhood a few years ago. In the excitement to hurry and find the eggs, Joey attempted to jump over a large air-conditioning unit beside their house. Joey fell and cut his knee to the bone and had to be rushed to the hospital emergency room. Joey was an agile and athletic little boy, and he thought he could jump over the air conditioning unit. If he had asked his mother, she would have told him, "No Joey, do not try to jump over it." She would have had some prohibitions - in fact some commandments! Why? Was it because she did not want him to have fun? Did she want to spoil her son's enjoyment? Was it because she did not want him to find the Easter eggs he was in such a hurry to find?

No, of course not. Carol had hidden the eggs, invited neighbor children over. She wanted them to have fun! But she could see farther than her son could see. She knew eight year old legs were not long enough to jump over air conditioners. She could also see dangerous places on top of the air-conditioner. Air conditioners are not made for jumping over.

> *God's rules - God's commandments - are rules to increase our pleasure - to increase our happiness, our joy!*

God's rules - God's commandments - are rules to increase our pleasure - to increase our happiness, our joy! The greatest lesson in life is that God is in charge here. If we are smart, we will obey the rules God has, in his greater love, set down for us - even those rules that we do not understand.

A few years ago, I bought a book by Elton Trueblood entitled, *A Place to Stand.* I read it over and over because of the many insights that spoke to me. He had entitled the book *A Place to Stand* using a phrase from Archimedes who said, "Give me a place to stand, and I will move the earth." Archimedes was the inventor of both the lever and the pulley.

As a philosopher, Trueblood points out that humankind, in our lostness and separation from God, cannot find ourselves because we do not have a place to stand while we search for ourselves.

It is in finding Christ that we have a place to stand because Christ becomes our central postulate. Only in finding God, a firm place to stand, can we find ourselves. Only by seeing ourselves through the eyes of God, can we find the self-image and the firm place to stand that we need for the living of life.

The activists in Hollywood, as well as other enemies of righteousness, have managed to convince some of our people that "religion" is a "private matter", that people who witness outside the church are "fanatic and intolerant." But if our fore parents had kept their faith a private matter, we would never have had the "protestant work ethic" and the progress and prosperity we have enjoyed in this country.

We do not have to reinvent the wheel of morality. Yet we have people expecting our teenagers to go out into the world to make up their own rules for life as they go along. No direction - no absolutes. As a result, many are messing up their health and their lives with alcohol, other drugs and sexual experimentation because they are expected to live without direction. They are expected to experiment, to invent, to imagine and re-imagine and to decide through trial and error when a God of love has already written out clear directions for a way of life that works.

This belief in one God set the Israelites apart from other ancient religions. Before God gave this first commandment, He identified Himself: "I am the Lord your God who brought you out of the land of Egypt, out of the house of bondage."

The basis of this commandment is that we are told that the "Lord our God is a jealous God." This statement puzzled me as a young woman because I tend to connect jealousy with envy and pettiness. But "jealous" in this passage comes from the Greek word that means "emotional." It means God's care for each one of us is personal and emotional. God is not indifferent to what we do and how we live just as we cannot be indifferent to our children or those we love.

A man complained to me about his wife getting upset when he "took a drink," but he said she didn't seem to mind at all if other people drank alcoholic beverages. How many of you understand this wife?

We have concern about those we love - not only concern about what they do but who they are! There is a fine line here. That is why couples sometime have a hard time understanding one another. However, a marriage is not in as much trouble when the couple fights as when they become indifferent to one another.

The God who brought the Hebrews out of slavery wanted to keep them and wants to keep us out of an even greater bondage. He simplified the rules of life down to ten - one for each finger.

1. No other gods. No idols.
2. God's name is important.
3. We are to bless not curse.
4. For our own sake, we are to stop working one day a week and remember we are more than our possessions or what we do.
5. Honor our parents. They are our roots.
6. Don't murder - life is precious.
7. We are not to play around with our marriage vows. Keeping our covenant with one person is our best chance of growing up.
8. If we take what belongs to another, we are the loser.
9. Speak the truth. When we twist our words, we limp through life.[8]
10. The tenth commandment telling us not to "covet" comes silently after the booming "thou shall not" about lying, stealing, adultery and murder.

Our community was shocked, in fact it made news all over Georgia and beyond, in July of 2004, when a respected youth leader in a large Baptist church in Rome was accused of the murder of a fellow church leader. We were later dumbfounded when it was alleged the murdered man's wife was in an affair with the alleged murderer and an accomplice in planning the murder.

Probably none of us were more shocked than this man and woman now in prison for murder. When we begin the hidden sin of coveting, we never know how far down the slippery slope it will take us. It seems so harmless when we first engage in a flirtation that might lead to adultery. It seems so harmless when we first

---

[8] Barbara Brown Taylor, *Gospel Medicine*, p. 57

engage in perhaps soft core pornography that requires more and more explicit materials and often leads to acting out, according to statistics.

These "little" offenses are only revealed when an overt action like adultery or murder brings it into the limelight. Jesus tells us sin begins in the heart with hidden lust and anger.[9]

To covet means to wish for or desire that which belongs to another. To covet is dangerous because it is silent and hidden. We do not see "covet." There are no civil laws against covetousness. It is even hard to pronounce so we do not denounce it!

Yet this tenth commandment about covetousness covers the other nine. Covetousness is deceptive and goes hand in hand with discontentment, lies, lust and hate. We are not to "covet anything that belongs to someone else - house, spouse, or anything that belongs to our neighbor."[10]

The awesome message of these commandments is that a God of love has given us guidelines for a successful life. He has given us guidelines for what it means to be a civil and liberated human being as well as what it means to be a covenant person and a follower of Jesus Christ.

I have found God's laws to be the liberating directions on the road of life. Someone has said, "When in doubt read the directions." God's directions in the form of the Ten Commandments[11] are the gift of God's boundless love and amazing grace fulfilled in Jesus. Amen.

[9] Exodus 20:17
[10] Matthew 5:22-27
[11] Exodus 20:1-17

The Two Sons

Luke 15:11-32 (see full scripture at end of chapter)

"But when he came to himself, he said, 'How many of my father's hired servants have bread enough and to spare, and I am dying of hunger! I will arise and go to my father, and will say to him, "Father, I have sinned against heaven and before you, and I am no longer worthy to be called your son. Treat me like one of your hired servants."'
~Luke 15:17-19 (NRSV)~

One of the most effective methods Jesus used in teaching was the parable. The parable is a way to interpret abstract truths in concrete terms. Or, as we learned as children, "A parable is an earthly story with a heavenly meaning" or "a parable begins in the 'here and now' to get to the 'there and then.'"

Today we are looking at what we know as the "parable of the prodigal son." This parable has been called, even by secular literary critics, one of the greatest short stories ever told. The father is the only character who appears throughout the story. So we could well call it "the parable of the loving father."

This famous scripture lesson is often used on Father's Day as a story of an ideal father. In giving us this parable, Jesus has given us the powerful illustration of the amazing grace of God - a grace that is greater than all the rebellious sins of any wayward son or daughter.

God has given us freedom to follow our impulses and desires. We have even been given the freedom to say "no" to God. But there comes a time of accounting.

Our lesson today could also be called "the parable of the two sons." This father had two sons, and the story is presented in two scenes. The first scene focuses on the younger son and the second scene focuses on the elder son.

According to Jewish law, the younger son would inherit one third of the father's estate at the father's death or it could be received as a gift from the father in his lifetime. This younger son asked for and received his inheritance early and left for the far country to do his own thing.

The younger son got his inheritance in cash. When he got into the far country, it seems he was quite unprepared for its flattery and seductions. So, little by little, everything he had was used up. This young man seemed to have been swept off his feet and away from his common sense. We are told all his resources were soon depleted in riotous living. The boy took his inheritance and went out and spent it. He reached bottom and had to take a job feeding swine which no self-respecting Jew would do.

He had thought he was having a good time, but it ended when his fair weather friends left him after his party money ran out. The young prodigal was homeless, alone, hungry, feeding pigs and eating husks.

Then a wonderful thing happened! Jesus tells us that the young man came to himself. Four simple words; "He came to himself." William Barclay said Jesus paid sinning humanity the greatest compliment it has ever been paid when he said, "He came to himself."

Jesus believed that so long as we are away from God, we are also away from ourselves. When we are against God, we are against ourselves. We are not truly ourselves when we are away from God. This young man came to himself, so he started home.

> *We can only find ourselves when we find God, for in finding God, we have a place to stand while we look for ourselves.*

People keep saying they want their children to "find themselves." The prodigal son was truly himself when he was on his way home. We can only find ourselves when we find God, for in finding God, we have a place to stand while we look for ourselves.

This scripture teaches that God is not opposed to our having a good time. In fact, it is not our seeking a good time that God is concerned about. God wants the very best for us as we want the best for our children. The laws of God are the rules of the house and are to bless us, not to deprive us. God's concern is that we are missing the great time God has planned for us.

This is the emphasis in this story of the prodigal. When he finally came to himself, he was willing to humble himself by returning home to be a hired hand. He realized he no longer had a legal claim to his father's estate. He realized he had sinned against this father, and he was wise enough to know that a sin against another human being is also a sin against God. This is brought out again and again in the Old Testament as well as the New Testament.

So the young man started home, and in his wildest dreams he could not have imagined what would happen next. Imagine the joy of this hungry boy when he again felt his father's arms of forgiveness around him. There was a party when the prodigal got home. The story has a happy ending. Verse 24 tells us, "They began to be merry."

When the boy "came to himself," he had a right relationship with himself. Very simply; happiness (or blessedness) requires the acceptance of ourselves - truly finding or knowing ourselves. We need a right relationship with others. We also need a willingness to forgive and to practice non-condemning love toward others. This is not always easy to do.

C.S. Lewis tells us there is one person we have always practiced non-condemning love toward: ourselves. We easily forgive ourselves for our thoughtlessness or temper tantrums. We say, "I was mean today because I did not sleep well last night." We say, "I lost my temper because I had a headache." We say, "It is that Shaw temper or Baird temper." We have no problems finding excuses for our own bad behavior, but we tend to make others toe the line.

Then we need a right relationship with God. We need a relationship with Christ who helps us to love and forgive others as God has loved and forgiven us. Christian morals are for the purpose of protecting and fulfilling us, not for the purpose of limiting life.

As the parable of the two sons tells us, the lost are not always the down and out people. They are the people who are trying to make it without the Father, without God!

We can be as lost in the executive suite as we can be when homeless on a park bench. Being lost has little to do with whether or not we are rich or poor, educated or uneducated, young or old.

In the parable about sheep, Jesus said a rather strange thing. Jesus said, "I say to you that likewise there is more joy in heaven over one sinner who repents than over ninety and nine just people who think they need no repentance." This is a correction to the Pharisee's religious snobbery. The Pharisees thought and taught that there was joy in heaven when those who provoke God perish from the earth. They seemed to think God was out to zap the sinner!

We never outgrow our need to repent.

The Pharisees, like the elder son, missed the joy of the Lord and the Father's party because they had lost their need for God. They were as lost as those they judged so severely. We never outgrow our need to repent. The Greek word for repentance is "Metanoia," which means an "afterthought," a "change of mind," a turning around and moving in a new direction.

Did you notice that just as the father left the house to meet the returning younger son, he also left the house to go out to the elder son and to "entreat him" to come in and join the celebration?

The father called for rejoicing because he knew that only when the elder brother could rejoice in the return of his brother would he be free from a life of calculating rights and wrongs and comparing levels of righteousness.

I am thankful we are not given the responsibility of judging people! We are called to love - not judge. Christ is our example of what it means to be an authentic elder brother. We, like the elder brother that stayed home, realize that it is only by the grace of God that we are not in the hog pen with the prodigal.

So the parable begins with the younger son lost in the far country and ends with the older son equally lost in self-righteousness.

All the sins and excesses of the younger son did not keep him out of the father's party because he came home repenting. All the virtues and good behavior of the older son did not get him in as long as he, in his self-righteous indignation, refused to join in the celebration.

God is still seeking all of us. As a woman seeks a lost coin, as a shepherd seeks for a lost sheep, as a father seeks a lost son, so God invites us all in and runs to meet us with outstretched arms while we are yet a far way off! Amen.

Luke 15:11-32 - Then He said: "A certain man had two sons. And the younger of them said to his father, 'Father, give me the portion of goods that falls to me.' So he divided to them his livelihood. And not many days after, the younger son gathered all together, journeyed to a far country, and there wasted his possessions with prodigal living. But when he had spent all, there arose a severe famine in that land and he began to be in want. Then he went and joined himself to a citizen of that country, and he sent him into his fields to feed swine. And he would gladly have filled his stomach with the pods that the swine ate, and no one gave him anything.

"But when he came to himself, he said, 'How many of my father's hired servants have bread enough and to spare, and I perish with hunger! I will arise and go to my father, and will say to him, 'Father, I have sinned against heaven and before you, and I am no longer worthy to be called your son. Treat me like one of your hired servants.' And he arose and came to his father. But when he was still a great way off, his father saw him and had compassion, and ran and fell on his neck and kissed him. And the son said to him, 'Father, I have

sinned against heaven and in your sight and am no longer worthy to be called your son.'

"But the father said to his servants, 'Bring out the best robe and put it on him, and put a ring on his hand and sandals on his feet. And bring the fatted calf here and kill it, and let us eat and be merry; for this my son was dead and is alive again; he was lost and is found.' And they began to be merry.

"Now his older son was in the field. And as he came and drew near to the house, he heard music and dancing. So he called one of the servants and asked what these things meant. And he said to him, 'Your brother has come, and because he has received him safe and sound, your father has killed the fatted calf.'

"But he was angry and would not go in. Therefore his father came out and pleaded with him. So he answered and said to his father, 'Lo, these many years I have been serving you; I never transgressed your commandment at any time; and yet you never gave me a young goat that I might make merry with my friends. But as soon as this son of yours came, who has devoured your livelihood with harlots, you killed the fatted calf for him.'

"And he said to him, 'Son, you are always with me, and all that I have is yours. It was right that we should make merry and be glad, for your brother was dead and is alive again, and was lost and is found.' "

Just the Facts

John 20:11-23

Then, the same day at evening, being the first day of the week, when the doors were shut where the disciples were assembled, for fear of the Jews, Jesus came and stood in the midst, and said to them, "Peace be with you."
~John 20:19 (NKJV)~

My husband served as pastor of Epworth Methodist Church, in Atlanta in the 1970s.[12] The "Workers Class" at Epworth went to Wesley Woods Health Center (near Emory University) once a month to assist patients by taking them down to the main floor for the Sunday morning worship service. They invited me to go with them to Wesley Woods on several occasions.

We would go from room to room offering to assist any of the residents who needed help. One Sunday morning, I went into one of the rooms and asked the lady on the bed if I could help her get ready and take her down for the service. She told me, "No" and explained that she had gone to church much of her life, but now she said, "I've had enough of it." It occurred to me that she was regarding church as some kind of prison sentence, and she had "done her time."

We went from room to room and helped many other residents get dressed and into their wheel chairs and to the morning worship service on the first floor of the building. We stayed for the service to help residents back to their rooms. As I sat down beside the last Wesley Woods resident I had rolled into the gathering room, I looked up and saw Miss Layona Glenn, who had been a missionary to Brazil for over fifty years. Miss Glenn was over 100 years old at the time and had a front seat so as not to miss a single word.

---

[12] My husband Charles C. Shaw (member of North Georgia Conference) was pastor of Epworth United Methodist Church on McLendon Avenue (Little Five Points) in Atlanta 1970-1974.

Georgia people and others might remember that Layona Glenn could bend down and touch her toes at age 100 and was invited to visit President Johnson in the White House and demonstrate this skill which was broadcast on WSB television.

When I saw Miss Glenn on the front seat at Wesley Woods, I thought, "Miss Layona has never had enough of it." I thought of the contrast between the woman back in her room alone and Miss Layona Glenn, hymn book in hand, singing the praises of God and seeking to learn and praise and witness to her faith in Jesus Christ, even in her old age.

I read about a little boy who was on his way to church on Easter Sunday and was not too happy about it. He wanted to stay home and play with his toys, but his parents said, "We're going to church." The child replied, "Well, it's just going to be the same old story." Like the elderly lady at Wesley Woods, he thought he had heard enough.

Some of you are here every time the church doors are opened and never tire of hearing and telling the "same old story." We love to tell and hear the story of the incarnation at Christmas, the story of the cross during Lent, and the story of the resurrection at Easter. Like the hymn writer, we "love to tell the story because we know it's true. It satisfies our longing as nothing else can do."[13]

The Easter celebration is not just a day but a season. Today and every Sunday until Pentecost are Sundays of Easter. The resurrection is the cornerstone of the church.

In John 20:19 we see three different reactions to the empty tomb. We see John, the beloved disciple, who believed with no evidence but the empty tomb. When John saw the empty tomb, he remembered what Jesus said about rising again in three days. And John believed.

A different reaction was given by Mary Magdalene and the other women. After the Sabbath day had passed, they took seriously the

---

[13] Hymn, "I Love to Tell the Story," by Katherine Hankey

responsibility to minister to Jesus one more time by anointing his body with spices to counter the smell of decay. They were dejected wondering who would roll away the stone for them. When they arrived at the tomb, physical proof of the resurrection began to unfold before their eyes. They saw that the massive stone has been rolled away. Then they saw that the tomb was empty, and there was an empty bench and an empty shroud.

Their reaction was one of alarm. They believed that someone had desecrated the grave. Jesus had been falsely accused and crucified between two thieves, buried, and now someone must have stolen the body. What else awful could happen in one week? It was only when Jesus called her name, that Mary Magdalene knew that Jesus was alive again.

So John remembered and believed when he saw the empty tomb; Mary Magdalene believed only when Jesus called her by name. And Thomas? Thomas's faith would only come with difficulty. He could only be sure after physical contact with the risen Jesus. Thomas's attitude was, "Let's not rely on faith alone. What are the facts?"

Thomas said, "I understand what you are saying about seeing the Lord, but what are the facts here?" Thomas was not with the other disciples when they first saw the Lord, and he certainly was not going to take their word for it without seeing for himself.

Jesus appeared to all the disciples except Thomas, and Jesus bestowed His peace in verse 10. And then in verse 21, He commissioned them to continue the work that God had given Him through the Holy Spirit.

Thomas was absent, and he had trouble believing all this. As a result, he has been called "Doubting Thomas" because he said, "I will not believe until I see the nail prints in his hands and the wound in His side."

But when Thomas placed his own hands in the nail prints and in the wound in the side of Jesus, he believed! Thomas then made the strongest confession of faith of all of them. Thomas said, "My Lord and my God."

Jesus pronounced a blessing on Thomas but also on all who came after Thomas who did not see the nail prints in His hands or the pierced side and who believed through the word of the Apostles and the word and witness of the church.

In other words, even two thousand years distant from the time and place of the resurrection, we believe because of the witness to the facts handed down to us today, through the New Testament, the church, through reason and our own experience. In other words, when we accept Jesus Christ into our lives, our faith begins to grow because of our own experience.

I read a story about Richard Baxter of Kidderminster, England. He was one of the hardest-working ministers ever to pastor a church. He preached with great earnestness, wrote with untiring zeal, and served his parish with great love and care. In his final illness, he was in great pain and once said to one of his friends, "I have great pain, but I have found peace." Later when he was asked how he was, he said through his pain, "Almost well." Then he died. What the resurrection took away was the sting of death.

On my last Palm Sunday as pastor of East Point Avenue Church where I served for four years after mandatory retirement age, I conducted the funeral of George Haney, the chair of the Administrative Board and the right hand of the church for many years. During George's final illness from cancer, I would visit and pray with George at Our Lady of Perpetual Care in Atlanta. When I would walk into his room and ask how he felt, George would answer early on, "Oh, just so-so." This went on for weeks. The last day I visited him, the day before his death early the next morning, I walked into his room and asked him how he was feeling. George Haney's strong answer was "Fine."

George would not want to be held up as a saint. He was well aware of his human frailties, but he gave me plenty to say at his funeral service. The nearer George Haney got to heaven, the better be became.

<blockquote>
*Death has never been the same since the day
it took on Jesus Christ.*
</blockquote>

When I stood up before a huge crowd of church and community people (he had been an officer in the Lion's Club and other community organizations) to conduct the funeral service by celebrating the life of this good man, I spoke of his wonderful Christian witness during a painful and fatal illness. George and the other men at East Point Avenue United Methodist Church treated me like their special sister, and they were indeed my special brothers in Christ Jesus.

Death has never been the same since the day it took on Jesus Christ. With Jesus as our Savior we will step out of this life into another world as different from life as this one is from our mothers' wombs. Paul tells us that that bit of transparent computer-like information or DNA or whatever is the "real me" and the "real you" will be transformed into another kind of body. Jesus walked out of that airless dark grave. He was raised in a transcendent, indestructible body – one that was recognizable. It was also a body that could walk through doors and be ascended into heaven.

This is the good news. This is the story! These are the facts! These are the facts I never get tired of proclaiming. Jesus conquered death and came that we might have life abundantly – and eternally. Amen.

Holy Ground

Exodus 3:3-14   Luke13: 6-9

"Do not come any closer," God said. "Take off your sandals, for the place where you are standing is holy ground."
~Exodus 3:5 NIV~

The first book of our Bible, Genesis, closes with the death of Joseph. Joseph, who had been sold into slavery by his jealous brothers, had finally become Prime Minister of Egypt and was so honored by the king that Joseph was able to bring his father, Jacob, his eleven brothers and their families to an honored place with him in Egypt.

The second book of our Bible, Exodus, informs us in the first chapter, "There arose a new king over Egypt who did not know Joseph." (Exodus 1:8)

The new King became fearful that the descendants of Israel would become larger in number and more powerful than his own people so he decided to "deal shrewdly" with them and place harsh taskmasters over them. (Exodus 1: 10-11) Part of this king's plan later was to kill all the boy babies born to Hebrew mothers.

The second chapter of Exodus tells of the birth of Moses and how his mother hid him for three months. Then when Moses became too old to hide, his mother built a little ark of bulrushes for him, dabbed it with asphalt and pitch, put Moses in the basket ark and laid him in the reeds by the river's bank. (Exodus 2:1-3)

When the king's daughter and her maidens came down to bathe in the Nile River, they found the baby. So Moses became the adopted son of the daughter of the Pharaoh, and he grew up in the king's court as the grandson of the powerful king of Egypt.

When we get to today's Scripture lesson, Moses was 80 years old. He had fled Egypt after killing a man and was living in the land of Midian some 200 miles across the Sinai Peninsula. Moses had settled down in Midian, had married Zipporah, the daughter of Jethro, the priest of Midian, and had a son, Gershom. It is here that Moses was confronted by God.

Moses was not confronted by God in a worship service with candle lights and a cushioned altar, but in an uncanny fire - an uncommon light out in the middle of nowhere, and when he least expected it. The burning bush was an odd fire! Moses kept watching and did not see any ashes fall off. It was burning but was not being consumed. So Moses decided to take a closer look. Moses turned aside, and to his astonishment noticed the bush was not immediately reduced to ashes. It was burning but not burned. It was a mystery. It was uncanny - awesome.

Moses was like people who are wise enough to think or say, when they see a church building, "Someone has built an awesome sanctuary. There may be something to this Christianity after all." When they turn aside to investigate, they learn that this Christ has made a difference in Western Civilization and more. Changing time from B.C. (before Christ) to A.D. (Latin for after Christ) is only the beginning.

When the Lord saw that Moses had turned aside and was paying attention to the miracle before him, it was then and only then that God spoke to Moses. When Moses turned aside from his daily task, the Lord spoke to Moses out of the burning bush. God called Moses by name and told Moses to take off his shoes.

The Lord tells Moses that He has seen the oppression of the children of Israel and has chosen Moses to bring them out of their slavery in Egypt.

Moses was just about as reluctant a leader as some of the rest of us. We are not the first people to say, "I've done my time." Moses, in effect, said the same thing. "Lord who am I that I should bring the Israelites out of Egypt? Lord, I am just now learning to lead sheep. Now you want me to lead an entire nation?"

The Lord does not offer Moses much reassurance - at least not the

> *God did not tell Moses that he would be safe.*
> *God said to Moses, "I will be with you."*

kind of assurance most of us want. God did not tell Moses that he would be safe. God said to Moses, "I will be with you," as if that would be all Moses would need. What really mattered was "who God is" and that God had chosen Moses for the great task of bringing the Israelites out of their slavery in Egypt.

Moses asks for God's name! Not directly, because to know a person's name was to know their essence and, in a sense, to have some power over that person. So Moses asked God indirectly. Moses replied to God; "You know, God, if I go and tell these people that God has sent me to lead them out of Egypt, and they ask me His Name, what do I tell them?"[14]

And God said to Moses, "I am who I am." Not much of an answer. God seems to be letting Moses know that there is no controlling Him. God told Moses "I am that I am." God's answer was not clear to Moses, and it is not clear to us. The rest of the story is that Moses went on to lead the children of Israel out of Egypt, and he became one of the heroes of the faith.

The way that Moses responded to God's call in the burning bush is interesting. Moses answered with what appears to be the self-confident, "Here I am." Moses had lived long enough to believe that he was fairly capable. Many of us would conclude the same.

Maybe we are just a bit too self-confident when we cannot tell that

---

[14] In a very real sense, this text in Exodus 3 is one of the most important in the Bible. For it reveals the name of God. In antiquity, to know the name of another was to have insight into the self-hood and character of the other. What does it mean to say God is "I Am Who I AM." To use the verb "to be" in the name of God may be misleading. In Hebrew, the verb "to be" calls attention, not to being itself, but to presence and activity. Thus this name "I am who I am" emphasizes God as the only existent who is present and active in each and every historical moment. In a sense, the rest of the Bible tells how God is present and active. Isaiah 6:5-10

---

the sacred has invaded our secular world. It could be that a good self-image has blinded us to our need to take off our shoes and fall in humility and reverence before a Holy God. God told Moses, "Do not come any closer. You are standing in a place you've never stood before. Take off your shoes; you are in the presence of the God of your fathers."

Suddenly Moses, who had earlier said to God, "Here I am," in humility replies, "Who am I?" It seems that knowing who the creator is and who the creature is can be an enlightening as well as a humbling experience for some of us.

God's answer seems to put Moses in his place - a place of listening to God for direction. Being chosen of God to do a task is no bed of roses. It is not a comfortable place to be. God's presence and power is offered to all, but it is not forced on any.

Consider the character of God as portrayed in this passage. The God who speaks to Moses from the burning bush is mysterious, uncanny, holy, and near. He is deeply concerned about injustice and oppression.

The Lord said; "I have indeed seen the misery of my people in Egypt. I have heard them crying out because of their slave drivers, and I am concerned about their suffering. So I have come down to rescue them from the hand of the Egyptians and to bring them to a good and spacious land - a land flowing with milk and honey. (Exodus 3:7-8)

All this is great news to Moses! But in verse ten, God tells Moses; "So now go! I am sending you to Pharaoh to bring the Israelites out of Egypt."

"I am that I am" is God's answer to Moses's question of God's name. It is God's own definition, and it is a short one. It confounds mortality that dared to question God. Indeed God is the only "Is." All the rest of us "have been" or "will be" God is! God is the forever Now!

There is also a practical application of the meaning of the mysterious name, "I Am." If the name of God is "I Am," it seems to follow that only through what I am, can I worship God aright.

Isaiah, in the year that King Uzziah died, saw the Lord high and lifted up and heard the singing, "Holy, holy, holy is the Lord Almighty." He worshiped, saying, "Woe is me for I am a man of unclean lips and I dwell among a people of unclean lips." Then Isaiah said in amazement, "My eyes have seen the King! Not King Uzziah but the King of Kings, the Lord God Almighty." [15]

Moses decided to believe God, and although Moses never saw more than the backside of God again, after many such encounters with the God of the Burning Bush, his own face begins to shine with such an uncanny light that at one point he had to wear a veil over his face.

I have entitled this message, "Holy Ground," but as H. L. Ellison reminds us, it was the belief that **every place where God was revealed is holy**. Of course this is true, but it needs to be kept in balance. The place of God's revelation to Moses at the burning bush is an unidentifiable spot.

The words of Cowper's hymn:
> *Jesus, where'er Thy people meet,*
> *They there behold Thy mercy seat:*
> *Where'er they seek Thee, Thou art found,*
> *And every place is hallowed ground.* [16]

Amen.

---

[15] Isaiah 6:5-10
[16] *The Daily Study Bible*. Exodus. Page 17

The Nightingale of the Psalms

Psalm 23

The Lord is my shepherd. I shall not want. He makes me to lie down in green pastures. He leads me beside the still waters. He restores my soul. He leads me in the paths of righteousness for his name's sake. Yea thou I walk through the valley of the shadow of death, I will fear no evil. For You are with me. Your rod and Your staff, they comfort me. You prepare a table before me in the presence of my enemies. You anoint my head with oil. My cup runs over. Surely goodness and mercy shall follow me all the days of my life; And I will dwell in the house of the Lord forever.
~Psalm 23 (NKJV)~

If you were asked to name the one Psalm in the entire Psalter that expresses a perfect model of peace and tranquility, it would be Psalms 23. The Shepherd's Psalm is a psalm of green pastures, still waters, divine protection, a table of plenty and an overflowing cup.

Psalms 23 has been called the "Nightingale of the Psalms." The nightingale is a bird known for its melodious singing in the nighttime. It is often in the nighttime that we need songs and a psalm! That is why this Psalm is so appropriate and the one most used for funerals. At the February 19, 2000 funeral of my brother, Tom, my nephew read Psalm 23 and expounded on it. I have never used it as the basis of a message before, but have read Psalm 23 at the graveside of nearly every one of the many funeral services I have conducted.

> *If we are ever to appropriate this great salvation for ourselves, there must come a time when our parents' and our grandparents' God or our neighbors' God becomes our God - becomes my God!*

This passage of scripture is the best-loved single passage in the Old Testament because of the comfort and assurance it brings. Its images of serenity and loving care are timeless.

It is a personal Psalm, and it begins with a personal confession of faith. "The Lord is my shepherd!" God is Israel's God, but He is also the God of Abraham, Isaac and Jacob. God is known for His individual relationships. If we are ever to appropriate this great salvation for ourselves, there must come a time when our parents' and our grandparents' God or our neighbors' God becomes our God - becomes my God!

Psalm 23 starts off with "The Lord is my Shepherd!" It is not my father or my mother, but it's me, O Lord, standing in the need of prayer.

The mother of a child dying of cancer taught him the 23rd Psalm by having him repeat the five words of "The Lord is my Shepherd" on his five fingers. To teach him about his personal relationship to the Lord, she had him to hold that finger in his fist, symbolizing the personal pronoun. When he died, he was found holding his ring finger. He woke in the Shepherd's arms because his mothers' shepherd was also his shepherd. The Lord is MY shepherd; I shall not want; he leads ME in the paths of righteousness.

In John's gospel, Chapter 10, the first part of the chapter talks about the shepherd, the door, thieves and robbers. Verse 11 focuses on the contrast between a shepherd and a hireling. Jesus is the Good Shepherd – the model shepherd that is the pattern for other shepherds. This model in the early church was held up before pastors urging them to care for the church flock in spite of the dangers of false teachers.

We are all called to be shepherds to one another. In I Peter 5:1-2, Peter appeals to the people using the shepherd terminology, as a "fellow elder" and a witness of Christ's suffering, for them to be "shepherds of God's flock."

The paths for grazing in the Holy Land have always been a maze of paths, and sheep can easily become confused and lost in the maze of pasturage. Many paths lead to nowhere. The wilderness is always only a breath away.

Paul and Peter would remind us that we, too, are in danger. We must rely upon the Good Shepherd so that we do not take a fatal turn. Jesus is the One who leads us beside the still waters and restores our souls and leads us in the paths of righteousness for His name's sake.

The word "shepherd" is often applied to God in the Old Testament, and Israel's kings are also called shepherds. David was called the Shepherd King partially because of being the poet who wrote this masterpiece. But David would tell us that God is the author of this Psalm and it is the Lord who is our shepherd.

Philip Keller, who worked for about eight years as a sheep herder, has written a book called *A Shepherd Looks at Psalm 23*. In this book he tells about going out at night to walk under the stars to remind himself of God's majesty and power. He talks about looking at the star-studded sky of at least 250 million stars, each one larger than our sun. He talks about planet Earth being only a speck of matter in space. It is said that if we could transport our most powerful telescope and set it up on our nearest star and look back this way, the Earth could not even be seen.

We remember that each of us is only a tiny mite on the tiny little ball of Earth, and that the God who created this vast universe deigns to call Himself our personal Shepherd and invites us to consider ourselves His sheep. We are the special object of His love and affection. So even though I am only a tiny speck on a tiny ball called Earth, the creator God is my shepherd, my caregiver.

Regardless of how we interpret Psalm 23, the general picture is quite clear. The Lord is with us. This Psalm assures us that the Lord is with us.

This revered Shepherd's Psalm presents a faith that is rooted in trust. He leads me beside the still waters; He restores my soul; He leads me in the paths of righteousness. Like sheep that have faith in the good shepherd, our security is grounded in the goodness and mercy of God. The flow of the Psalm guides us each step of the way to a higher and higher plateau of trust. We move through the glen where we discover the inner joy of existence, through the gorge where we experience peace even in the midst of death, and finally toward the elevated peak of glory.

At each plateau we are led by the loving Shepherd, Jesus. The Good Shepherd guides us from the glen, through the gorge, and toward the glory.

Moffat's translation of verse 3 says: "My road may run through a glen of gloom, but I fear no harm for Thou art beside me."

> *. . . crisis and tragedy serve an important function in our lives. They bring us back to the recognition of our limits and mortality.*

The sheep of Israel are easily frightened in the glen of gloom and may scamper toward higher ground that could lead to a precipice. The good shepherd prevents such an escape by careful guidance. Sooner or later, we all pass through the glen. There is no detour around. Death is only one of many generators of grief. Separation, divorce, moving, loss of employment, aging, sudden or ongoing serious illness of a parent, and changes in our own health – all of these expressions of change or separation lead us into phases of grief.

Crisis situations are always good times for thinking about God. Perhaps, given the way we are, crisis and tragedy serve an important function in our lives. They bring us back to the recognition of our limits and mortality. When we have no shepherd to guide us, when we are in the glen of gloom, we are easily lost in the wilderness. It is Jesus, the Good Shepherd, who can guide us to paths of righteousness that we may be restored by the still waters.

The mother of five-year-old Angie Harris tells about their pediatric neurologist diagnosing her daughter's brain tumor as inoperable.[17] She tells of all their prayers, "O God, please make Angie well

---

[17] *Guideposts*, April 1997

again." She said that Angie was pure sweetness, goodness, pure innocence. She felt if this could happen to Angie, nothing made sense anymore; nothing felt safe or sure – not even God.

She said she thought, "God, how could this happen to Angie? I've been so careful with her. I've been a good mother. God, how could You abandon us this way?' Little Angie had begun chemotherapy in January just before her fifth birthday. They had a party for her with balloons, birthday cake, and numerous friends. But her condition continued to deteriorate, gradually causing her to lose the use of her limbs.

Mrs. Harris said her faith wavered. Where was God in all this? Mrs. Harris said that as much as her faith wavered, she somehow believed that in heaven Angie would be healed, safe, and whole again. She clung to that tiny thread of faith and made one more appeal to God, praying that the Lord would help her comfort Angie.

That night as she tucked Angie in bed, Angie asked her mother to read the story of the *Runaway Bunny* again. The mother tells how one of Angie's favorite stories was "the bunny book" about a runaway bunny. So she read to Angie the familiar story of the spirited bunny who tells his mother he is going to run away. The mother bunny says that she will run away with him. The little bunny tells the mother that he will become a fish in a stream, and the mother tells him that in this case she will also become a fish in the stream. Whatever the little bunny decides to disguise himself as, the mother bunny steadfastly assures the little bunny that she will be with him.

In the midst of the story about the bunny and his mother, Angie brought up the subject of death. She said to her mother, "Mother, when I die, will you die also?" With her heart racing, Mrs. Harris took Angie's hand and finally knew what to say. She said, "A part of me will die when you die, Angie; and the part of me that you need will go with you wherever you go." And Mrs. Harris said to Angie, "You remember, the same as in the story, no matter where the bunny went, his mama followed him." Then little five-year-old

Angie spoke of her death with more courage than the bravest of men or women could display. And when she asked about heaven, Mrs. Harris told her that in heaven she believed Angie would walk and run and dance again.

Mrs. Harris said that over the months she had cried, "O God, where are You in all this?" At that moment, she said, she finally knew where God was. God was with Angie, giving Angie the strength and courage she needed, and He was also with Mrs. Harris giving her the words her daughter needed to hear.

Catherine Marshall tells a similar story of a Mrs. McDonald who lost her only child, a son, when he was fifteen years of age. When her son asked her one day, "Mama, how does it feel to die?" she ran to the kitchen to "check on something on the stove," praying, "O God, tell me what to tell my child." She came back to her son and said, "Kenneth, remember how you used to play so hard and be so tired some nights that you would go to sleep in our bed and be surprised the next morning when you woke up in your own bed? This was because your daddy would, with his strong arms, come in the night and carefully pick you up and carry you to your own room. This is what it is to die. We go to sleep down here in a room that is not our own; and our father God, with His gentle and strong arms comes and carries us to our own special room."

It seems to be true that God becomes most real when we see that life as we know it in this world is not forever!

She said that after this, Kenneth never feared death, and even though the Lord did not give them the gift of healing, the Lord gave them an even better gift, which is the gift of God's self. As much as we pray for and often get a gift of healing, physical healing is always temporary. The greatest gift of all is the gift of salvation, the gift of the Giver of eternal life through Jesus Christ our Blessed Savior.

This amazing Psalm 23 presents the human condition of pain, loneliness and death. We are all terminal; yet the Psalm declares God as protector and affirms tranquility even amid the harsh realities of a fallen world. It seems to be true that God becomes most real when we see that life as we know it in this world is not forever! It seems to be natural for us not to think very much about God when things are going smoothly and easily for us. But when we think our days are limited, we get a different perspective.

I remember going to the hospital emergency room one Saturday night with severe stomach cramps when I was pastor of East Point Avenue Church.[18] The diagnosis was finally diverticulitis. I have learned that if I watch my diet and drink plenty of water, it doesn't bother me much. Many of you know that in the emergency room you sit a long time. They check your vital signs, and if there are no signs of immediate demise, you sit awhile. I was there all night. That was somewhat encouraging – at least I knew that they thought I was not in immediate danger. I kept thinking that if I did not feel any better by morning, I would come home and call the district superintendent for someone to preach for me at the church.

However, toward morning, they checked my blood and then checked it again. They decided that the blood count was very low and wanted me to check into the hospital. I told them I was feeling better and needed to get home to get ready to go to church. They finally agreed telling me to go to my doctor the next day.

I picked up on their concern for my low white blood count because my brother, Bill Baird, had died a year earlier with leukemia. So I drove home and got ready for church thinking my diagnosis was probably leukemia and perhaps I only had a few months to live. So I did some extra praying and did not call anyone to preach for me since it was already Sunday morning, and I was sure the Lord, who called me, wanted me to preach that morning.

---

[18]I served as Pastor of East Point Avenue Church in East Point, Georgia for 4 years - June 1993 to June 1997.

I am glad it didn't work out for me to have leukemia and go out as rapidly as my brother Bill did in 1993; but we all need to somehow learn to face death. As the 23rd Psalm tells us, "Yea, thou I walk through the valley of the shadow of death, I will fear no evil. For thou, O Lord, art with me. Thy rod of power and thy staff of mercy shall comfort me."

In the play, *Shenandoah*, I loved the song, "Papa's Gonna Make It Alright," and loved hearing my son, Terrell, sing it in his beautiful tenor voice. But there comes a time when Papa cannot make it alright. We, as parents, try with all within our power to make it alright for our children, but there comes a time even the most loving of papas and mamas stand helpless at bedsides or before tragedies. Even the finest of doctors and nurses come to the end of their knowledge and power, and we are left in the hands of God.

I sat in the room with my brother, Tom, after he had died, holding his hand and stroking his brow for nearly 30 minutes before his wife and daughter could get there.[19] They had left just an hour earlier thinking Tom was better. I asked the nurses and doctor what they did when my dear brother suddenly took a turn for the worse. They said that they massaged his heart and did all medical science could do.

Loving wives and daughters, sisters and brothers, fathers and mothers can only go so far. Medical science can do only so much. Then we are left to the mercy of God. How wonderful that our God is a God of love and mercy and absolute power!

We are gathered here today in this place of worship and around our Book of Faith - the Holy Bible - because we know that our God is a God of love, boundless forgiveness, and absolute power. We know that when our dearest loved ones and our most-efficient medical personnel have done all they can do, the Lord will carry us all the way home.

---

[19]Hospital is in Rome, GA where I have lived since December 1997. My brother Tom and his wife lived in Cedartown, twenty miles from hospital. We gave the nurse my number to call in emergency.

The closing verse of psalm 23 affirms that goodness and mercy - like faithful sheep dogs following the sheep, like protective secret-service agents following a head of state – goodness and mercy shall follow us closely all the way home. Amen.

Don't be Afraid of Christmas

Luke 2:8-11

For there is born to you this day in the city of David a Savior, who is Christ the Lord.
~Luke 2: 11 (NKJV)~

I read an interesting story recently about a lady who suddenly realized it was only a few days before Christmas and she still had not bought Christmas cards. So she hurried down to the nearest store. Most of the cards were already sold, but she located a box depicting a nice Bethlehem scene and bought them immediately. She hurried home, addressed the cards to family and friends, stamped them and rushed to the nearest mailbox, congratulating herself on having completed the task in one day.

While she was relaxing, she glanced over and picked up the one remaining card in the box and realized in all the rush she had not taken time to read the card. To her unexpected horror, the card read, "This simple note is sent to say…a little gift is on its way."

This story is amusing because we recognize this is not the sentiment this lady intended to convey.

> *This first Sunday of Advent is to remind us*
> *that God's gift of love is on its way.*

But this is the message of Advent. This first Sunday of Advent is to remind us that God's gift of love is on its way. Every Christmas we celebrate the historical event of the birth of Jesus Christ, and we "re-en-act" it during the Advent season. The heart of Christmas is God's gift to the world. God has sent and is sending his Gift of amazing grace through Jesus Christ to all who will receive.

In Luke 2 we read: "And the glory of the Lord shone round about them and they were sore afraid (greatly afraid) and the angel said unto them, 'Fear not, for behold I bring you good tidings of great joy, which shall be to all people.'"

This birth account of Jesus tells us the "glory of the Lord shone all around them," and we might expect the next words to be, "They rejoiced." We might expect the next words to be, "They were filled with great joy." We would think they would surely be filled with great thanksgiving to have the glory of the Lord shining all around them - not just Christmas lights shining - not just lighted Christmas trees - not just beautiful advent candles, but the glory of the Lord shining bright!

But the scripture does not say, "The glory of the Lord shone all around them and they rejoiced and shouted praises to God." Verse 9 tells us that "They were greatly afraid." They were afraid of the glory. They were afraid of this Christmas revelation. The NIV tells us, "the glory of the Lord shone around them and they were terrified." Terrified! How often we are afraid of new discoveries - new knowledge.

When I was in grade school, we learned that the smallest possible particle of matter was the atom. Then a few years later, in 1945, we were shocked to learn that this smallest particle - this microscopic atom - could actually be split, and that inside this smallest particle - this atom - is power beyond human comprehension. The power in one atom bomb can destroy whole cities. We react to this knowledge with fear.

We all know how easy it is to become fearful or to become depressed. Just last week I was told about a young man who committed suicide. The person who told me said that this young man was depressed and added, "You know many people get depressed during the holidays." During a season that has the theme "Joy to the world, the Lord is come," why do we get depressed? I find it so interesting that God has told us, "Don't be afraid," three hundred and sixty-five times in the Bible! That is one time for every day in the year!

James Wall (of *Christian Century*) wrote, "Is Secular Christmas Drowning the Religious?" He said, "Two Christmases travel on parallel tracks, but offer dramatically different perspectives. The secular Christmas never acknowledges a basic contradiction in its approach because no gift ever delivers what we long for because what we long for is a connection to the eternal."

This connection to the eternal is something no train set or bicycle or diamond bracelet or houseboat or new house can provide.

We keep wishing each other a merry Christmas; yet we can't quite pull it off. All the partying, all the gifts do not work. And like children who are crying from too many sweets, too much excitement, or not being able to open all the gifts at once, we are frustrated and we do not quite know why.

We still have that God-shaped void in our lives that no amount of holiday activity can fill. As Augustine put it, "Our hearts were made for Thee, O God, and they are restless until they find their rest in Thee." The celebration of a religious event for secular purposes is bound to leave the human spirit unsatisfied.

Nevertheless, society works energetically to uphold the secular Christmas and crowd out the religious version. A recent article entitled "Beating the Blue, Blue Christmas" points out that some of the frustration that makes us think or say, "I'll be glad when it's over" is from being burned out by the over-commercialization of the season. We are led to believe that we should feel more of a sense of fulfillment, joy and family harmony, and that leaves us disappointed.

I did not watch the *Brady Bunch* series when it was on TV, but I did see the Christmas reunion show a few years later when the father was trapped in a building that collapsed. The Brady family was distraught. Then the younger daughter remembered the year when their mother was sick and she said, "Remember we asked Santa Claus to let mother get well enough to sing at the Christmas service." So they asked Santa Claus to get their daddy safely out of the building.

Although they sang Christmas carols praising the newborn king, they were praying to Santa Claus. I don't know who wrote the silly script, but they could not even bring themselves to say the word, "God" or make the program "religious." They were afraid of the Glory of Christmas - afraid of the Christ Mass.

The word that God loved us enough to become human is so beyond the secular mindset that it must be greeted with an all-out defense of the secular version of honor, goodness and truth.

Madeleine L'Engle[20] called Christmas "the irrational season."

This is the irrational season, when love blooms bright and wild.
Had Mary been filled with reason, there'd have been no room for the child.

The Christmas truth invites us to a kind of irrationality - an irrationality that is not against reason, but beyond reason. The truth is, in responding to the mystery of God's historic revelation in Jesus Christ, we either accept the gift and stand in awe that God loves us, or we vigorously deny even the possibility that God could love us enough to come down to us."

The sad truth is that our increasingly secular society has pushed Christianity so far into the background that nearly everything but Christianity is permitted.

Who would have believed just a few years ago that we would see the tragic drug problem and damaging and life-destroying multi-billion pornography and alcohol problems even in our elementary schools?

Who would have believed a few years ago we would see the ACLU seeking to legalize the "Man Boy Love Association"? Who would have believed we could now have a large number of grandparents raising their grandchildren because of the widespread alcohol and drug addiction of young mothers?

---

[20] Madeline L'Engle is the popular author of many books for children and adults.

In the birth of our nation, we have some wonderful words that came with our Christian roots. "We hold these truths to be self-evident, that all men are created equal, that they are endowed by their Creator with certain unalienable Rights."

These unalienable rights come from our Creator. Our forebears - my parents and many of your parents - in their acceptance of this Christ of Christmas, learned that we are "endowed." And it was like finding buried treasure: We may be "poor as church mice," but we have an endowment.

God came down at Christmas to endow us. An endowment (an inheritance) is better than any material Christmas gift (gold, diamonds, new car, houses or land) we could ever receive. Do not be afraid of the Gift. Accept Jesus Christ as your Savior, your inheritance from a God of love.

In the history of humanity's struggle to be free, our American Bill of Rights is unprecedented. The concept of freedom and justice for all came from the Bible. Even our due process tradition of presumed innocence came from that Christ Child of Christmas that the ACLU works to keep off our Court house lawns or in any public place.

Captain Gerald Coffee was taken prisoner during the Vietnam War. On Christmas 1968, his third year as a POW, the Vietnamese unexpectedly distributed candy bars to the prisoners - 3 pieces of candy each. The candy bars were wrapped with foil, red on one side and silver on the other.

Coffee took the wrappers and flattened them and began to fold them. The first wrapper he folded into a swan, the second one he folded into a rosette. He said he lay there alone in his cell, and he heard the guards outside his window laughing and talking as they celebrated the holiday. He heard a little boy, the son of one of the guards playing with a toy truck. It reminded him of how he missed his own sons.

He took his last candy wrapper and began to fold it - not sure what it would be. It ended up as a star, and he thought - the star of Bethlehem. He then took three straws from the broom in his cell and attached the ornaments to the straws and stuck them in cracks in the cell wall. He sat there watching them in the light of the yellow light bulb that always hung in his cell. He sat there thinking about the simplicity of Christ's birth and what it had meant to his own life. He said he realized anew that it was his faith in Christ that had sustained him during those long years as a prisoner of war.

Captain Coffee wrote: "Here there is nothing to distract me from the awesomeness of Christmas. No commercialism. No presents. Little food. I was beginning to appreciate my own spirituality because I had been stripped of everything by which I measured my identity - rank, uniform, money, family." Yet he continued to find strength within and realized, although he was hurting and lonely and afraid, that night just might be the most significant Christmas of his life.

I was pastor of East Point Avenue United Methodist Church in Atlanta for four years. Every Christmas our church bought poinsettias to give to each shut-in. I delivered many of them each year. When I would visit one special couple in the church, both bedridden, her mind started working about what I could hand her, take away or do while I was there. Of course, I was more than glad to help her out.

The day I took the poinsettias, I had done several little chores - brought in their mail, taken her to the bathroom, got fresh water for both of them and a warm wet wash cloth. When I started to leave, I was painfully aware of their frightful situation. They were each on one of the twin beds in their bedroom in their small house. I knelt down between the two beds and took one of each of their hands to pray for them.

She spoke for both of them and said, "I told John this morning that we are so much better off than many people, and best of all, the Lord is with us."

Those words "the best of all, God is with us" are said to have been the last words spoken by John Wesley.

> *Our Merry Christmas is not dependent on what is happening around us or to us but on what has happened inside us.*

And I remembered all over again - Christmas tidings of great joy that replaces fear in our lives does not come from escaping reality or being protected from the shocks of life, but from looking life squarely in the face and seeing the countenance of God. Our Merry Christmas is not dependent on what is happening around us or to us but what has happened inside us.

My husband preached his last sermon on the first Sunday in Advent in 1986. All I wanted for Christmas that year was to hear Handel's *Messiah* sung by a church choir! I looked in the newspaper but could not find that any of the College Park or South Fulton church choirs had planned it. Then on Sunday night before Christmas I turned on the television just as the Atlanta Symphony with Robert Shaw directing was being televised. I sat down to listen to Handel's *Messiah*. It was wonderful, and when they got to the "Hallelujah Chorus", although I am not a musician, I stood to my feet and sang with the best soprano voice I have ever used - "For the Lord God Omnipotent reigneth. Hallelujah!"

In spite of any disappointment, sickness, grief or fear that clouds our eyes from seeing clearly the beautiful and the true, the message of this first Sunday and all of Advent and Christmas is like the North Star, that gives us direction under all circumstances. The Light of Christmas is still shinning in the darkness; and the darkness will never be able to put it out! Amen.

Christmas Means God Loves Us

Luke 2:1-7

And she brought forth her firstborn Son, and wrapped Him in swaddling clothes, and laid Him in a manger, because there was no room for them in the inn.
~Luke 2:7 (NKJV)~

"Christmas Means God Loves Us" is a thought that often gets lost in the Christmas rush. Some of us complain about people refusing to celebrate Christmas or to even say the words "Merry Christmas" in schools and/or public places for fear of offending people of other religions or of no religion.

But the truth is, many of us celebrate Christmas more and more as a "holiday" and less as a Holy Day and a Christ Mass.

One of Norman Rockwell's *Saturday Evening Post* illustrations a few years ago pictured a sales girl in one of the department stores. The date on the calendar is December 24. The clock points to 5 minutes after 5 P.M. The lady is slumped over a pile of toys. Her hair is down in her eyes. Her eyes are rolled back in her head. She has just made it through another great American commercial Christmas.

This was a popular Rockwell painting because most of us know a little about how she feels. We get tired with making lists and checking them twice. We get very tired of all the Christmas rush. Looking around, we hear, "I'll be glad when it's over" or "All I want for Christmas is two more weeks to prepare. "

In our country we start advertising Christmas before Halloween. Some of us go on a giant shopping spree. Most businesses of trade say that if they do not make it financially at Christmas, they have to get out of business.

Many of us preachers feel that if we cannot tell the story of God's gift of Jesus to the world at Christmas, we might as well stop trying. But the activities of what we call "Christmas" cause some to stay home from church. But the activities of what we call "Christmas" cause some to stay home from church and miss hearing the glorious and true message of Christmas.

A British missionary to Tibet was a captive of Chinese communism for 3 years. He tells of an experience on December 24. He had spent a long tiring day crossing a mountain pass and stumbling down the other side in heavy winds. His captors brought him to a group of houses late in the afternoon. He was given a meal and then ordered to go downstairs to give hay to the horses. Going down the stairs meant climbing down a notched tree trunk to the lower floor which was given over to stabling the animals. It was dark. The missionary said his boots squished in the mature and straw on the floor, and the putrid smell of the animals was nauseating. He felt his way among the mules and horses expecting at any moment to be kicked.

As he groped his way in the darkness, he suddenly remembered that it was Christmas Eve. For a moment he stood still in that oriental manger and thought about the first Christmas.

He thought about Jesus coming all the way from heaven to some wretched Eastern stable. And he said to himself, "Just think he came for me." Christmas means God loves us. He came to earth to be born in a smelly stable, not like the olive wood Nativity scene we bought in Bethlehem to display on a table in our living room. Not like the collection of small Nativities we display on a bookcase.

Because God loves us, he came to earth to die on a bloody cross. Not the kind of gold cross I wear around my neck or the cross we display on the altar in church.

Verse 7 in Luke 2 tells us, "She brought forth her firstborn son and wrapped him in swaddling clothes and laid him in a manger." Some of us have heard the story all our lives. I memorized it from both Luke and from Matthew long ago as a child.

We know the story, but do we have any idea of what it means? We just take little bits and pieces of it and hear it preached if we happen to get to church a few Sundays of the year. Many of us do not get to all four services of Advent and when we do, we are sometimes thinking of all the things we have to do to celebrate the "holidays."

Today let us take a few minutes to bend over the manger of Bethlehem and take a look at the helpless nursing baby Jesus - count the fingers and the toes - as we try to understand that Christmas means God loves us.

We behold in a smelly cradle, Christ the king of the universe unable to hold his head up without assistance from human beings. This is what God decided to be because "God so loved the world that he gave his only begotten son that whosoever believes in him should not perish but have everlasting life" (John 3:16).

> *The history of our love relationship with God is pretty one-sided.*

The history of our love relationship with God is pretty one-sided. Sad to say, it is the repeated story of our sin and God's forgiveness.

Have you even seen a couple or a parent and child and you feel like all the love and concessions are on one side? One gives and gives and gives. The other one takes and takes and takes.

Counselors advise us to break that cycle with "tough love." Tough love is a love that will not stand back and enable the loved one to drink or drug himself/herself to death. The term is "intervention." The term was used when the family of Betty Ford got together and confronted her with the fact that she was drugging herself to death. They intervened.

Let me paint this picture for you. Here is the Savior, the one whom John called "the Word." That is to say the very heart and mind of God; the Bible tells us "God in human flesh." Look at the stable. Not as we like to see it through the eyes of medieval artists whose colors made angels and shepherds and the wise men from the east glitter with glory but like the missionary prisoner did that Christmas

Eve, as he waded in smelly compost in an Eastern stable. See a young woman giving birth to her son. See the young family becoming refugees in Egypt to escape the wrath of King Herod. All of this and more is involved when we talk about God becoming man and of God loving us enough to intervene on our behalf. He wants us to know the joy of abundant and everlasting life.

When love came down at Christmas, God met humanity's most basic need - the need for love. This love of God facilitates human love. Statistics show that men and women who truly love God can find love with one another better and more lasting.

We are without excuse. The Christ who saved me will save anyone as soon as he or she gets tired of being lost and decides to turn to Christ.

A doctor told the story of a young woman who had surgery on her face to remove a malignancy. A nerve had to be cut that caused her mouth to be disfigured in a kind of impish way. The doctor was there to remove the bandages. The young woman was sad when she looked in the mirror and saw her lips twisted in such a pitiful way. Her husband was standing nearby and smiled at her and said, as he bent over to kiss her "I think it is kinda cute." The doctor said he was standing near enough to see how the young husband twisted his own lips to accommodate her lips - to show her that their kiss still worked.

Christmas means God loves us. Jesus loves us so much he not only came down to become one of us, he was twisted on a cross to save us and to bring us back to God. Not a saccharine kind of love that just parrots the right words, but tough love, agape love that fills our lives with joy and helps us to grow in Grace. Amazing grace!

He came all the way down from the throne of glory to save us. Christmas means God loves us! Amen.

You're Nobody 'til Somebody Loves You

I John 3:1-7

Behold what manner of love the Father has bestowed on us, that we should be called children of God! Therefore the world does not know us, because it did not know Him. Beloved, now we are children of God; and it has not yet been revealed what we shall be, but we know that when He is revealed, we shall be like Him, for we shall see Him as He is. And everyone who has this hope in Him purifies himself, just as He is pure.
~I John 3:1-3 (NKJV)~

On the bulletin board over the copy machine in our work room at East Point Avenue Church, someone put a poster with a little ragamuffin boy saying, "I know I am somebody 'cause God don't make no junk." This is the very truth of God! God don't make no junk. We are somebody because God loves us! We are made in the image of God, and God Himself breathed into us the breath of life. The Bible tells us we are made in the image of God. In fact, we are told we are somebody so important that God's own son, Jesus the Christ, died for us.

Nevertheless, in times of trouble, it is sometimes easy to forget our divine inheritance and to feel pretty low. There is an old romantic love song that begins, "You're nobody 'til somebody loves you. You're nobody 'til somebody cares." I do not remember any other words of the song, but, in a world of couples, sometimes individuals feel as forlorn as the words of this song suggest.

A man, whose wife of 53 years had died, said, "Oh, if I could have only died with her. I don't have anything to live for anymore."

A young woman named Sarah, in the throes of divorce - which was the last thing in the world she ever expected to happen to her – said, "It's a living death. I wish I could just curl up and die."

An older woman who was going through cancer surgery and painful therapy said, "Life isn't worth living. I am just about as low as I can get. Will I ever be myself again?"

Sooner or later, most of us go through times when we feel like we are at "the end of our rope," so to speak, and the end of our hope. Coming to the end of our rope is not always a negative thing. It is sometimes positive.

Paul frequently said, "In my weakness, I am strong." Paul tells us that often we are strengthened to the degree that we are aware of our weaknesses.

I can assure you, if I ever stepped up in this Holy place, feeling that I had it altogether without dependence on the Lord, I would quickly know how weak I am. My constant prayer is, "Lord, I cannot do this except as I am enabled by You."

Even when starting out to visit in hospitals and nurse care places, I know my need to take time to pray that the Lord would guide me into praying and saying His will and blessings to those with whom I would minister.

Knowing our own limitations is important. Putting ourselves into the hands of God is important. Knowing how much the Lord loves us is important. Knowing how much the Lord wants to make us strong and effective is important.

This is not to say that God sends these life threatening experiences. I remember visiting an older man in the hospital - a successful business man - who told me, "I had to get flat on my back before I could look up and see God! "

God does not necessarily put us on our backs. We bring some of our problems on ourselves by habits and lifestyles we know are harmful. Other things we may do or fail to do because we do not know better. We all make mistakes and are sometimes the victims of the mistakes of others. We are living in a fallen, a "full of sin," world. There is Scripture that indicates that it is not God but the Evil One who sends sickness and disease.

But God can also use the difficult places to mediate his saving grace. The Psalmist said, "Before I was afflicted, I went astray." It is indeed easier to look up when we are flat on our backs.

So regardless of our present situation, whether we have some other person who loves us or not, God loves us and has offered to come into our lives with all the blessings we need for joy unspeakable in this life and the next.

Today's passage of scripture is a message of hope for the hopeful and hope for the hopeless. It is a message of love for the loved and love for the loveless!

Just reading the first verse is hope set to music: "Think how much the Father loves us? He loves us so much that He lets us be called His children." One translation tells us, "He lavished His love on us so that we can be called the children of God." The good news is that we can be birthed by God. He labored on the cross to re-birth us as his children.

> *Easter . . . is the amazing good news of what this Savior can mean to us in the nitty gritty circumstances of everyday life.*

Easter, then, is the amazing good news of a risen Savior and more. It is the amazing good news of what this Savior can mean to us in the nitty gritty circumstances of everyday life. And this is where his good news really becomes meaningful - on a sick bed, in a funeral home, at the police station, in a prison, in places beyond our control and sometimes beyond our understanding.

Someone has said, "Our gospel of Jesus Christ does not leave us on a dark and lonely hilltop called Mount Calvary but in the sunlight of Easter Morning.

The message of the Cross and Resurrection is that we do not have to be "drug down" by sin and despair. We do not have to continue in addictions. We can be lifted out of the miry clay of despair.

A few years ago, a lady told me she read my "butterfly poem" every morning, It is a little poem about being lifted above negative circumstances:

Life with Wings

God made the butterfly
and I
stand on earth
and watch it fly.
And see that God
has fashioned wings
For even earthbound,
creeping things.

I'm sure that God
intended wings
for you
and me.
Oh, my heart sings.
I've found my wings
and even I
Can over circumstances
fly!

~Ruth Baird Shaw~

Our scripture lesson for this third Sunday of Easter is that the resurrection of Jesus is the antidote to the despair and confusion in our lives because it puts us in touch with our true identity. We are somebody! We are the children of God!

In the book of Acts, Doctor Luke begins by summarizing his book of Luke as "an account of all that Jesus began to do and to teach." He then tells his readers in Acts that the risen Christ is still at work. Luke wants us to know that the great love that God has lavished on us is still at work but now in a different form.

The book of Luke is the Acts of Jesus and the book of Acts is the Acts of the Holy Spirit. All that Jesus began to do in the books of

Matthew, Mark, Luke and John, he continued to do in the book of Acts and in an even greater form in the abiding presence of the Holy Spirit.

In the last recorded words of Jesus (Acts 1:8) Jesus himself lays out the plan. He tells us, "You will receive power when the Holy Spirit comes on you, and you will be my witnesses in Jerusalem, in all Judea and Samaria and to the ends of the earth."

The book of Acts faithfully follows this outline. The first seven chapters show the church in Jerusalem. The next five chapters focus on Judea and Samaria. The rest of the book of Acts follows the spread of the gospel to the outposts of Roman civilization.

Peter, who had been a coward who denied Jesus when the going got rough, after his experience with the resurrected Jesus, became a tireless and powerful witness. But Peter also had a certain humility because he knew where the power was, and he knew the power was not in Peter but in Jesus! It is Jesus who brings newness and wholeness to our lives.

I often say, "The most important event of the week is what happens in church on Sundays when we gather around the Bible for a word from God." The reason we are not always aware of this truth is that sometimes we are sowing seed that will bear fruit later. Sometimes this truth is readily available but is taken for granted.

We hear a lot of talk these days about the "dumbing down of education." We are also dumbing down Christianity. We are taking the power out of it because we are not willing to repent.

Jesus tells the story of the simple Publican and the proud Pharisee. The Publican was so humble he could not lift his eyes but bowed low saying, "God be merciful to me, a sinner." Jesus said the Publican went out of the temple justified while the proud Pharisees went out the same way he came in.

Easter opens new doors with its hope to bring new life to those who were "dead in their sins."

I started off this message by telling about people who had lost a spouse through death or divorce or who had lost a body part or who were learning that, as we grow older, life can be a series of losses. I was invited to teach a seminar on "Handling Grief's Tentacles" a few years ago, and I learned as much as I taught. Our grief reaches out even beyond the loss of lifelong friends and family members, the loss of youth, loss of looks, loss of strength, and on until finally the loss of physical life itself.

And Easter comes to us in the midst of this reality telling us that loss is gain. Paul says over and over in one way or another, "For me to live is Christ and to die is gain." (Philippians 1:21)

> *Jesus did not go to the cross for us to continue in our sins but for us to have new life and life eternal.*

I had a friend whose son went through a bad stage, and the mother told him, "I didn't bring you in the world for you to throw your life away." This is the message of God in our text from the pen of John. God did not call us His children for us to drag through life as orphans and strangers. Jesus did not go to the cross for us to continue in our sins but for us to have new life and life eternal.

When I was the pastor in Grantville, we finally got some young couples in our church. One of these young mothers and I got the idea of starting a "Mom's Morning Out" program for the young mothers in the congregation. This called for some research and guidelines. One of the things we had to do in preparation was to learn CPR (cardio pulmonary resuscitation) for children. A nurse came out to teach us how to get down on the floor and breathe into the child's lungs and pound on his/her chest in case of an emergency that might require it. We had life size dolls to practice on. Blessedly, we did not have such an emergency that required CPR.

The message of the resurrection is that we who are weak and

discouraged and drowning in sin and despair can be resuscitated, renewed, re-birthed.   We do not have to continue in our old sins. We can be re-birthed into a new life as God's children. John tells us, "See what love the Lord has lavished upon us to bring us to new life as children of God." Amen.

A Long Line of Love

Ruth 1: 1-22

But Ruth said: "Entreat me not to leave you or to turn back from following after you; For wherever you go, I will go; and wherever you lodge, I will lodge. Your people shall be my people. And your God, my God."
~Ruth 1:16 (NKJV)~

Some of you may remember the once popular county music song entitled, "A Long Line of Love." It tells about a young man who is getting married. His sweetheart asks if he thinks they can stay in love and stay married, and he answers her by telling her "yes" and adding, "I come from a long line of love." The young man goes on to talk about his parents' marriage and his grandparents' marriage, and at the end of each refrain he sings "Forever is in my heart and in my blood. I come from a long line of love."

I saw a great example of "A Long Line of Love" recently when I attended a gathering for retired pastors, wives and widows at Simpsonwood in North Atlanta. The first day one of the pastors and his wife came with flowers celebrating their golden anniversary.

This caught the attention of the woman who was in charge of the meeting. Then we learned that most of the couples attending had been married 50 years or more! All the couples got together for a group picture. It took a wide lens camera to snap a picture of that long line of love and marriage! A fifty-year marriage is especially good news in our day when nearly half of all marriages end in divorce.

The book of Ruth in the Bible is only four chapters long. It begins with a man named Elimelech, his wife Naomi, and their two sons, Mahlon and Chilion. A famine swept through their land so Elimelech and Naomi packed up and moved to the land of Moab.

In Moab, both sons grew up and married women from Moab. Elimelech died, so Naomi was a widow. Then, sadly, both of the sons, Mahlon and Chilion died. Naomi was grief stricken because she had lost her husband and sons, and she was also disturbed because there was no opportunity for women alone in those days, and especially in a foreign country. So Naomi decided the only hope for her and her daughters-in-law was to return to Bethlehem to try to find some place among her relatives in her hometown.

Naomi and her two widowed daughters-in-law, Orpah and Ruth, started out for the land of Judah. Soon Naomi realized, as much as she and her daughters-in-laws loved one other, the younger women would be better off with their own kinsmen.

Orpah finally agreed to stay in Moab, but Ruth chose to go with Naomi. We read Ruth's beautiful reply in verse 16 - a passage often quoted at weddings: "Entreat me not to leave you or to turn back from following after you. For wherever you go, I will go; and wherever you lodge, I will lodge. Your people shall be my people. And your God, my God."[21]

This was the turning point in Ruth's life, and Ruth was brought to it along a path of disappointment, suffering and grief.

There is a saying, "When you're at the end of your tether, remember that God is at the other end." Ruth's loyalty to Naomi was shown to have its roots in her loyalty to Naomi's God. At the end of verse 16 she said, "Your God shall be my God." Ruth placed her pain and grief within the structure of God's sovereignty and learned that faith can cope with the uncertainties of life. For God is the God of covenant, love and faithfulness.

So Naomi and Ruth walked from Moab to Bethlehem. We do not know how long it took, but when they arrived, Naomi's old friends came out to greet her happily saying, "Naomi is back home!" However, Naomi told her old friends that she was no longer Naomi but was now "Mara" which means bitter. She told them about her affliction and misfortune in the death of her husband and both sons.

---

[21] Ruth 1:16

Naomi and Ruth arrived in Bethlehem at "barley harvest" time. Ruth took a job and worked long hours in the grain fields and each day brought grain home for her mother-in-law. Their desperate situation was soon to change because Ruth was working in the field belonging to Boaz. Boaz was a powerful land owner and, more importantly, from the same clan of Elimelech. Even more importantly, Boaz was also a kinsman-redeemer.

I read a little about what a kinsman-redeemer does and learned it is another great thing about our Judeo-Christian heritage! A kinsman-redeemer is a man who is responsible for protecting the interests of members of his extended family who are in need of help.

When Naomi learned the Lord had lead Ruth to the fields of Boaz, who might serve as their kinsman–redeemer, she was greatly encouraged!

In Charles' and my early days and in days of decision making, Charles would often say, "The Lord is still on the throne." Naomi, who felt like a bitter Mara, was to learn that the Lord was still on the throne and had not deserted her, which meant God's long arms of love were at work. This did not mean Naomi was to sit down and do nothing. Instead, she was to listen and seek God's guidance and blessing.

In the 3rd chapter of Ruth, we find Naomi instructing Ruth about how she was to go down to the threshing floor when Boaz was there and let him know she was available for marriage. Ruth listened carefully and followed Naomi's "strange to our ears" instructions.

The bottom line here is that Boaz accepted Ruth's proposal. Boaz told Ruth she was recognized as a woman of character who could marry any of the younger men as all had noticed how Ruth cared for Naomi. So Boaz gladly set about taking care of the details for his marriage to Ruth.

In Ruth's story, we see another example of God's love reaching all the way down to anyone in need, even to a Gentile woman like Ruth, who was not raised in the Jewish faith but was to become the great-grandmother of King David, Israel's greatest king and an ancestor of Jesus!

In October 2010, I got caught up in watching the dramatic rescue of 33 miners from Chile who had been the victims of a mine disaster that cut off their exit to the outside world for 69 days. For the first 17 days it was assumed they were dead. Then it was learned they were alive but had little food and were trapped in one small room, 2000 feet underground surrounded by 700,000 tons of rock - very unstable rock - a frightful, impossible situation.

But on October 14, 2010, the impossible became possible when we saw 33 men pulled up to safety one by one in a bullet shaped, life-sized capsule devised by some of the best minds in the world, working together.

The news media did not make much of it, but most of the men, as they stepped out of the capsule, immediately dropped to their knees in a prayer of thanksgiving! Then most of them turned to their wives. As I watched, I joined them in their tears of pure joy to again be joined in the arms of their wives, then to the arms of other family members and finally to the arms of the President of Chile.

I am not a person to cry easily, but my tears of joy flowed a little more when I realized we were getting a tiny glimpse of what heaven will be like. Just a tiny glimpse of our rescue from the grave to the arms of the special one whom we loved and lost and then to beloved parents who told us about Jesus and then "safe in the arms of Jesus" as one of Fanny Crosby's old hymns tells us.

Probably many of you who watched the rescue of the Chilean miners noticed the tan T-shirt they were wearing. On the left sleeve was the word JESUS. On the front of the shirt and above the Chilean flag were the words "Gracias Senor!" which translates to "Thank You Lord!"

When we hear these words, "A long line of love," we thank God for the long blood line of our family history but also, and more importantly, the long blood line of love that goes all the way back to the cross of Jesus Christ.

It is a historical fact that the Christian faith is the father or the grandfather of almost everything fine in Western Civilization. Take Christianity out as the root, and the fruit will wither and die. The major factor in the amazing progress of civility in Western civilization is this truth. One small example: the first words ever spoken on a telephone recognized God with the words, "What hath *God* wrought?"

There is really no combination of words to express God's love, but "A Long Line of Love" seems a good way to try to express love at its best.

We see God's long line of love acting through Ruth, a gentile - the usual target of rejection by the Jews. It was God, not chance, that determined history's course.

> *The commandment here is really a single commandment: the commandment to love.*

The commandment here is really a single commandment: the commandment to love. John tells us that if we say we love God and hate our neighbors, we are liars and the truth is not in us. For he says, "How can we love God whom we have not seen if we do not love our neighbors whom we have seen." For human beings, love takes on tangible forms. It is about what we do to our neighbor. Its testing comes in specific application. To proclaim, "I love everybody" is easy.

Most of us can identify with Linus in a *Peanuts* cartoon. Lucy was fussing at Linus, telling him that he would never amount to anything because he did not love mankind. Linus was just standing there with his thumb in his mouth and holding on to his security blanket while Lucy fussed. Finally Linus took his thumb out of his mouth and said, "I do love mankind. It's human beings I can't stand."

But when this long line of God's love gets in our hearts and in our blood, we can truly love as God has commanded us. As John reminds us, "If we love one another, people will know that God abides in us and His love is perfected in us."[22]

This long line of love theme goes all the way back to the cross of Jesus Christ. It reaches from that blood-stained cross on down to the deepest need of the last and the least of us. This is true regardless of what kind of love our parents or our grandparents or we had or have. Jesus said, "This is how much I love you." And he "measured" out His love by stretching out his arms on a cross and died for you and for me. We come from a long line of love! Amen.

---

[22] 1 John 4:14

The Communion of Saints

Matthew 26: 17-20, 26-30

And as they were eating, Jesus took bread, blessed and broke it, and gave it to the disciples and said, "Take, eat; this is My body." Then He took the cup, and after giving thanks, gave it to them saying, "Drink from it, all of you. For this is My blood of the new covenant, which is shed for many for the forgiveness of sins. But I say to you, I will not drink of this fruit of the vine from now on until that day when I drink it new with you in My Father's kingdom." And when they had sung a hymn, they went out to the Mount of Olives.
~Matthew 26:26-30 (NRSV)~

The two sacraments in our church, Baptism and Communion, symbolize the entire Gospel of Jesus Christ. Baptism is the beginning of new life in Jesus. We believe and are baptized. Water baptism is a one-time experience.

Holy Communion symbolizes the constant feeding of the soul that has been begotten unto a spiritual life by the power of God.

As in most churches, we celebrate Holy Communion (the Lord's Supper or Eucharist) often - at least once a month. Holy Communion symbolizes the constant feeding of the soul that has been begotten unto a spiritual life by the power of God. The bread and the fruit of the vine indicate spiritual nourishment. As we come to communion, our three "Rs" are to remember, repent and renew.

The early invitation to Communion affirms: "Ye that do truly and earnestly repent of your sins and are in love and charity with your neighbors, and intend to lead a new life, following the commandments of God and walking from henceforth in His holy ways; Draw near with faith, and take this Holy Sacrament to your comfort, and make your humble confession to almighty God."

Life is filed with beginnings and endings. Life is full of all kinds of occasions and celebrations. When Jesus told the disciples at their last meal together, "Do this in remembrance of me," he was saying, in effect, "Keep up this custom. Let the meal of fellowship be a sacred bond between you and all believers and between all believers and God." This is the joy and beauty of the Communion service - Communion with the Eternal God, our Heavenly Father, with Jesus Christ our Savior and communion with one another and with all Christian believers.

I heard a story of a farm boy telling about the time when he came out of his house and heard a commotion in the chicken coop. He ran quickly to find a hen being savagely attacked by a large hawk. As the hawk flew off, the hen collapsed. The boy looked sadly at the dying hen wondering why the hen had not flown to safety in the chicken coop that was only a few feet away. Then suddenly he knew why. Out from under the wings of the hen emerged four little chicks, and on each one was the mark of blood - the blood of the mother hen that had sacrificed herself to save her chicks.

We come to communion, "not weighing our merits," but praying for the "pardoning for our offenses" through Jesus Christ our Lord. When we take the bread and the juice, it is a symbol. But it is more! We are not merely displaying or enacting symbols of remembrance. This is why we speak of the service as "communion." No perfect symbol is merely a symbol.

This is true all through life. We use symbols to represent realities. But they do more than create, they also increase realities. For example, family love needs expression - birthday presents and wedding anniversary celebrations. These symbolic occasions not only express love, they also rekindle and even increase love, preventing love from dying for lack of expression.

Most of us are not willing to be like the man who had been married for twenty years. One day his wife said, "Do you realize you have not told you loved me in twenty years." He looked at her in surprise and said, "I told you I loved you the day we were married. If I ever change my mind, I will let you know."

Love can die from lack of expression. Celebrations expressing the love we have for one another rekindle love. How often men and women have been reminded of their vows to faithfulness by symbols - a ring, a photograph on a desk or in a billfold.

We are to remember who we are. We did not evolve in a dish. We were created in the image of God, and we are so important that Jesus Christ died for us.

In our world where people are sometimes treated like robots and we sometimes act like animals, we need to be reminded that we are made in the image of God. We are to remember God loves us and has a wonderful plan for our total lives.

When we look at this passage of scripture, we must remember that when Jesus said, "This is my body. This is my blood," he was sitting there in his physical body and with blood still running in his veins. In the Communion service, his body is broken for us and his blood of the new covenant is shed for us for the remission of sins. We have a symbol of the crucified and broken body of Christ on the cross.

In the remembering and in the act of caring enough to celebrate, the celebration itself renews our vows. Our covenant rekindles our love, and in the act of Communion, we find the presence of the living Christ.

We need to be aware, also, that the communion service is a link with the church of the past. In the Apostles Creed we affirm, "I believe in the **Communion of the Saints**, the forgiveness of sins, the resurrection of the body and the life everlasting."

This thought about the importance of the **Communion of Saints** first came to me when I was serving as pastor of the East Point Avenue United Methodist Church for four years after I reached mandatory retirement age.

It was the week in our church when we lost a beautiful young wife and mother, Valerie Nabers, to leukemia. It was also the week my nephew, Bobby Baird, died after a brief illness. I believe and thus I wrote: "I believe that when my nephew, Bobby Baird, and our precious Valerie Nabers died, both confessing Christians, when they closed their eyes for the last time here on earth Monday morning, they opened their eyes in the presence of Jesus and their loved ones.

A woman from our congregation, Barbara Chambers, who had known Valerie as a child, stood at Valerie's graveside and said, "I like to think my Daddy (Barbara's Dad had been Valerie's pastor when she was a child) is probably showing Valerie around in heaven right now."

I thought how my father, a witnessing Christian Lay Leader, who died when his grandson, Bobby Baird, was a few weeks old, could very well be showing Bobby around heaven.

My mother told me how, when a newborn Bobby was brought to my father's bedside just days before his death, Papa took Bobby in his arms and said, "You look like you are going to be our preacher." Bobby moved his little hand toward Papa and Papa said, "Oh, so you want to shake on that." Bobby was not a preacher but was a witnessing Christian leader and father. Both Bobby's sons became preachers.

I praise God for the "Communion of the Saints," celebrated in scripture and in our church. For I am aware that on Communion Sunday at Trinity (the church I now attend) I am kneeling at the same altar where my husband knelt as pastor and where many dear Trinity "saints" whom I knew from the past have knelt. So we are not just communing with Christ and with one another but celebrating communion with all Christians of previous generations - our parents, grandparents and many we did not know. We believe in **the Communion of saints**!

The Communion service is also a link with the church universal. We say, "I believe in the holy catholic church." This, of course, does not mean the Roman Catholic Church, although it does include Catholic Christians. What we are saying is that we believe in the holy church, period! We are not communing only with Methodists or Baptists or any other denomination or any single congregation. Holy Communion in the Methodist church is open to all Christians. In Holy Communion, we join in prayer and fellowship with all Christians - some with different understandings of Biblical truth than ours.

In Acts 2:42-47, Luke tells us that "day by day" the early disciples "broke bread in their homes and partook of food with glad and generous hearts, praising God." Some of these meals were the sacrament of Holy Communion, while others were meals together, much like our church suppers today.

This passage is an amazing testimony of the power and grace of the Gospel![23] The early church was composed of both Jews and Gentiles. Not only did Jews and Gentiles not eat together, Jews and Gentiles were sworn enemies who had nothing to do with one another. They lived in separate neighborhoods. They did not even walk on the same side of the street. If a Gentile happened to wander into a Jewish household while a meal was being served, all the food would have to be thrown out. A Gentile's mere presence in the house would make the meal unclean and untouchable.

So when Luke tells us in Acts 2 that members of the early church - Jews and Gentiles - ate together, he is reporting a great wonder! What in the world happened to make this momentous change? In short, Jesus was the reason! Jesus changes our way of looking at one another!

People sometimes ask about what Maundy means in the Maundy Thursday observance of Holy Communion? Maundy comes from the word, "commandment" and is used in recognition of the commandment that Jesus gave his disciples at the Last Supper. Jesus summarized the essence of the law: to love the Lord your God with all your heart, soul, mind and strength and your neighbor as yourselves.

I like to quote G. K. Chesterton's statement that slavery was

---

[23] Acts 2:42-47

defeated when Jesus died, but it took the church a long time to become strong enough to defeat the powerful slave trade.

> *In other words, we first experience the grace of Christian love through the love of Jesus for us, and then we love each other as we are loved.*

The last supper depicted all barriers broken down between Jew and Greek, male and female, slave and free.[24] In other words, we first experience the grace of Christian love through the love of Jesus for us, and then we love each other as we are loved.

Sunshine Camp is a camp for adults with special needs.[25] Most of the campers are age 50 or older. These "special needs adults" are served Holy Communion after the sermon each Sunday. The pastor explains, as simply as possible, what the ritual of Holy Communion means to us as Christians, and all are invited to participate.

One Sunday after the sermon, one of the campers, "Joe," came through the Communion line and told the minister, "I've never been to Communion before, but I love Jesus and I'm hungry."

The minister broke off a larger than normal piece of bread and smiled to himself as Joe dipped the bread in the juice and ate it with a big smile on his face. What the minister did not know was that Joe, instead of going back to his seat, continued around to the back of the church and got in line again. When he got back to the minister, he bent over and said, "That was so good I decided to come back for more."

At lunch, the talk among the counselors was all about Joe taking communion twice! They wondered if some of the campers did not

---

[24] Galatians 3: 28

[25] This story of the Sunshine Camp comes from the Alabama-West Florida Conference of the United Methodist Church. The Sunshine Camp for special needs adults is an Advance Special Ministry.

understand what Communion was about. Should they re-think serving communion at Sunshine Camp in the future? After the discussion, they agreed that people come to Christ in different ways, and they should continue providing the opportunity for all Sunshine campers to participate in the service of Holy Communion.

When Joe was leaving after lunch on Sunday, he gave all of the people hugs and smiles and told them how much he loved Sunshine Camp. Joe died three days later. The pastor writing the story said, "When we received word of Joe's death, we were all sad at the loss but eternally grateful that Joe had come to Sunshine camp and that he had been able to so joyfully receive the sacrament of Holy Communion."

All of us are invited to come to Holy Communion just as we are, and, just as Joe came, "because we love Jesus and we're hungry." Amen.

What Child Is This

Luke 2:41-52

And when Jesus was twelve years old, they went up to Jerusalem according to the custom of the feast.[26]
~Luke 2:42 (NKJV)~

Much has been said about the seven last words of Jesus from the cross. We have as our scripture lesson today the first recorded words of Jesus. Luke lets us know the importance of home and church in the family life of Jesus. We see the home and the temple as formative institutions in Jesus's development.

The Law of Moses was kept at every point: Circumcision on the eighth day, Mary's purification and Jesus's dedication. And in today's lesson in Luke 2, we have the family's pilgrimage to Jerusalem for Passover.

Some people do not understand our church's sacrament of infant baptism. We ask the parents, "Will you keep this child under the ministry and guidance of the church until he or she, by the power of God, shall accept the gift of salvation for himself or herself?"

We baptize babies, to over-simplify, testifying that they are "saved" until they reach the age of accountability. The christening part of the ceremony is when the church names the baby. That is why we refer to our given names as our "Christian names." For example, my Christian name is Sarah Ruth, given to me when I was baptized as an infant.

Sometimes people use infant baptism as merely a christening or naming process – or even a "cute ceremony" or magic formula. And some few rarely take their child back to church, even though they had promised, by precept and example, to keep their children under the ministry of the church so they could accept Jesus as their personal savior for themselves.

---

[26] Feast of the Passover

When we find the syllable "bar" in the scripture, it means "son of." Bartimayus means "Son of Timayous." Bar Mitzvah means "son of Moses" or "son of the law." So in verse 42 we read that Jesus, being at the age of 12 - the age of the Bar Mitzvah, accompanied his parents to Jerusalem for the Passover feast (Luke 2:42).

When Charles and I were in Jerusalem in 1969, one of the most moving things I saw was the bringing of twelve-year-old boys out to the old Jerusalem wall for their Bar Mitzvah ceremony and the opening of the scripture, the law of God, for these young boys to read for themselves.[27]

Jesus lingering behind at the temple is an indirect testimony to the deep faith in the family and the fulfillment of the act of dedicating the child to the Lord earlier in Luke 2:22-23. These verses (22-40) that I read this week and first thought to use today are very moving verses in which the old prophet Simeon came up to Mary and Joseph and took the baby Jesus in his arms and prophesied that Jesus was to be a light to the Gentiles and the "Glory of Israel." Next we read about the 84-year-old prophet Anna who came up and also prophesied to all who were looking for the redemption of Israel. So Simeon and Anna both testified that day to the special relationship of Jesus to God.

In today's lesson, Jesus is 12 years old and is claiming for Himself that special relationship to God which was symbolized in His dedication as an infant.

Up to this point in scripture, all signs of the unusual nature of Jesus and his mission as the Messiah of God had been through the testimony of others.

The angel Gabriel testified telling Mary that she would have a Son and he would be the "Son of the most high God." Mary testified, "My soul does magnify the Lord." Elizabeth testified to Mary about the divinity of Jesus. The wise men testified. The shepherds

---

[27] In Methodist and other churches, following the teaching of the New Testament, we have both boys and girls 12 years of age in Confirmation classes.

testified. Simeon and Anna testified. All these testified to the divine uniqueness of Jesus. But now, in today's passage, we see Jesus in the temple claiming this for himself.

He had gone there for the feast of the Passover. The Passover was the Jewish festival celebrated each spring in commemoration of the account in Exodus when the Lord passed over the firstborn Israelite slaves in Egypt when the Egyptian firstborn had been slain. The last supper was a Passover meal, and our Communion service was instituted at Passover time.

As Christians we see the crucifixion of Jesus as the fulfillment foreshadowed by the Passover. It was the aim of every Hebrew sometime in his lifetime to attend the feast of the Passover in Jerusalem. Actually it was laid down by law that every Jewish male who lived within 20 miles of Jerusalem must attend. A Jewish boy became a Son of the Law at age twelve. Jerusalem, the holy city, the temple and the sacred ritual were important. As a child, Jesus must have studied the scripture.

Much has been written about when Jesus realized his true identity and mission on Earth. This brief vignette of the boyhood of Jesus is the only record about Jesus between His birth, babyhood, and manhood. This scripture wants us to know that Jesus was nurtured in His obedience and worship, and He was unwavering in His observance of the demands of home, synagogue and temple.

Jesus had gone to the temple with Mary and Joseph and other neighbors and kinspeople. When the feast of the Passover was over, Mary and Joseph traveled in a caravan back to their home, thinking that Jesus was in their company. This was not as unusual as it might be thought. Usually the women in the caravan went ahead, and so Mary thought Jesus was with Joseph, and Joseph thought He was with Mary.

One of the most amusing stories in our family is about the time that we left our daughter, Deborah, at a service station in Ohio! Debi said that when their family moved to Rome in 1989 and went to church at Trinity, a woman who was introduced to her said, "Oh, you are the one they left at a service station?" Our son Terrell and his wife Sheila had been members at Trinity for several years and had told this dramatic story to some people at the church.

We were on a camping trip through Kentucky and Ohio. We stopped for gas at a station in Louisville, right at the bridge that crosses the Ohio River. All the children had been to the bathroom and were back in the station wagon. Deborah suddenly remembered that she had left a hair barrette in the rest room. She slipped out of the car to go back to get it. I was feeding baby David in the front seat. Charles came back from paying the bill and started the car. He turned the few yards onto the long bridge that spanned the Ohio River. Carol saw a huge ship on the river and said, "Look, everybody. Look, Debi! Mama, where's Debi?" I panicked. We all panicked, but we could not make a U-turn on the bridge. If there had been any physical way to turn around on that bridge, all of us who knew Charles Shaw know he would have found it. I was ready to get out of the car and run back to the service station. But we could not even stop on the bridge because of the heavy traffic. Charles pulled the 9-passenger Chevrolet station wagon into the first place across the bridge to turn around, and right behind us, much to our relief, was the service station man bringing Deborah to us.

Debi later told the story to her children in her own dramatic way. She says that the man in the service station probably thought, "These Georgia crackers have probably been dropping off children all the way from Georgia; but they are NOT leaving one here." Anyway, when Deborah came out of the restroom to see us crossing the bridge, the service station owner put Debi in his pickup truck and brought her to us. I will never forget the joy of seeing her little head in that truck and the kindness of the station owner.[28]

---

[28] Our child had slipped out of the car so quietly, even her seat mates, Carol and Terry, had not noticed. Do you think she needed a spanking? We were so happy to see her and she was so cute and happy to see us, we thought only to hug and kiss her.

Children have a way of keeping you on your toes, and apparently Jesus was no exception. In the hymn "Away in a Manger" we have the phrase, "The little Lord Jesus no crying He makes." But the baby Jesus was fully human as well as fully divine. One of the glorious truths of the Christmas message is that the infinite God so loved the world of finite human beings that He came into the world as a helpless baby, unable to hold His head up without help. So I am sure that Jesus, as a baby, developed His lungs by crying as other babies do.

When Mary and Joseph discovered Jesus missing, they turned around and went back. They found 12-year-old Jesus talking with the learned men in the house of God.

Barclay[29] reminds us that we must realize that during the Passover, it was the custom of the Sanhedrin to meet in public in the Temple. Here they would discuss, for all who cared to listen, religious as well as theological questions. So this scripture is not telling us that Jesus, as a boy, was dominating a crowd of seniors. "Hearing and asking questions" is a regular Jewish phrase for a student learning from his teachers. The Bible tells us that Jesus was hearing the teachers and asking questions.

The reply of Jesus to Mary and Joseph has gone down in history as expressing an early awareness of his special identity. He replied that they should understand that he must be about the business of his Father in heaven. He must be about God's business. Mary said, "Your father and I have been searching for you." Jesus takes the name "father" and gives it to God. "Did you not realize that I must be about my Father's business?" The Father may have revealed to Jesus at this early age His role as Savior and Redeemer. But there is another part of the "Father's business" in this scripture lesson – "going home with Mary and Joseph" and "being subject to them." Another part of the Father's business was increasing in wisdom and knowledge and in favor with God and man. In this scripture, Jesus said, "I must be about my Father's business." God's business then for Jesus was that He went home and was subject to Mary and

---

[29] William Barclay (1907-1978) was a Scottish scholar who wrote many commentaries on Christian theology.

Joseph. The Father's business for Jesus at age 12 was not preaching and working miracles but remaining at home and developing in wisdom and stature and in favor with God and people.

There are times in the life of each person when he/she must submit to the discipline of preparation. There are times for the discipline of studying the scripture under the guidance of the Holy Spirit, and not coming to the Bible with preconceived ideas and unloving attitudes. Sometimes there is the discipline of waiting or the discipline of staying in the background. I certainly had done much of this for years before I was called to stand in a pulpit.

Paul was not converted one day to sit down and write the amazing and beautiful theological book of Romans the next. Paul was already well-versed in scripture and the classics, but we read that Paul was led in the wilderness for three years to be taught by God after his encounter with Jesus on the Damascus Road.

It seems that the devil likes to get new converts side-tracked into thinking that they have all the answers and do not need the discipline of Bible study, church attendance, and prayer as well as the study of classic literature and church history. God performed many miracles in the life of Paul and in others through Paul; but God also required some years of preparation from Paul.

> *Why did Jesus become human when He could have stayed God? Why was He crucified when He could have saved Himself the grief and pain?*

This is a mystery as great as the mystery of the incarnation and the Christmas mystery. Why did Jesus become human when He could have stayed God? Why was He crucified when He could have saved Himself the grief and pain? Why was He crucified when He could have called ten thousand angels? Because He loves us. Because He has come to lead us through the waters of life and death into life eternal.

In *Pilgrim's Progress*, the man named "Christian" arrives in his journey at the heavily-guarded palace. It will be a battle to seek entry. A man sits at the door to take down the names of those who would dare to enter. Many are hanging back, reluctant and afraid; just as today many hang back from making a firm decision for Jesus Christ. It may seem easy to those of us raised in a church and who accepted Christ when we were young, but even walking into a church building is difficult for some people. Many are reluctant to stand up and be counted as a Christian.

I have never had difficulty in identifying myself as a Christian, but I have had a hard time identifying myself as a preacher. I know how people set you apart and expect you not to act human. I found it hard enough to be identified as a preacher's wife. Some people are uncomfortable around preachers. I have never felt it is important to volunteer the information in a social situation; but I finally came to the conclusion that I might as well be tarred with the same brush as the rest of the preachers. For, as Paul says, "I am not ashamed of the Gospel of Christ. For it is the power for God unto salvation, for all who believe."

In John Bunyan's classic book, *Pilgrim's Progress*, Christian is standing near the gate of the palace, reluctant and afraid. But then, with a stout countenance he makes a decision. He walks up to the guard at the gate and says, "Set my name down, Sir."

"Set my name down, Sir." This is what baptism and public confession is. It is setting our name and our life on the line for Jesus Christ and His Kingdom. It is taking a stand for Christ and His church. It is identifying with the people of God. Amen.

Mount Moriah

Genesis 22: 1-14

After these things God tested Abraham, and said to him, "Abraham!" And he said, "Here am I." He said, "Take your son, your only son Isaac, whom you love, and go to the land of Moriah, and offer him there as a burnt offering upon one of the mountains of which I shall tell you."
~Genesis 22:1-2 (RSV)~

This text is too big to handle. Abraham is bigger than life here. Who could agree to take a child, bind him and offer him up as a sacrifice - a burnt offering? Who could offer up even a pet as a burnt sacrifice?

Mount Moriah is beyond my experience or even my imagination. I only stand in the foothills and gaze up. But for a little while I want us to walk around Mount Moriah and point upward and let the message speak to us today

God's directions to Abraham were unreasonable. The whole thing probably did not make sense to Abraham either, even though he was living in the midst of a culture that practiced child sacrifice to their gods. We notice Abraham did not try to explain it.

The immediate prelude to this compelling story is the birth of Isaac.[30] Isaac is the child of promise. Finally Abraham and Sarah are given this son in their old age. Sarah is well past menopause, and Paul describes Abraham much later in our Bible "as good as dead."[31]

We first met Abraham in Genesis 11, while he was still Abram, the son of Terah, a descendent of Shem, one of the sons of Noah. The latter verses in Genesis 11 tell of his birth and his marriage to Sarai and the fact that Saria was barren.

---

[30] Genesis 21:1-7
[31] Hebrews 11: 8-12

In Chapter 12 we hear the first promise to Abram. The last verse of chapter 11 tells us Abram's father, Terah, has died. The first verse in Chapter 12 tells us the Lord spoke to Abram with directions to leave his country and his father's house and go to a land the Lord would show him. The promise is to make of Abram a great nation, a great name, with blessings to Abram and his descendants and the blessing of God to all people through Abram. This was God's blessing, not only to the Hebrew people, but also to all the peoples on the earth through Abraham and Sarah!

Abram set out, as directed. In Genesis, Chapters 12-15 we have the traveling, the dishonesty, and the Sodom and Gomorrah story. Then in Chapter 16, Sarai took matters in her own hands and had Abram father a son, Ismael, by Hagar, Sarai's Egyptian slave girl.

There was more talk of covenant and promises. Finally in Chapter 18 there was a name change, and from there on out, it was Abraham and Sarah. They both still had much to learn, but Sarah finally conceived in their old age and they both laughed in joyful disbelief.

We think we have to get to the New Testament to see the love of God or at least get to the book of Jeremiah or Hosea. But there in the first book of the Bible, we see Abraham who got a glimpse of God who loved him enough to give him the son he had promised - a God powerful enough to enter into covenant but also powerful enough to keep his promises. The God who brought joy and laughter into Abraham's life with the birth of the promised son was the God Abraham was prepared to keep following.

So when we get to today's lesson, we realize this was not the first time God had tested Abraham but it was certainly the most difficult test! A supreme test! A final exam, if you please.

Today most Christians seem to think God's agenda is the same as ours. We seem to think God's main purpose is to make us feel good about ourselves. The idea that God might initiate a test is foreign to the way we see our "esteem builder" God. God certainly loves us and has a wonderful plan for our lives, but that does not exempt us from trials or tests!

> *It seems faith is strengthened and matured through the experience of stressful testing in the same way the cardio-vascular system is strengthened through exercise and the muscles are developed by pumping iron.*

The Epistle of James puts it in perspective when he writes, "Count it all joy when you fall into various trials, knowing that testing of your faith produces patience. But let patience have its perfect work, that you may be perfect and complete, lacking nothing." (James 1:1-2) It seems faith is strengthened and matured through the experience of stressful testing in the same way the cardio-vascular system is strengthened through exercise and the muscles are developed by pumping iron.

This Scripture lesson in Genesis states just the bare facts. There is no attempt to tell what Abraham was thinking or feeling when the Lord called him to take Isaac up to Moriah and offer him as a sacrifice. There are some feelings and some encounters that are unexplainable. I have lived long enough to get a faint glimpse of why Abraham did not try to explain his action in response to the call of God.

I have learned that calling and commitment are not always reasonable or explainable. There are just no reasonable words to tell of struggling with convictions and callings that grip you.

When Charles Shaw gave up a good job to go back to school to prepare for ministry, a member of our church confronted him and said, "Charles Shaw, you are crazy. What about your children?"

Many of us read Hebrews 11 before we read Genesis 22 and we remember that by faith Abraham, when he was tested, offered up Isaac. We know the rest of the story. We have seen the back of the book. Yet we still look at Abraham, an old man trudging up Mount

Moriah with his son Isaac by the hand because God told him to offer Isaac as a burnt offering to God. We feel the drama of the moment. We know that both he and Isaac will come back down the mountain. What did Abraham know?

The promise of God required that Isaac should live, and now the command of God decreed that Isaac should die? How is God going to work it all out?

When Isaac asked his Dad how they were going to sacrifice without a sacrificial animal, Abraham replied with amazing confidence. In verse 8 we read, "My son, God will provide for Himself the lamb for the burnt offering."

So Abraham pressed on toward Mount Moriah and thus reminds believers of all generations that faith in a faithful, promise-keeping God will sometimes stretch us beyond our limits - far beyond the limits of our physical, emotional, social, intellectual and spiritual limits. But the stretching will expand our capacity to know God and in the knowing to discover the vast potential of life lived by faith.

When the church friend said to Charles, "What about your children?" she certainly hit a nerve. As parents, we say, "What about our children?"

Yesterday I was thumbing through some old booklets and ran across an article by William H. Willimon who was at one time a Chaplain at Duke University, a Bishop in the United Methodist Church and later a professor at Duke Divinity School. In commenting on Abraham's being willing to sacrifice Isaac, Willimon told about having Milliard Fuller, the founder of Habitat for Humanity, to speak at their chapel one Sunday.

Millard Fuller told how he and his wife decided to move out of their comfortable, affluent suburban existence to a poor neighborhood in Americus, Georgia and begin to build homes for the poor - one house at a time.

Later, two college students asked Willimon how old the Fuller children were when their father made this decision. Willimon realized that these seminary students were thinking that it was all right for the Fullers to have some religious experience and move wherever they wished, but it was not all right to drag their helpless children with them. These students thought this violated the freedom and dignity of the Fuller children.

So the question is not if we are willing to sacrifice our children to God, but which god will have the lives of our children?

Willimon said one of the people who had asked the question was a man whose daughter he knew had been on birth control pills since age 16 and whose son was in a second series of drug treatments. Willimon concluded, "So maybe the question is not, 'Will we sacrifice our children?' but 'Upon whose altar will we sacrifice?'" We are busy laying our children on some altar. So the question is not if we are willing to sacrifice our children to God, but which god will have the lives of our children?

In verse 12, when Abraham arrived at the top of Mount Moriah, as he bound Isaac up and stood over him with the knife, with his heart breaking and his faith stretched to the breaking point, God spoke, "Do not lay your hand on the lad, for now I know that you fear God since you have not withheld your son." As someone has said, "God intervened and acted not a minute too soon or a minute too late."

Abraham had left his home in Ur to follow God. He went out in faith not knowing where the journey would end. Abraham had been in covenant with God since the day he went out from Ur not knowing where he was going. This supreme testing time came on Mount Moriah, but Abraham came down from the mountain with Isaac.

It is not easy to leave a "sure thing" for a leap of faith with no tangible map. Abraham did. By faith, Abraham went when he was called, obeyed by going out, not knowing where he was going. Abraham did not know the rest of the story.

We know the rest of the story by looking in the back of our Bible. (Hebrews 11) Yet this is not an easy story to swallow. In our kind of world it leads us face to face with the reality that God is God. It leads us face to face with the mystery of God. God is not a saccharine kind of God, patting us on the head saying, "I'm OK and you're OK." As Father Abraham tells us in Genesis 22, God can be a "tough love God." You will remember that when Job's friends began to question him about the testing time that came his way, Job said, "The Lord gives and the Lord takes away; blessed be the name of the Lord." (Job 1:21)

So the question we ask is, "Does God really test us in this way?" The premise of this passage is that he does. In our sophistication and pride, the whole idea of "testing" is bothersome. In fact, that is one thing we may have disliked about school. During my years of school, I would have preferred to write five papers than take one test. Blessedly for me, in seminary at Candler School of Theology, we were assigned many more papers than tests.

God's directions may not seem logical or even explainable, but when we know who is giving the directions, we go.

The idea that God would test Abraham in such a way is difficult to understand. We are like the little boy who asked, "Was this before God became a Christian?" But the same issue is clear in the New Testament. Every Sunday we pray the prayer in which Jesus taught his disciples: "Lead us not into temptation." What we are saying, from the original translation, is "Don't bring us to the test."

We learn the difficult lesson that God does not measure time in the same way we do. I turn to Psalm 90 to read that "A thousand years in God's sight are like a day that has just gone by and like a watch in the night."[32] What can we learn from what we think of as "tragic and untimely deaths" of fine young people?

---

[32] Psalms 90:4-6

This is something of what living the life of faith is all about; going, yet not always knowing. God's directions may not seem logical or even explainable, but when we know who is giving the directions, we go.

And when we look in the roll call of the saints in Hebrews 11, none help us more vividly than Abraham's experience on Mount Moriah. We are reminded that our Lord Jesus Christ, for the love of each one and all of us, climbed all the way to a place we now call Mount Calvary. It was that awful Friday we now know as "Good Friday." It is a good Friday because, only three short days away, very early on Sunday morning, Jesus laid aside his grave clothes and is alive forever more! Amen.

For Jesus's Sake

II Samuel 9:1-11

And David said, "Is there still any one left of the house of Saul, that I may show him kindness for Jonathan's sake.
~II Samuel 9:1 (RSV)~

Recently we remembered with great respect and honor D. Day - June 6, 1944 - when so many men and women "for freedom's sake" were willing and did give their lives for liberty.

I remember D. Day very clearly! I was a young mother of two little girls, with a husband in the South Pacific and a brother in the Army in Europe and another brother in the Army Air Force in the South Pacific. My husband and I had married in our teens. We were blessed with the birth of our first precious daughter only 10 months after our marriage and our second equally precious daughter only 2 years and 5 months later.

I could not hold back the tears Monday as I watched TV and they showed row after row of white grave markers. Most people my age remember young soldiers who gave their lives in World War II for freedom's sake. Four of my school classmates were killed during World War II: James Homer Cook, Quinton "Red" Cole, Carroll Adams and J.W. Rye. I call their names in blessed memory of their sacrifice as young soldiers. God bless their memory!

Some years ago, I read an article featuring "ordinary people doing extraordinary things." They told the story of a man in his seventies, a World War II veteran, who had gone through several battles as a squadron leader and had lost many of the men in his squadron in one battle.

Each year on Memorial Day, this man drives some distance to the Veteran's Memorial Cemetery to put flags and flowers on the graves of the soldiers. He was interviewed and explained he did it for the sake of and in appreciation for his buddies who had died in battle. For the sake of his buddies who died in battle, this soldier took this action. This soldier said the same thing I heard my husband Charles say many times - that the men in his unit were like family. I am sure the veterans in this congregation would agree. Soldiers become very loyal to those who fight alongside them.

This is what each anniversary celebration of D. Day is all about: taking action to show appreciation and loyalty for the memory of those who have gone before us and especially for those who, in the words of Abraham Lincoln, "gave the last full measure of their devotion."

Communion is also a Memorial Service. For Jesus' sake we take this action in remembrance and in ceremonial gratitude for what Jesus did for us on the Cross of Calvary, and in loyalty for the salvation God has provided.

In our marriage ceremonies we say, "I require and charge you both, as you stand in the presence of God, to remember that love and loyalty alone will prevail as the foundation of a happy and enduring marriage." Love and loyalty are the foundation of a happy and enduring marriage.

In today's passage in II Samuel, the Hebrew word, "hessed," meaning loyalty, is used three times. As David said, "Is there anyone left in the house of Saul that I may show him kindness for Jonathan's sake?" I thought about giving this message the title "For Jonathan's Sake." King David, after learning of the death of Jonathan, knowing he could do nothing else for Jonathan, sought out a child of Jonathan's to help "for Jonathan's sake."

For the Memorial Day just past and the D Day theme, it occurred to me to call this message "For America's Sake." We love our country. We want to see it continue and thrive. But we hear so many conflicting messages and proposals. It is difficult sometimes to know what to believe and how to vote. The very freedoms we enjoy sometimes cause conflict.

A friend and I were in a Christian bookstore recently, and my friend saw a book by someone running for office and said, "He's bad news." I said, "If we are to believe the Atlanta newspaper, that is true, but personally, in this case, I do not agree with the newspapers." The friend quoted Will Rogers by saying, "All I know is what I read in the newspaper."

And in a sense, that is true. We get much of our information from the media, and it is difficult to know who to believe in a world in which we do not have a great deal of time to read or listen to all sides of all issues.

Just as in a democratic church where every member has a right to speak, it is sometimes problematic. I always dread our United Methodist General Conference that meets every four years with an equal number of ministerial and lay members voting. In recent years we have had controversial issues up for vote. The media has the general public thinking the United Methodist church is filled with radical activists. They seem to always look for the most radical persons present to interview. Some political activists who are not delegates or even Methodist come to our General Conference and appear on the Conference floor to talk to the media.

We can title this message "For Jesus's Sake" because this is what we are all about. This is the message of the gospel. What we do "for Jesus's sake" boils down to the last prayer of Jesus before the crucifixion. Jesus prayed in the beautiful prayer we read in John 17: "For their sakes I dedicate myself."

This is a prayer I remember praying at the bedside of my four children in 1950 when Charles was struggling with the call to preach after coming home from the South Pacific during World War II. What we do "for Jesus's sake," we do for one another, for our families, for ourselves, for our church and for our land.

There are a familiar few lines of poetry that go something like this: "Be there a man with soul so dead, who never to himself has said, "This is my own, my native land."[33]

---

[33] Sir Walter Scott, "The Lay of the Last Minstrel"

There is something compelling to us about our own land, our spot on earth, our own home; whether a little house on the prairie, a cottage in a small village or countryside, or a mansion somewhere. Sacrifices have been made and wars have been fought for "the land's sake." We do this and that "for the land's sake," which has been shortened to the exclamation of "Land's sake."

> *Christians are to take care of each other, our environment, and our land - for the sake of each other and for future generations and "for Jesus's sake."*

In fact, the Christian faith is about our relationship to God, to ourselves, to others and how we relate to others, to our environment, and to the land. Christians are to take care of each other, our environment, and our land for the sake of each other and for future generations and "for Jesus's sake."

When we study the books of Genesis and Exodus, we know that the God that Jesus called Father was the God that gave them the land and taught the Hebrews how to care for the land and for each other. Land and "the land of Israel" is a central theme of Biblical faith.

This yearning to belong, to have a safe place, is still the yearning of many.

The story of Jonathan and David's friendship goes back to their youth. Jonathan was the son of King Saul. Saul became insanely jealous of David when the people responded to David with admiration after David killed the Philistine giant and defeated the Philistine Army. Jonathan saw the injustice of the situation and when King Saul sought to kill David, Jonathan saved his life. They became friends for life.

When King David heard that this friend Jonathan had fallen in battle, his grief was very real.[34] In II Samuel 9 we read about his

---

[34] II Samuel 4: 4 David's grief for Jonathan's death

kindness to Jonathan's crippled son Phibosheth "for Jonathan's sake."

On D. Day, we honor the memory of soldiers fallen in battle. But we also honor men and women, our forefathers and fore-mothers who built this land and who endured much "for our country's sake and for "our sake."

During World War I they were fighting a "war to end war." In World War II it was to make "the world safe for democracy." The Vietnam War was to try to destroy the lust for power and to protect the freedom of small nations against the tyranny of communist expansion. During the Gulf War it was to stop aggression in the Middle East. The wars we are involved in now are in response to the Islamic terrorist attacks and the terrorists that are plotting and who continue fighting to take over Western civilization.

Probably most people who have served in armies, if they were asked to give a reason would not say, "to make the world safe for democracy." They would say, "to save our homes and those we love." They would say, "to keep our land free, for 'our land's sake.' "

How can we pay the debt we owe to the men and women who have lived and died for America? Some of us remember when our history books told thrilling stories of heroic action by our ancestors. Events and persons in American history may have been over idealized, but let it be said that generally speaking, most of them were persons that should have been admired and trusted! Over idealization is better for us and for our nation than the constant debunking and underrating of our national heritage.

It is interesting that some historians and educators who spend so much time debunking everything American and Christian and seem to be trying to take away our political and Christian heroes, have given our youth new heroes of sports and film and rock stars.

When we have no one left to admire and look up to and stop loving our ancestors, we stop loving our contemporaries, our children and life in general. It is possible that child abuse and abortion problems relate to the lack of respect for our ancestors and the country. It is not trite to speak and sing about "the land of the free and home of the brave." For our country's sake and for all the Jonathans that went before us and will come after us, we uphold the freedom that is a part of our inheritance as Americans.

David was a man of loyalty. Saul had sought to kill him. David had to run for his life and on one occasion could have easily killed Saul. But David remained a man under oath. He vowed loyalty to Jonathan, and for the sake of Jonathan and for the sake of all that was important, for his God's sake and his people's sake, and for his land's sake, he was loyal to King Saul.

The bottom line of our lesson in II Samuel is about the keeping of promises. At our best, for our own sake and for the sake of those we love, for "God's sake, and for Jesus sake, we are all keepers of promises to God, to others and to ourselves.

Prayer: Our Father, we are thankful for this lesson from King David and pray we may apply it to our own lives "for Jesus's sake." Amen.

Inquiring Minds Want to Know

Acts 9:1-6

So he (Saul) trembling and astonished, said, "Lord, what do You want me to do?" Then the Lord said to him, "Arise and go into the city, and you will be told what you must do."
~Acts 9:6 (NKJV)~

Saul's conversion to Jesus Christ is fascinating and important to know about, not just because people are interested in wanting detailed accounts of people who have become great or famous, but because Saul who became Paul is possibly the greatest man who ever lived, outside of Jesus Christ who was the divine Son of God.

I suppose the tabloid newspaper, *The National Inquirer*, is still in business. I have not seen or heard anything about them lately. But they used to advertise by saying, "Inquiring minds want to know." In a real sense, we all need to have "inquiring minds." There are many things we want to know and need to know.

Our scripture lesson today is about Saul of Tarsus and his conversion into the great Apostle Paul. I want to talk about Paul's conversion and ours.

Some pastors have inquiry rooms where, at the end of a church service, people who are interested in learning more about Christ and the church or in accepting Jesus into their life as Savior are invited for prayer and counsel instead of up front of the church or at the altar. So the "altar call" was an inquiry room call. I believe the great evangelist D.L. Moody[35] used an inquiry room where great crowds of people would go to have a Christian counselor pray with them and answer any question they might have about the Christian faith or the church.

---

[35] Dwight Lyman Moody (1837 - 1899), also known as *D.L. Moody*, was an American evangelist and publisher.

In this context, inquiring minds are not interested in the latest gossip about famous people but are inquiring about how to become a Christian.

The truth that Paul encountered on the Damascus Road is the greatest good news the world has ever heard. This great news is that the eternal God who created the universe will, at our invitation, come into our lives and save us. When we truly believe this and accept Jesus as our savior, ask Him to come into our hearts and lives, we are changed as surely as the Saul who was killing Christians became the great Apostle Paul. It was the apostle Paul who gave his life to carry the Gospel of Jesus Christ to the Gentiles and into the then known world.

We look at things like the Islamic terrorist attack on 9-11-01 and we ask, "How can human beings be as evil and cruel as to cause so much suffering, death and waste to other human beings?" We need to know that seeds of evil can be in the hearts of all of us.

The Bible teaches that God so loved all of us in the world that he sent his only begotten Son, Jesus, that all of us who believe in him will have eternal life. Jesus walked the earth teaching and healing. We saw the evil and tragedy of sin when evil and complacent people killed the loving and innocent son of God.

> *Saul learned that in fighting against the God of creation, he was also fighting against himself.*

In the blinding light on the Damascus Road, Saul met the Jesus that he had been trying to stamp out. The light of God's presence shown all around Saul so brightly that it blinded him. Saul learned that in fighting against the God of creation, he was also fighting against himself.

On the road to Damascus, Saul heard his name called, and the risen Christ appeared to him. Saul saw himself as he was, devastated and helpless! He was suddenly and finally brought to the end of his own resources - to the end of his pride and his learning. The once-proud Saul had to be led by his hand to Damascus because he was blind. When Saul opened his eyes three days later, he had a new vision.

The proud Saul had sat at the feet of the greatest teachers. He knew much about God and religion, and he had been certified about big important ideas and big important people. But Saul was rendered as helpless as a baby and had to be led by the hand and at the mercy of strangers and had to be instructed by the very people he once looked down on.

There is a strange path of enlightenment in which we progress by regression and go forward by falling backward. There was confusion, speechlessness, hunger and childless crawling toward light.[36]

Saul's turnaround was so dramatic and he was so completely changed by the voice of God that even his old name would not do. He was now Paul, the Apostle of Jesus Christ![37] The conversion of Saul of Tarsus was so remarkable and so fascinating, it is told in Chapter 9 of Acts, in Chapter 22 and again in Chapter 26. Dr. Luke, who wrote the book of Acts, is known for brevity, but he considers the conversion of Saul of such importance that he tells it three times. Paul gives his personal testimony before the church in Jerusalem in Chapter 22 and before King Agrippa in Chapter 26.

Paul became the great missionary to the Gentiles (us). Someone has said this has to be one of the greatest surprises in the entire Bible. Paul had been relentless in his determination to stamp out the Christian movement and was one of the greatest persecutors of the followers of Jesus. Saul was both a Hebrew Pharisee and a man of the world. At an early age his parents' resources had enabled them to win for Saul the privilege to studying under Gamalier, the greatest Hebrew intellectual of the time. Saul spoke fluent Greek, Hebrew and Aramaic. Saul was just the man God needed to lead the church of Jesus Christ.[38]

---

[36] Willimon, Pulpit Digest. Mar-Apr 1993
[37] Ibid
[38] Lloyd Ogilvie, Page 166

I heard a man give his testimony recently. He had been in trouble with the law and with drugs, alcohol and violence since his teens. He had married and had a child but continued having periods of rage and getting into trouble with the law. He had spent years in prison.

One night he was fresh out of prison and was hitchhiking when a Christian man picked him up. This hitchhiker was looking for trouble, and he thought how foolish this man was to pick him up. When he got in the car, the Christian man turned to him and asked, "Has anyone ever told you how to be saved - how to become a Christian?" Suddenly this man, who had been in trouble all his life, wanted very badly to know how to become a Christian. He became an inquirer. The Christian man told him, "Tell Jesus you are tired of going your own way. Invite Jesus into your heart as Lord and Savior. Then worship, pray, read the Bible and hang out with Christians." This hitchhiker's life was dramatically changed. It became filled with love and concern for others.

When Saul met the risen Christ on the road to Damascus, everything about his life was changed. In Acts 9:17 we meet Ananias, the first Christian Saul saw after his conversion. I love that the first word of Ananias to Paul was "Brother." Ananias said to Paul, "Brother Saul, the Lord, even Jesus, has sent me to greet you."

The last commandment Jesus gave us is to love. Love is the badge by which people are to know us. Jesus said, "A new commandment I give you, love one another. By this all shall know that you are my disciples if you love one another."[39]

Christians like Ananias make goodness attractive. Others in the church are stumbling blocks in the way of the sincere inquirer. Sometimes people become Christian because of us, and some people become Christian in spite of us.

---

[39] John 13:33-35

Barbara Brockoff[40] said she became Christian in spite of poverty when she was growing up. She was embarrassed because of her poor home and poor clothes. Barbara tells about one Easter when she was 13 or 14. They had no money for clothes she badly needed, but her mother had made her a dress from some material she had. Her mother knew she had cardboard in the bottom of her shoes, and the cardboard had gotten about as big as the bottom of her shoes. Somehow her mother managed to scrape together enough change to make a dollar. So she told Barbara to go downtown to the Brokerage (a discount store) and see if she could find a pair of shoes on the dollar rack. Barbara said she was very excited when she finally found a pair of red shoes in her size. She had never had red shoes before, but they seemed wonderful to her. She was happy to think of getting to wear the new shoes with no holes to Sunday school and church the next day.

Barbara said to this day, she still hurts when she remembers the pain and embarrassment she felt when a woman at church looked at her feet and said, "How could you have the nerve to wear red shoes to church? You look like a Jezebel. Only harlots wear red shoes!" (I suppose this hate-filled woman did not know that popes wear red shoes). Barbara said she was cut to the quick because she did not see anything wrong with wearing red shoes, and she could afford no others. In spite of this negative encounter in her church, Barbara, with her "inquiring mind" and personal experience in Christ, went on to become an outstanding and effective Christian minister of the Gospel. Happily, the love and positive witness of many dedicated pastors and lay Christians outnumber the mean-spirited ones.

The church has survived and thrived in spite of church people like that woman and like some of us who call ourselves Christian. We need, according to Jesus, to be in the business of loving and affirming one another, not condemning and finding fault! Amen.

---

[40] Rev. Dr. Barbara Brockoff, a popular minister of Ruth Shaw's generation.

The God Who Gave Us Life, Gave Us Liberty

Galatians 1:13-25

It is for freedom that Christ has set us free. Stand firm then and do not let yourselves be burdened again by a yoke of slavery.
~Galatians 5:1 (NIV)~

The first time I was privileged to visit our nation's capital was in the late sixties. My husband was pastor of Trinity Methodist Church in Rome. That year we took a two-week vacation and made it a camping trip with our five younger children, between the ages of five and sixteen. We had five days in Washington D.C. and then a few days on the outer banks of South Carolina before heading back to Georgia.

Our oldest son, Terry (Terrell), had gone to Washington with his West Rome High School band; so we appointed him to work out our District of Columbia itinerary.

Our schedule included visits to the Washington Monument, the Lincoln Memorial, the Smithsonian, the FBI building - just about all the important buildings and monuments in Washington. We even attended church at the Washington Cathedral.

But one of the highlights of this visit for me was the evening we sat on the steps of the Capital Building and listened to the Navy Band and Chorus sing, "The God Who Gave us Life, Gave us Liberty at the Same Time."[41]

This is the foundational theme of these United States of America - the theme of "Life, liberty and the pursuit of happiness." We can't forget the famous words of Patrick Henry: "Give me liberty or give me death!" Real life is real liberty, and both are a gift from God.

---

[41] This song was written by Randall Thompson for the Virginia Glee Club to celebrate the bicentennial of the birth of Thomas Jefferson. The text for the work was taken from Jefferson's writings.

This is the message Paul would have us know in this scripture lesson from the letter to the church in Galatia. Paul would have us know that the God who, in the beginning said, "Let there be light," and there was light, is the God who, in Jesus Christ, will come into our life to bring each one of us life and liberty. He will save us "to the uttermost" and bring abundant life and liberty.

Galatians has been called Paul's "freedom letter." Paul is telling these new Christians (and reminding us also) to retain the freedom given to us in Christ. Paul is telling us that the God who in the beginning breathed into us the breath of life has given us liberty! Paul is telling us the Christ who said, "I am the way, the truth and the life" is the same God who has given us liberty - freedom! It is God's new life in us that gives us liberty at the same time that we receive this new life in Christ.

> *Grace is God's love expressed in Jesus Christ, a love that gives and suffers, but also fully conquers and delivers.*

Paul wants us to know in this passage and others that the God who gives us grace also gives us freedom. Throughout the book of Galatians, Paul makes the point that salvation is a grace – a gift from God. He tells us we cannot earn this great salvation, but we are justified - that is, we are made right with God - by God's grace. We are made right, even though unworthy, by our faith response to God's amazing grace! Grace is God's love expressed in Jesus Christ, a love that gives and suffers, but also finally conquers and delivers.

When Paul gets to chapter five, our text today, he lists the practical implications of the gospel of liberty and grace!

Paul talks about Christian freedom, which is freedom from sin, death and hell. He emphasizes freedom from the restraints of the law. As Christians, we are not required to fulfill the letter of the law but to live by a new commandment, the commandment to love one another as Christ loves us. This freedom is so wonderful in that we are not given the job of judging one another!

This is the secret of a life of joy and peace. This takes ethics to a new and higher level than the law could ever do. Some people have asked, "If this is a gospel about the gift of grace and not works of righteousness, does Christian freedom and liberty give us a license to sin?"

Many years ago, in our little town there were two churches, a Methodist and a Baptist. They were right across the street from one another and often had joint services. During a revival meeting at the Baptist Church one night, a man known as the "town drunk" went up at the invitation at the close of service and professed to accept Christ as his savior. A little over a week later, he got drunk, staggered in front of a moving car and was killed instantly - a sad story of human weakness. The pastor of the church, in celebrating this man's life, alluded to the night when he came forward to repent of his sins. This was a part of his story. But God wants to save us from our sins, rather than "in them."

Romans 6:1 reads; "Shall we continue in sin that grace may abound? Shall we go out and sin as much as we can so that God's grace will be in effect more and more?" Paul quickly says; "God forbid. How can we who are dead to sin, live therein?"

On every Fourth of July we celebrate the birthday of our great nation. When our forefathers declared their independence from England, they also declared their dependence on Almighty God. The Declaration of Independence says that liberty is from God who endowed us with certain inalienable rights. Behind our Declaration of Independence is the birthright of dignity of human beings made in the image of God.

And the best news of all is the way God values each one of us in the gift of His Son, and the willingness of Jesus to die for each one of us. Augustine reminds us that God loves each one of us as though we were the only person to love. Even if I were the only person needing salvation - even if you were the only person needing salvation, Christ would have given his life that each one of us might have life abundant and the liberty that comes with this gift of grace.

Recently we have heard talk about our birthright as Americans, but there is also a level of freedom that is uniquely Christian. It is the internal freedom of the spirit that enables us to live with dignity and meaning even in the midst of suppression and oppression.

We have seen this in Christian African-Americans, many of whom endured segregation and discrimination with love and dignity. We see this in nursing homes where people who are sick and disabled still find joy and dignity in the midst of loneliness and pain and the inability to take care of themselves.

I heard an African-American police officer talking to a group of high school boys. He told them about thousands of men and women who died on slave ships bound for America. The policeman told the young men, "The very fact that your great-grandparents survived and that you are here shows a great inheritance. Don't forget what many of them went through to give you freedom. Don't make yourself a slave to alcohol or other drugs to make your grandparents' gifts be in vain."

Paul puts it this way in the first verse of our text, "Stand fast in the liberty with which Christ has made us free, and do not be entangled again in the yoke of bondage."

Liberty also brings responsibility. In verse 13 we are called to freedom, but then we are told, "Do not use your freedom as an opportunity for the flesh, but through love be servants of one another."

Then Paul goes on to list some of the sins of the flesh that follow when liberty is perverted: fornication, impurity, licentiousness, idolatry, enmity, strife, jealousy, selfish ambition, and dissension. Paul is telling us that we have been given freedom, but that when we take these negative things - these sins - into our lives, we lose our freedom and become entangled again in the yoke of bondage.

Mother Teresa's Missionaries of Charity bought two old dilapidated buildings in New York City and spent $100,000 to restore them for shelters for the homeless. But some of the New York bureaucrats told the nuns that the New York access law mandated that they must have a $50,000 elevator to accommodate homeless men who might not be able to walk up the stairs. Although the Sisters explained that in India they had carried such men up the stairs, the bureaucrats said this would insult the dignity of the homeless men. In the end, the missionaries had to abandon the project.

One person's liberty is sometimes another person's indignity. Examples of this kind of reasoning could be given over and over. Do you think that sometimes we need to lose our dignity and our pride and humble ourselves before the Lord and before one another? We have lost many of the Biblical values that made this country great and the moral values where each person took responsibility for his/her behavior. Too many of us take our moral values from Hollywood and the entertainment industry.

Several years ago I went with a friend to see *Forrest Gump* movie that had been highly recommended by his pastor. It was a good movie, but in the Viet Nam War scenes, the loud profanity and vulgarity was so out of place, it put a damper on what could have been a warm and good story.

You say, "Well they are just trying to be realistic." No! They are setting standards, and impressionistic people are being influenced, and our world is becoming more and more insensitive to this kind of language. Doug Larson of United Features Syndicates said recently, "It took only 50 years for the movies to go from silent to unspeakable!"

We cannot walk around Washington without realizing the Christian foundations on which this nation was built. At the Jefferson Memorial written in stone around the statue of Jefferson, every phrase and Bible verse attests to the nation's belief in God.

The final verse in our scripture today is verse 25, "If we live in the spirit, let us also walk in the spirit." Paul is urging us to remember that, as Christians, we have received the spirit of Christ; therefore we are to walk in this spirit. When he says, "Let us walk in the Spirit of Christ," the implications are that we can. We do not have to continue in sin and self-defeating behavior. Christ has set us free.

This is what freedom is about - being set free from anything that is dragging us down. Paul tells us over and over that the Spirit is more than the manifestation of supernatural power (as important as that is). The Spirit is more than the giver of dramatic gifts. The Spirit is the daily sustaining, inspiring and guiding power in the Christian life.

"The God who gave us life, gave us liberty at the same time." This is the kind of liberty Christ wants to give each one of us. Not absolute freedom that makes us run roughshod over other people's freedom. Not freedom without responsibility. Instead He wants to give us freedom rooted and grounded in the death and resurrection of Jesus Christ.

This is the freedom of knowing our sins are forgiven. This is the freedom of knowing that to be absent from the body is to be present with the Lord in heaven. This is the freedom of knowing that death does not have the last word.

This Sunday message is that Christ walked out of the grave saying, "Because I live, you shall live, also." I thank God for the liberty we enjoy as Americans. Even more, I thank God for the liberty we have in Jesus Christ.

"The God who gave us life, gave us liberty at the same time." Stand firm then and do not let yourselves be burdened again by a yoke of slavery. Amen.

Working for Bread

Matthew 20:1-16

For the kingdom of heaven is like a landowner who went out early in the morning to hire laborers for his vineyard.
~Matthew 20:1 (NRSV)~

This parable about equal pay for unequal work was totally unexpected – a shocking concept really. It was unacceptable to early laborers. It is unacceptable to us. It just goes against the grain of our sinful selfish natures. We believe in the Judeo-Christian work ethic. We don't believe people who work only one hour in the day should be paid the same as those who worked all day. But there are several important truths that we need to learn from this parable.

First, let me say that the men who were sitting around the marketplace were not depicted as lazy. This was the place where individuals were supposed to go when they did not have a regular trade or job or did not own land. The marketplace was the place for workers to gather who wanted to work – a labor pool of sorts – a place where people could go to find work to support their families.

But this parable does not focus on economics, though some people have tried to press it in that direction. This is a parable about grace. It is about the boundless grace of God! It seems that many people are struggling through life aimlessly because they are uncertain about their relationship with God! They have never accepted the grace of Jesus Christ.

A couple of years ago I attended the North Georgia Conference of the United Methodist Women meeting at the Ben Hill UMC. The program consisted of many inspiring services, and in a final program on ecology, we were urged to recycle and preserve our environment. It was described as a matter of life and death. But from my long years of observing life, the major thing I've seen that could change a person from the kind of self-centered life that is ruining our environment is a personal relationship with Jesus Christ. Even our ecology problems are spiritual problems.

I heard Bryant Gumble say on television one day that all ocean and sea life is paying a high price for decades of pollution. This is true, and we must be concerned and do something about the pollution of our environment. I thought, as I listened to Gumble, that it is even truer that our children and all of us are paying a high price for the pollution of our minds and emotions.

As concerned as I am about the pollution that is ruining our environment, I am even more concerned about the increasing amount of pornography, gambling, alcohol and other drugs that are polluting and affecting the environment in which our children are living.

Oh, how we need to know about grace in our kind of world! Oh, how our world needs to know about the grace of God! John Wesley once said that men and women could, by becoming Christians, learn grace without the benefits of a dance master.

In Wesley's time, dance was different from much of the dancing done in our time. It was a matter a propriety rather than the cheap way some of it has become in recent years. People who could afford to do so sent their children to dance classes to learn manners and grace.

It is not an accident that the word "grace" (*Caris* in the Greek) is the word used in polite society to describe a lady or a gentleman. Wesley believed, and I believe, that if the grace of Jesus Christ is at work in a person's life, he/she is "gracious." Gracious people are ladies or gentlemen. They learn manners and grace in the new birth that Jesus offers. The new birth that Jesus offers fills us with love and respect for one another. It fills us with grace.

During Wesley's time, the dance master, or the finishing school, taught gracious behavior. The new birth tends to rub off the rough edges because we are filled with love and concern for others. In other words we become "civilized" and thus "more civil."

We desperately need this in any society. The lack of grace is polluting our Earth and waters and is also polluting our children and our adults too – even our old people.

As I studied today's scripture lesson, I was excited again about grace – the boundless grace of God.

At one time, the people on the Atlanta Board of Education were wringing their hands about a student who shot and killed another student at Harper High. The story was on the front page of the newspapers, and it was the lead story on the television news. As a result of this incident, they decided to allocate another million dollars for metal detectors! Someone did finally come forth and say we have to somehow change the children inside before our schools can become safe again. We are sadly spending time and money trying to teach our children manners and morals and ethics and gracefulness without the grace that God freely gives!

In this passage of scripture, it is interesting to observe the attitude reflected in the men who had worked. Some of the men were angry because they thought they should have received more wages. Many of us can relate to that in work situations today. We might hear someone say, "He gets a lot more pay than I do, and yet he does half the work."

When I was employed at the Internal Revenue Service Center, I was interested to hear people in the mornings complaining about how little work the "night shift" did the night before. Nearly every day someone was sure to look at all the documents left to be processed and say, "They sure must have played all night. Just look at all this work they left for us to do." The night shift probably complained about what was done or not done by the day shift workers.

The truth is we all feel our own sweat and our own weariness, and we see others around looking cool and comfortable, not realizing that we may look cool and comfortable to them. It is difficult to put ourselves in another person's place. Yet, as Christians, we are asked to do just that – even commanded to do so.

Jesus said, "See that you love one another." We can only truly love our neighbors as ourselves by God's grace, and we can indeed love and respect our neighbors by an imaginative extending of our own rough edges, sins and mistakes in the direction of the rough edges, sins and mistakes we encounter in our neighbors.

For example, Keith Miller pointed out that while he had never stolen $100,000, he did one day bring a stapler home from his office. We can somehow "identify ourselves among the transgressors" by realizing that while we may not have done the big sins, we have dabbled in sin at some level.

I suppose my past is pretty much an open book. One does not give birth to and raise seven children and have a lot of time to get into trouble. So, like Keith Miller, I have never stolen $100,000 or even one dollar that I know of, but a few years after my last day as a tax examiner, I saw a U.S. government ball point pen on my desk. I never actually took a handful of pens, and I can actually rationalize that there was probably little ink left in this pen when it somehow got from my desk at work to my desk at home. But, by extending all the feelings in my own imagination I can understand another thief better because technically I am also a thief if I even take a paper clip that does not belong to me.

I think that the key to the most helpful attitude for a Christian in truly loving others as Jesus commanded us and thus producing creative change in our work is to realize that in some ways we can all walk in almost anyone's shoes as Jesus walked in our shoes. Jesus, the only sinless person who ever walked this Earth, walked in the shoes of the vilest sinner – all the way to the cross! And He said over and over in one way or another, "Neither do I condemn you. Go and sin no more!"

As Christians we can, in some measure, learn to respect people and identify with them in the midst of their sins, stupid mistakes and self-destructive behavior, which, in the eyes of God, are not much different than ours.

C.S. Lewis says that while some of us only nibble at sin and others gorge themselves, we all give it some sort of try. For all have sinned and fallen short of the grace of God. And because we are personally experiencing the healing forgiveness of God, we have this to bring to others. We can honestly say, "Let him that is without sin cast the first stone." This does not mean that we are to wallow in our sins and say that sin does not matter. Sin matters. Sin matters so much that Jesus hung on a cross to save us from our sins – not in our sins. And sin is anything that hurts and damages us or anyone - anything that keeps us from attaining our best. I am sinning when I overeat because I am hurting my body. By the same token, we may hurt ourselves by under-eating to meet current standards of female beauty.

The Lord wants to save us. The Lord wants to rescue us from our sins. Because He loves us, He wants the best for us. He wants to lead us into lasting changes in our lifestyles. Lasting changes will bring us the joy of the Lord.

On Labor Day weekend, we seek to celebrate the privilege of work and the benefits and respectability of any honest work. All through scripture we are admonished to work. Jesus admonishes us to toil, not just for the bread that perishes, but also for the Bread of Life.

As the writer of Ecclesiastes 6:7 reminds us (RSV) "All the toil of man is for his mouth, yet his appetite is not satisfied." Jesus knows what will satisfy us. It is not just physical bread but the bread of heaven.

To work for nothing but physical food is an absurdity, yet people do it all the time. Our suburbs are filled with working couples, both working to pay for a house but so exhausted by their work that they have little time for one another or their children. We all know people paying for a nice house but having no time to make a home.

Jesus told this parable right after Peter and the other disciples had wanted to know what rewards they would receive for following Jesus. "We have left all to follow Thee. What then will there be for us?" (Matthew 19:27) For those who labor long and hard this parable might seem unfair. I've heard people say that it doesn't seem fair that some people sow their wild oats, live it up, and then get saved and have all the rights of those Christians who have spent their entire lives in service for the Lord.

> *The point is that we cannot pile up merit with God. Our relationship to God is not purchased. It is a gift.*

There is one example of a last-minute conversion in the Bible. One of the thieves on the cross beside Jesus asked for and received forgiveness. This lets us know that there is always hope but only one example to help us know that we are not to count on it! Jesus teaches here that we cannot say that only those who work for a long time count with the Lord. The point is that we cannot pile up merit before God. Our relationship to God is not purchased. It is a gift. We are saved by grace, by faith in Jesus Christ, not by works. And we save ourselves a lot of misery when we realize that we are not supposed to look around and judge other people's work or life.

As I was meditating on this passage of scripture, I kept coming back to the words of Ecclesiastes 6:7 "All the toil of man is for his mouth; yet his appetite is not satisfied." And to the words of Matthew 4:4, "Man shall not live by bread alone, but by every word that proceeds from the mouth of God." In other words, the worker who gets paid the most for the least work is not necessarily the better off. The gracious employer in this parable illustrates the acts of God, sending laborers into His vineyard all through the day as He finds them in the marketplace.

Jewish law in Leviticus 19:13 required that payment be made at the close of the work day so the family could eat. "Thou shall not defraud they neighbor, neither rob him. The wages of him that is hired shall not abide with thee all night until the morning."

The employer had agreed with the earlier laborers for a full day's wages of a certain amount of work; but he gave those who came the last hour the same wage. He did this because, in his compassion, he recognized that it took as much bread to feed their families as it did the families of those who had worked the whole day. The "gracious" employer in the parable emphasizes God's graciousness.

Grace – God's steadfast love and mercy extended to all alike. There is a profound democracy in creation, things that we all inherit - God's steadfast love and mercy extended to all alike!

I learned this as a child of eleven, sitting in a Methodist church with a congregation singing, "At the cross, at the cross where I first saw the light." My father had died when I was nine; my mother took in boarders and worked in a textile mill to support us, but I learned that God's grace extended to me, just as it did to the owner of the mill. And God's grace changed my life.

The scripture lesson today illustrates that not all people respond alike to God's goodness. Some compare and evaluate their own goodness and thereby fail to understand God's graciousness. "God, I only stole one ballpoint pen and you call me a thief, same as the guy who stole a million dollars." The fact that all of us alike are sinners places us together without distinctions or degrees and all in need of God's gracious acceptance.

You see we all need and we all have the glorious privilege to partake of this "graciousness" so that we don't strut through life looking down our noses at people or holding grudges. The kids in our high schools need to partake of this grace and learn graciousness. We may laugh at bumper stickers like "I don't get mad; I get even," but this "get even" attitude is a miserable existence.

Equal pay for unequal work was totally unexpected and unacceptable to the laborers and to us. It just goes against the grain of our sinful selfish natures. "Lord, I've sweated here all day; you could wring a gallon of sweat out of my clothes; and you are going to pay this cool Johnny-come-lately the same pay that I'm getting? It's not right. I'm going to make myself and everyone else miserable the rest of the day and grumble about it."

No one had been denied; no one had been cheated; no one had been given less pay than agreed upon. The offense was in looking around and seeing that someone else got more for less.

This parable in Matthew 20 is about grace. Paul put it this way, "Where sin abounds, grace that much more abounds."
Marvelous grace of our loving Lord - grace that exceeds our sin and our guilt - freely bestowed on all who believe.

I first got a glimpse of that marvelous grace and made the decision to accept that grace as a child of eleven sitting in church. I pray that if there is someone here who has not made the decision to believe Jesus Christ, he or she will decide to accept this marvelous grace! It is the most important decision you will ever make. Amen.

A Legacy of Love

Philippians 1:1-11

I thank my God upon every remembrance of you.
~Philippians 1:3 (KJV)~

As I was reading the book of Philippians, this first chapter preached itself to me. We could read it and go home and have an important message from the Lord.

The third verse says something important that I want to say to you. In the words of Paul, "I thank my God upon every remembrance of you." And I want to come back and lift up other things from this important passage in God's holy word.

Today is Father's Day. So I want to say something about fathers to the dear men in this congregation and to all of us. As I said about mothers on Mother's Day, "We all have or had a father." We all come to Father's Day thinking about our own dad or the man or men who influenced our young lives, rather than thinking about some honor due us if we happen to also be a father.

In *USA Today* newspaper, I read an article entitled, "A Father's Death Leaves Love Behind." William Maddox wrote about his father-in-law, a man he never met because his wife's dad died when she was only three. Nevertheless, this father, who would have been his father-in-law, had a profound influence on his daughter.

Her dad had been a musician who sang in a quartet and had cut a few records. William Maddox said his wife's father's legacy lived on because his words and deeds and music had a deep influence on his wife's upbringing. The father had died young, but he did indeed leave a legacy of love behind. As a child, his wife loved to go to the church where her father often sang, and she became interested in finding her father's God.

I was interested in this story that so paralleled mine, because, as I have mentioned before, my father died when I was nine. I remember as a young child missing my Dad so much I would pray that I would see him in a dream. My father had a profound influence on me as a serious-minded and shy child.

I would hear other children say, "I want to be a nurse" or "I want to be a policeman," and I would think, "When I grow up I want to be a Christian like Papa." My father's Christian influence was a greater legacy for me than any amount of money or property he could have left me.

My mother's dad died when she was a baby. She said when other children would wear a new dress or shoes and say, "My papa bought them for me," she would feel sad and think, "If my papa was still alive, I would have new things."

I am glad for movements like "Promise Keepers" and other movements among men to help men and to help us all realize how much men are needed in each and every child's life and how rewarding it is for men to grow old with the love and respect of children because of the love and care their children received in childhood.

My father was a devout Christian and did not want to leave his wife and children. But as heart disease weakened his body, he was so certain of heaven that he looked forward to death as one would anticipate a long awaited vacation. Wilson Baird knew that what we call "death" does not have the last word over what God calls "life."

At a memorial service at our North Georgia Church Conference a few years ago, Bishop Bevel Jones preached, and one of the things he said was about Aristotle Onassis, who, amid his millions, never had a cause he supported. Jones said, "To leave no estate is not a disgrace, but to leave no legacy is a tragedy."

The influence of a father cannot be over-emphasized. Studies have shown that when a father is missing (absent from the home or ineffective in the home) there is a great hole in the child - especially in a son - that cannot quite be filled.

Fortunately the Bible teaches that there is one remedy. Many of the great leaders of past generations have filled that void with God. Some have filled the space left by an absent father with the Heavenly Father. The psalmist David said, even "if my father and mother forsake me, the lord will take me up."[42] God is able to take all kinds of tragedy and bring about good when we commit our lives to him.

This is what the gospel is all about because we are living in a fallen world. Life at best is short and is a preparation place. When we invite Christ into our lives, God can use all things to work for our good with "beauty for ashes," and joy in the midst of sorrow and life eternal in the midst of death.

David Blankenship has written a book, *Fatherless America*. He writes that when a father dies, his fatherhood lives on in the head and heart of the child. If and when family and friends keep the father's memory alive and when they find ways to help compensate for the father's absence, his fatherhood survives. In this sense the child is still fathered.

Looking back, I was deeply influenced by my mother telling me about my father. She told me how he prayed for me. My mother told me how on his death bed he prayed for each child by name, that each would come to know Christ as Savior and Lord.

I hope I leave a legacy of love and prayer and good spiritual preaching and especially practicing what I have tried to preach. This is what I have been called by the Lord to do and, in the words of Paul, "I have sought to be true to that heavenly vision."

Paul, in our text from Philippians, is writing like a father to beloved children. He called them his "joy and crown." In verses 2-4, Paul writes, "Grace be unto you and peace, from God our Father and from the Lord Jesus Christ. I thank my God upon every remembrance of you. Always and in every prayer of mine for you, making all requests with joy."

---

[42] Psalm 27:10

The church at Philippi was Paul's joy and crown, even though Paul was no longer with them. Paul was writing this from prison, but he was thinking of the people at Philippi. Paul was thinking and praying for the churches he had served. So this letter throbs with personal intensity and with gratitude and joy.

Three times in the first two verses Paul speaks the name of Jesus, his Lord and Savior. These references to Christ are the cord binding Paul with the Christians he is writing to. These people are the friends who are participants with him in the gospel.

So even though Paul is writing to dear friends, he does not let his deep affection for them substitute for the central subject matter which is Jesus Christ. Paul's central subject is Jesus Christ! This is the bond he shares with the Philippian church. This is the bond we all share in Christ. This is our legacy of love as Christians.

In our lesson today, Paul reminds us that God has given us a new status "in Christ." In fact Paul gives them two addresses. They are in "Christ" and they are in "Philippi." Later he will tell them they are to "let their lives in Christ Jesus be evident in Philippi."

Paul reminds us all that we are called to be "in Christ" wherever we go. We are incorporate in Christ Jesus. We are privileged to be partners in Christ Jesus - incorporate with him! This is an exciting promise. The promise in verse 6 is "being confident of this very thing, he who has begun a new work in you will complete it."

> *"Joy" is the word we hear Paul saying over and over in this little epistle to the Philippians.*

This love brings joy. People who look at other people with suspicion and fear are miserable. "Joy" is the word we hear Paul saying over and over in this little epistle to the Philippians. Paul was writing from a prison cell, chained to a Roman guard. How in the world could Paul write about joy when his own survival was at stake?

How in such an environment could the emotion of "joy" survive and thrive? Because Paul had two addresses! Paul was in a Philippian jail but he was also "in Christ Jesus!"

Later in this letter Paul said, "Rejoice in the Lord always, and I say it again, rejoice, the Lord is at hand." Paul had been in the limelight. Now he was in the backwaters of life. How could Paul rejoice? Paul learned that even in prison "the Lord is at hand." Paul was in bonds in jail, but he was "in Christ Jesus!" Paul had a thorn in the flesh, but he was "in Christ Jesus!"

How does Paul say it? "To all the saints in Christ Jesus, grace to you and peace from God, our father, and the Lord Jesus Christ. I thank my God upon every remembrance of you!" Amen.

Jonah Running

Jonah 3: 1-5, 10

Now the word of the lord came to Jonah the second time, saying, "Arise, go to Nineveh, that great city, and preach to it the message that I tell you." So Jonah arose and went to Nineveh, according to the word of the Lord. Now Nineveh was an exceedingly great city, a three-day journey in extent.
~Jonah 3: 1-3 (NKJV)~

You have all heard about Jonah and the whale. Even people who do not go to church have heard stories about Jonah and the whale. Actually, the Bible doesn't call it a whale, just a big fish prepared by God. The Book of Jonah in the Bible is a book of four short chapters stuck between the Minor Prophets Obadiah and Micah toward the end of the Old Testament.

The story of Jonah is really a story about all of us. It is a look in the mirror. It is a story about me and about you and our story of running away from God and then running back to God. It is about our effort to make God bow to our will instead of submitting to the will of God for our lives.

God was in pursuit of Jonah, not out of anger but out of love. God was chasing Jonah in the storms of Jonah's life because of his love. The story of Jonah's encounter and struggle with God is power-packed with truth - with God's truth and with applications in the lives of all of us.

Like Jonah, we all tend to run away from God, if not all the time, at times we do. Then we often find ourselves running back to God in times of need, as finally did Jonah. The truth about us is that we are often much like Peter when he said to Jesus, "To whom else can we go? You have the words of eternal life." [43]

---

[43] I Corinthians 13:12

The book of Jonah is also a comforting book of grace and mercy. It is a story of grace and mercy for the reluctant prophet Jonah as well as for the pagan Gentiles at Nineveh.

> *Sometimes we also run ahead of God. We try to use our prayers to tell God to do our will instead of submitting to God's will and plan for our lives.*

So, like Jonah, we sometimes run away from the Lord. Then we run back in time of need and distress. Sometimes we also run ahead of God. We try to use our prayers to tell God to do our will instead of submitting to God's will and plan for our lives.

Most Christians say or think, "I know the Lord doesn't expect me to give up this or that or to do this or that. God knows I'm only human." We do not realize what we are missing by not seeking the guidance of a Father God who loves us and can see the whole of life and not just "through a glass darkly" as we do. [44]

We are told the book of Jonah is a didactic biography written about a historical prophet named Jonah who lived in the 8th century B.C. The young prophet is called by God to go to the wicked city of Nineveh (now northern Iraq) - this land of pagan Gentile "foreigners." They were not Jonah's kind of people. It seems God was interested in us "foreigners" early on before some of God's prophets found out about us or even wanted to find out about us.

Jonah had a better idea. We can identify! I can be full of better ideas. Our educational system, our culture, our popular media and our vested-interest advertisers are full of better ideas. Why? Why in the name of God and this old-fashioned book should we not take our cue for living from our surroundings and our culture?

---

[44] *The Communicator's Commentary*, Lloyd J. Ogilvie, The book of Jonah, pages 401-431.

And even though we are Christians, we tend to reflect the values and customs of those around us instead of setting Christ-like standards.

We all know it is sometimes difficult enough and time-consuming enough to go the second mile for our loved ones, our own family and friends. Isn't it "a bit much" to be expected to go to that much trouble for foreigners? In the name of common sense, Jonah just flat out didn't like the people of Nineveh, and he wanted no part of taking God's message to them. So, like a rebelling teenager, he didn't just stay home and refuse to go to Nineveh, he took off to Tarsus in the opposite direction!

Jonah went out and got on a boat going in the other direction as if he was trying to hide as far away from God as he could get. It didn't work. It never does. God followed him. It may seem to work for a while - even a long while. But it doesn't work in the long run. For Jonah and for me and for others, it did not even work in the short run.

Jonah did not get very far in the opposite direction. Like the "hound of Heaven" this story is about how God pursued Jonah. You know what happened. As I said, even people who do not go to church have heard about Jonah, but have you heard the whole story?

A few years ago someone brought out a soft drink and called it "The Big Gulp." Like the children's song about Jonah that goes something like this, "This is the fish that swallowed Jonah . . . gulp, gulp, gulp!"

Jonah's running away from God got him thrown overboard off the ship during a storm and swallowed by a big fish. After the fish got sick of Jonah and spewed him out, it was stress enough to make him run back to God and decide to try God's plan after all. Jonah got a second chance. We hear a good many people today talking about a second chance.

At the second command of God, Jonah finally went to Nineveh and preached repentance. Jonah shouted in the streets of Nineveh. Eight words are the only part of his prophetic sermon that the Bible gives us: "Yet forty days and Nineveh shall be destroyed."

And the biggest miracle of all happens - a bigger miracle than the fish swallowing Jonah and having him live to tell the tale. Miracle of miracles, those Gentile foreign people of Nineveh repented! The Bible tells us the people of Nineveh repented immediately. Most of us don't get that kind of quick results. Even the king of Nineveh repented, and he ordered a fast and led them all out in sackcloth and ashes.

Then the Bible tells us an amazing truth - God repented! Imagine that? God changed His mind and decided to spare them after all.

The King of Nineveh and all the people repented. God repented and did not destroy the city of Nineveh. Jonah did not repent! Jonah got mad. He didn't really expect nor want the people of Nineveh to repent. Jonah had no love for them. Jonah wanted these foreign Gentiles destroyed.

In Chapter 4, the first verse reports, "The people's repentance and God's repentance displeased Jonah." Jonah must have been a Pharisee. Jesus told us there is joy in Heaven when one sinner repents.[45] But the Pharisees thought there was joy in heaven when God zapped the sinner.

You heard the old story about the congregation that fired their preacher because he kept preaching hellfire and damnation. They got sick and tired of him telling them every Sunday they were all going to hell. So they got a wonderful new preacher. One of the members told her neighbor that he must come to hear this new preacher - that he was great, nothing at all like the old preacher.

The neighbor came to church and after the service he said, "I don't get it. You fired your other preacher who preached on hell, but this guy said the same thing. He said, 'You're all going to hell.'"

---

[45] Luke 15:7

The church member said, "Yes he did, but when he tells us that we're all going to hell, you get the feeling he's genuinely sorry about it."

Jonah was not sorry about it. He told the people of Nineveh they were on their way to hell's destruction, and apparently Jonah was glad. After all, they were not Jonah's kind of people. It was what they deserved. So when they repented and God forgave them, Jonah did not like it! Jonah wanted mercy for himself for his sins, but not for those Gentile sinners.

This message of God's love was not new with the book of Jonah! God told Abraham in the Genesis of our Bible that his people were to bless the whole world, but it was never a popular message then or now. Often the message of God's love for all got lost in the "formal" temple worship and the emphasis on the law. Even so, we see God's grace and love for the whole world in the Old Testament as well as the New Testament.

The message of mercy and grace was a stumbling block for Jonah and for many in the Old Testament as well as for many of the Jewish people in the days when Jesus walked the earth.

Paul said the message of salvation for "whosoever will" that leads to the cross was indeed foolishness to the Greeks and a stumbling block to the Jews; but to those who are being saved, it is the power of God.

The good news was not the exclusive message to Abraham or for Jonah, and it is not our private possession. Jesus is my personal savior but not my private Savior.

We make a serious mistake in our churches when we consider evangelism and mission as just one phase of the church's work. Evangelism and mission are the reason we do all the rest. They're the reason we are here and the reason we worship and teach. Evangelism and mission are the reason we have fellowship with one another and serve God - to find salvation and to tell others what we have found.

Evangelism is "one beggar telling another beggar where to find bread." Jonah did not see himself as one who had received mercy, received bread and received God.

These Gentiles at Nineveh were spiritual lightweights compared to the more spiritually mature Israelites. The Nineveh people were wicked because they did not know God, they did not know the Law of God, and they would never know God as long as the people who knew Him refused to go and tell.

I remember a lovely story in *Reader's Digest* a few years ago - just a brief paragraph. A lady with three children had married a man whose wife had died and left him with three children. One day someone told this stepmother, "I think you pay more attention to your stepchildren than you do your own." She replied, "I just have so much heart for these poor little motherless children."

The Lord wanted Jonah to have heart and feeling for these poor lost and wicked Nineveh people who had never heard about the true and living God. God is calling us to also have heart and love for those in our world who do not know God.

Stephen Neill said, "The only reason for being a Christian is the ever-growing conviction that the Christian faith is true." This happens when we meet Jesus Christ personally and experience his love, his mercy, and his grace. The hard inner core of our self-control surrenders to His control. When we invite Christ to live in us, we experience the power of His indwelling spirit and are free at last from our use of manipulative human power to evade His call.

When Christ comes into our lives in power, we put Christ on the throne of our lives. We know where the power is and it is not in our human flesh.

I heard an older person say, "If I'd known I was going to live so long, I would have taken better care of myself." That is one reason we need Christ in our life - because He alone can number our days. God alone can see into the future and we cannot. When we put our trust in Christ, He is full of surprises.

Space travel has labeled our planet that "little blue ball of earth." We thought it was big enough to hide us from our enemies. Now we know the truth of what Jesus knew and taught 2000 years ago. We have to learn to love our enemies if we want to survive. There is no place to run.

In the book of Jonah, as in other places in the Holy Scripture, we are given more than just security. We are given our marching orders - our commission, "Go ye therefore and tell the Good News." Amen.

The Red Sea Crossing

Exodus 14:19-31   Matthew 14:22-31

Then Moses stretched out his hand over the sea. The Lord drove the sea back by a strong east wind all night, and turned the sea into dry land; and the waters were divided.
~Exodus 14:21(NRSV)~

I first met Moses when I was a child in Sunday School. I loved to hear about how baby Moses was rescued from his little basket boat in the Nile River, where his mother had hidden him because the Pharaoh of Egypt had decreed to kill all Israeli baby boys.

The Bible introduces Moses, an Israelite, who is descendent of Jacob's son Levi in Exodus, Chapter 2. Before we leave chapter two he is all grown up as the adopted son of Pharaoh's daughter and thus was an Egyptian prince in the King's palace.

But Moses knew who he was, and one day when he saw his people being mistreated at the hands of an Egyptian. Moses killed the man who was brutalizing an Israelite man. The very next day Moses saw two Israelite men fighting, he was appalled and asked them why? Why, In the midst of all the violence against them, would the people of God fight among themselves? A good question for then and for now!

These two Israelite ruffians told Moses to tend to his own business, and furthermore they informed Moses that they had seen his violence against the Egyptians the day before.

Moses felt threatened and fled from Egypt to become a shepherd in the land of Midian. There he married Zipporah and became a father.

So we see Moses, who had been a prince in Egypt, tending sheep in the land of Midian, trying to forget that his Israelite people were slaves in Egypt. But in the last verse in chapter 2 of Exodus we are told the God had not forgotten. God remembered!

The third chapter opens with God coming down to Moses in the burning bush experience. God told Moses, in all those beautiful action verbs that are "power verbs for powerless people," God hears...God sees...God remembers...God knows... and God has come down. This is great news that God remembered and still loves the people of Israel.

The only problem was that God said to Moses, "Moses, I want you to go. Moses I have chosen you, called you. I want you to go to Pharaoh."

Moses's reply to God was, "Why me? Who am I that I should go to Pharaoh?" The gist of God's reply to Moses was, "It is not a matter of who you are Moses; it is who I am."

Moses did not want to go and he had some valid excuses. Moses and God worked on these excuses for the next few chapters in Exodus. It was decided that Aaron, the brother of Moses, would help him with the talking. So Moses and Aaron went to Pharaoh and told him all that God had said and done. They said that Pharaoh was to let the people go. But Pharaoh was not impressed with words or miracles. He turned up the heat on the Israelites, and things went from bad to worse.

Then there were the plagues. Moses and Aaron went before Pharaoh and told him to let God's people go. Pharaoh refused, and there were more plagues that just went on and on.

In Chapter 12, we see the exciting story of the actual narrating and celebrating of their sacred Passover before it took place. Then after the final plague of the killing of all the first born of the Egyptians, the Pharaoh summoned Moses to the palace and told him to go. Pharoah told Moses and Aaron to take all his people and get out of Egypt!

When we get to today's scripture lesson, the people begin heading for the Red Sea. However Pharaoh had another change of mind and began chasing after them.

This text concludes the account of Israel's deliverance at the sea which began in Genesis 13:17. This is an important text also for Christians and is paired with Matthew 14 when Jesus walked on the water. Both tell of God reaching out to people of faith on a dark night of helplessness, desperation and fear.

I read a story recently of a young man asking his teacher to teach him to pray. The teacher grabbed the student and held his head down under water for just the right amount of time and told him, "When you want to pray as desperately as you want to breathe, you will learn to pray."

As I read and re-read this Scripture text from several translations, I could not remember the first time, as a child in Sunday School, I heard this story, or the first time I saw paintings of Moses holding his hand over the Red Sea and splitting a path through the water as the people of Israel walk across the sea on dry land.

Some Bible commentaries have given this story the central place in the book of Exodus. This is the Exodus! But however we see this passage of Holy Scripture, we do see that all the various accounts of the event come together in the unqualified good news that God delivered the Israelites out of slavery.

It is a story of grace and not good works! The Israelites were confused and afraid! The Israelites were complaining and faithless! Just before this lesson the people saw the Egyptian Army closing in on them and they cried out, "What have you done to us, Moses? Were there no graves in Egypt, Moses? We told you so, Moses?" They were tired of Moses and tired of all his words about a God they couldn't see and whose ways they did not understand. They wanted a God in their own image - much like the Jesus in our United Methodist Youth Group Choir play, "Dive Deeper," a few years ago. They had a Jesus who kept patting everyone on the head, smiling and agreeing with anything and everything they said.

With the Egyptian Army behind Moses and the Red Sea in front, Moses made a speech. For a person who said he could not talk, he made quite an impressive speech for these terrified Israelites: "Have no fear; stand by and witness the deliverance which the Lord will work for you today! For the Egyptians whom you see today, you will never see again!" Significant, courageous words from the mouth of Moses. But they were in a voice that must have sounded like a cry because God told Moses, "Why do you cry to me? Tell the people to go forward."

In other words, God told Moses to tell God's people not to just keep a "stiff upper lip" but to take productive action. Tell them to move forward into the sea. Tell them to "fear not, to stand firm, and to see the salvation of the Lord."

As Americans and especially as Christian Americans, we love the drama of this moment in the history of Israel.

The presence of God in history means darkness to some and light to others.

Counting three, two, one, let the Doxology begin, "Praise God from whom all blessings flow." The Sovereign Father God is intervening on behalf of suffering slaves.

"And the angel of God and the pillar of cloud which went before them moved and stood behind them. And there was darkness and distance between the opposing armies." (Exodus 14:19) The very darkness was protection to the Israelites and confusion to the Egyptian army. The dark cloud to the Egyptians was danger, chaos and confusion. The dark cloud to Moses and his people was God.

The presence of God in history means darkness to some and light to others. So with the words of Moses ringing in their ears and Divine protection both in front and behind, we view amazing first steps; these cringing , complaining former slaves step off Egyptian soil into the sea!

Let the Doxology continue! "Praise God all people here below!" We are beneficiaries! These Israelite slaves still had a long road ahead. But they had started. The term, "Between the devil and the deep blue sea" probably can be traced back to that fateful day at the Red Sea crossing.

We know that a thousand mile walk starts with one step. On a night trip in a car we can see only as far as the headlights but one can make the whole journey that way. Hebraic legend extols the courage and the faith of that first person to step between the huge walls of water. Praise God above, all heavenly hosts!

Michael Fishbane[46] made this observation: "This Historical event is the consummate expression of divine power and national redemption as each generation looked to the first exodus as the expression of its own future hope." All the details are not clear but the bottom line is that God did exactly what Moses told them He would do. God delivered the former Israeli slaves across the Red Sea.

In Walter Brueggemann's *Israel's Praise:*[47] "All Egypt's crushing indignities cannot stop the relentless, God-given capacity for world-making." God's people continue to make this world what unbelievers do not want, do not permit and cannot stop. Israel saw the ruined chariots, the dead horses and the Egyptians dead on the seashore. The impossible happened. No one would have believed such a reversal possible. "Praise Father, Son and Holy Ghost."

The last verse in our text rightly makes a theological statement. God's act of salvation had led not only to Israel's trust in God, but also to Israel's trust in Moses as a prophet of God. Moses at first did not believe in himself. But believing in oneself is not a requisite for any of us. Moses believed in God!

---

[46] Michael Fishbane (born 1943, Ph.D., Brandeis University) is well known as a Hebrew Bible scholar.
[47] Walter Brueggemann, *Israel's Praise: Doxology Against Idolatry and Ideology*. Fortress Press, 1988.

The rest of the story, the rest of the Pentateuch, will define Moses in increasing detail as a prophet and deliverer and as one who bore the message of God.

The God of Israel's bottom line is liberation of His people. Never again will they identify God as only the God of Abraham, of Isaac and Jacob but as the Lord our God. Never again just the God of our fathers but the Lord our God.

This personal God is still in the business of lifting us up from the things that would drag us down to the very pits of hell and degradation. In our New Testament Scripture, Peter walks on water. When Jesus came to the disciples on water, Peter told Jesus, "If this is really You, let me come." When Peter stepped out of the boat onto the water, we might look on in amazement and ask, "Peter, have you studied yoga, have you studied 'surface tension?'" And Peter might have answered us, "It was when I took my eyes off Jesus and began to study 'surface tension' that I began to sink."

Faith focuses on Jesus who says, "Come." The Lord our God brings us up and out of our slavery to sin. The word is "come." Amen.

In Token and Pledge

Genesis 15:1-18a.

After these things the word of the Lord came to Abram in a vision, saying, "Do not be afraid, Abram. I am your shield, your exceedingly great reward." ~Genesis 15: 1 (NKJV)~

I love reading the book of Genesis! In Genesis 15:1-18a, we see Abraham, revered by both Christians and Jews, getting into covenant with God. The great central theme of our Bible, both the Old Testament and the New Testament, is God's covenant relationship with humanity.

After generations of dealing with rebellious people, God unfolds his plan of redemption for all people. In Genesis 12, God calls Abram to leave his home in Ur of the Chaldes and to travel to a distant but unspecified new land.

Abram responds in faith and obeys with nothing to cling to but the promises of God. Really, for Abram it was the long view. There was not much in it immediately or for a long time for Abram. How often we all see, in looking back over our life, that God took the long view.

The genealogists in the Bible take the long view with all the begats that we tend to skip over. I re-read Matthew this week and noted that in the family tree of Jesus, we know nothing about more than half the names. Some names, like Rahab and Bathsheba, we would just as soon not know about. Yet we see that even in the lineage of Jesus, God sometime uses human weaknesses to magnify divine power!

In the book, *A Different Kind of Strength*, Janice Crouse tells about how the five women in the genealogy of Jesus were used in God's own time in spite of their failures.[48]

---

[48] Janice Shaw Crouse, *A Different Kind of Strength*

Many of us have a problem with "God's timing." Ours is a "now" generation. We are into television dramas where a family crisis can be solved in thirty minutes and motion picture detectives can have justice roll down like waters in an hour. We do not like to wait. We want results immediately.

But in Genesis 15, we see Abram, who set out on his journey of faith in Chapter 12 still daring to believe God's promise for the impossible in God's own time.

In the fifteenth chapter of Genesis, he is just plain Abram. We have to get down two chapters later before God changes his name to Abraham. Abram believes God's promise about a son born to his wife Sarah. But it is not making much sense to keep believing when all the evidence is to the contrary. Most of us would have been cynical by now. We would have long since said, "This faith stuff is not working for me."

For several years when our children were young, we took a week each summer for a camping trip. As a mother, I think one of the most difficult things about rearing children is riding with them in an automobile! You are on a 4 or 5 hour trip and every few minutes one of them will ask, "How much longer will it be before we get there, Mama?" A minute later, "Daddy, how much longer before we get there?"

I heard about one little boy who was on a family vacation and kept asking this question and finally the father said, "Don't ask me anymore. I'm tired of the question. Please keep quiet about it!" The little boy got very quiet. Then, after a while, he said in a small whisper, "Daddy, will I still be alive when we get there?"

Abram must have wondered, "Will I live long enough to see God's promise fulfilled?"

So Chapter 15 in the Genesis of our Bible begins with God reassuring fearful old Abram that he and Sarah will have a son. In spite of the evidence to the contrary, God tells Abram that his descendants will be as numerous as the stars he sees on a clear night!

> *This basic attitude of trust is an inner attitude which puts a person in a right relationship with God.*

Verse 6 tells us that "Abram believed God and it was accounted to him for righteousness." This keynote comment defines the meaning of faith as implicit trust in God's character - trust in God's promise - even when proof is lacking. This basic attitude of trust is an inner attitude which puts a person in a right relationship with God. This is what righteousness means - a right relationship with God.

In a very real sense, Abram had repented. Abram had given up seeing reality as only something he could see and touch and manage. His faith was not grounded in the old flesh of Sarah nor the tired bones of Abram but in the "word of Almighty God."[49]

In Old Testament language, a covenant is cut - not spoken. We see Abram cut the larger animals in half and clear a path. This passing between the broken pieces of the animals symbolized the idea that within the very bodies of the slain animals, the parties of the covenant are united as one. This was their pledge to each other. By passing through the severed bodies of the animals, each party said, "May the same thing happen to me - may I be torn in half - if I do not keep my word." It is like children sometimes say, "Cross my heart and hope to die!"

Our ceremonies and pledges and covenants today seem colorless compared to this covenant Abram made with God on that dark night. We walk down carpeted aisles, kneel on a padded altar and repeat, "I accept Jesus Christ as my Savior and Lord." Or we stand in a comfortable courthouse and say, "I promise to tell the truth, the whole truth and nothing but the truth, so help me God." Or we stand with our beloved before a minister in an air conditioned

---

[49] Walter Brueggemann, *Interpretation Commentary.* Vol. 1, P.141

sanctuary and repeat, "In token and pledge of the vow and covenant between us made, with this ring I thee wed."

Abram did all he was told to do and walked - not down a carpeted church aisle or even a sawdust trail. Abram walked the bloody path between the animals to make his covenant with God. He even had to guard his part of the bargain by waving off the vultures that came down to eat the carcasses. After all the activity Abram fell into a fitful sleep. In the midst of such a sleep, Abram saw a pot of fire and a flaming torch pass between the halves of the slain animals. Abram saw and knew it was the Lord God keeping his part of the covenant.

Do you get the picture? The God of creation passed down a bloody path between severed animals! I vividly remember the first time I really studied this passage of scripture. I still read this text with great emotion because here we see a God of love, as Paul paints for us in the beautiful poem in Philippians, "emptying himself of his divinity and stooping down to make himself available for covenant with any man or woman!"[50]

This is the best good news I know! God loves us. God knows - and if we live long enough we will know - that we will need more than just a few religious Band-Aids to patch up our brokenness. No ritual "first aid" treatment can heal the grief-bruised and sin-sick soul. We need God for the challenges of life. Our best resources and finest minds are not adequate.

I heard a young preacher tell the story of when his wife became pregnant with their first child. He said it was an unplanned pregnancy. He was a graduate student, his wife was working, and they needed her salary. But even so, when the pregnancy was confirmed they were excited about the baby and accepted congratulations from family and friends.

Then a few days later, his wife began to have a threatened miscarriage, and her doctor said it was probably nature's way of terminating a pregnancy in which the baby was defective. The

---

[50] Philippians 2:6-8

husband called a doctor friend who listened to the symptoms, concurred with the first diagnosis, and consoled the young man that they could still have more children.

The husband came back and told his wife what the doctor friend had said. His wife did not reply and looked at him as if she did not hear him. He raised his voice and told her that perhaps they should be grateful because the baby could have been horribly handicapped and would lead a sad life. He reminded her that they could have more children.

He said he could not believe the horrified look on his wife's face as she screamed, "You don't understand how much I have come to love this baby in the 48 hours I have known of its existence. I want this baby, even if I have to spend the rest of my life taking care of it."

God loves us in a strange and wonderful way. What Jesus did for us reveals a love that is awesome, in spite of our handicap of brokenness and sin. God seems to have forgotten His own dignity and place and has given Himself to deal lovingly in covenant with us. The same God who came down to Abraham and walked between the animals said, "Cross My Heart and hope to die." In Jesus Christ he hung on a bloody cross to get to us and save us. He stretched out His arms on a cross and said, "This is how much I love you!" Amen.

A Question Mark?

Psalm 46

Be still, and know that I am God; I will be exalted among the nations; I will be exalted in the earth!
~Psalm 46:10 (NKJV)~

This has been a week of sorrow and grief and national mourning. President George W. Bush has declared the flags in our nation at half-staff in honor and in memory of the 32 innocent people who were massacred on the campus of Virginia Tech.

Bereavement, sorrow, grief and loss are this week's 24-hour news subjects. The flags in our hearts are also at half-staff as we listen to the details of this tragedy and see the tear-stained faces of parents and families of students and teachers who happened to be in the wrong place and whose lives were cut short when a psychopathic young man went on a shooting rampage.

I heard a telephone interview with the grandparents of a young man named Jeremy who was killed in the massacre on Monday. I sat in tears as they showed a picture of the young man whose grandfather described as "such a good little boy." Then the grandfather corrected himself and said, "Well, he's not a little boy anymore - he's 6 ft. 4." The picture reminded me of one of my grandsons, and so I was probably not the only parent and grandparent in tears as they talked about Jeremy. The grandmother told of getting up and after their morning prayers, they turned on the television and heard the news about the killings. "Why, that's Jeremy's school," she told her husband.

Then they began telephone calls to family. The grandfather mentioned how Jeremy had come and helped him plant 25 apple trees on their farm recently. Jeremy had said, "Grandpa, I'll be back and put a fence around them." The grandmother told how their son and his wife (the parents of Jeremy) and other family members were all in Blacksburg. They still had not released the body for burial.

The 23 year old college senior, Cho Seung-Hui, who conducted this one-man massacre of 32 students and teachers at Virginia Tech is said to have put a question mark in all the places where he was supposed to sign his name. What went wrong to make this young man feel he was nameless? What went wrong to make any young person feel he/she is only a question mark?

We, as parents, sometimes tell our children to remember who they are. Psychologists tell us that there is no more important process in childhood than the formation of the answer to the question, "Who am I?" The way we identify ourselves is important. Self-esteem is important. Television shows like *Oprah* and *Dr. Phil* focus on building self- esteem in people, especially in children. Teachers are taught to try to build self-esteem in their students.

I thought immediately back to my childhood during the Great Depression. I started to school in 1929, the year of the stock market crash. My father was in failing health and had lost his farm after the onslaught of boll weevils that took King Cotton off the throne as the major money crop in the poverty ridden south. He, along with other cotton farmers, took a job in a textile factory nearby where he worked as long as he was able. He died when I was nine.

So I was raised from age nine by a widowed mother who worked as a weaver in the cord weave shop in a textile mill. We were without many things but we never went hungry and always had time and money to share with others. My hard working, intelligent and Christian mother knew how to share with others as she "stretched dollars and pinched pennies."

> *The best good news we have ever heard is that God loves us and has a purpose and plan for the life of each one of us.*

My self-esteem was just fine! In church and at home and at school, I was taught that God loved me and I was so important that Jesus died to save me! There was no question mark about who I was. I was somebody! I was a child of God!

The best good news we have ever heard is that God loves us and has a purpose and plan for the life of each one of us.

Now our schools are supposed to be silent about God and especially the place of Christianity in our history as a nation and in Western civilization. So many of the kids, even from Christian homes, are being misled and cut adrift by the words or the implications of some professors that only the ignorant still believe in God. Quite the contrary. The most intelligent and well informed leaders in Western Civilization were Christian believers.

How many Christian parents have sacrificed to send their children to college only to have some misguided or arrogant professor waste precious learning time to ridicule the Christian faith?

In the aftermath of this deadliest college shooting rampage in United States history, Cho's college mates told the press that when they spoke to Cho, he would not reply. Most of his fellow students said they had never heard him speak.

Much has been reported since this horrible tragedy. These friends and family members of wounded and killed students at Virginia Tech in Blacksburg, Virginia, especially need our prayers. We have been shocked into remembering our purpose as the body of Christ is to pray for them and for one another.

The *Rome News-Tribune* reported on a meeting at Berry College here in Rome in which students and faculty gathered to pray for peace and comfort for all those at Virginia Tech who lost loved ones or whose lives were touched by the victims. The Berry students and faculty said they had also gathered to mourn with those who are mourning. [51] Berry's Chaplain led the worship service. He said he was "numb" when he first heard about the shootings. But his numbness ended, he recounted, when he heard his son and

---

[51] Berry College Chaplain, Dale McConkey.

daughter saying, "We live on a college campus. This could happen to us."

This has been the response from schools and universities all over the nation. Here in Rome, it was reported, "Our school systems have excellent safety plans in place, and training and exercising those plans are critical."

Thousands came together for a religious service to comfort one another. In addition to President and Mrs. Bush, the Governor and his wife and other officials in the state and community attended. They invited an Islamic priest who boldly spoke and prayed in the name of Allah. There was also a representative of Buddhism and two other women who stood to represent another religion. The last to offer some religious way to mourn for those who are mourning was a Lutheran pastor who tried to be as diverse as possible (as Christian pastors are often asked to do in public now so as not to offend any other religion). The pastor gave a good prayer but did not pray in the name of Jesus.

The sad thing about this is that these schools were founded and funded by Christians. So in a nation founded on Judeo-Christian principles where most of the founding fathers and mothers were active in Christian churches, the lack of a strong Christian voice in the memorial service was noticed. Even the secular world realizes that in times of crisis we all need the comfort of God. In our times of need, we all seek affirmation of God's presence and seek His grace.

After the 9/11/01 Islamic terrorist attack on the United States of America, Republican President George W. and Laura Bush and Former Democratic President William and Hilary Clinton all sat together in a worship service singing Christian and patriotic hymns.

Jesus addressed the subject of grief as he headed toward the cross. "In the world you will have tribulation, but be of good cheer, I have overcome the world.[52]

---

[52] John 16:32

Grief does not always relate to death and tragedies like the Virginia Tech massacre. We all face times of grief and sorrow. It is a part of the human condition. We all grieve over the crisis experiences of life. In Psalm 46 we are told that God is our refuge and our strength. Therefore we are not to fear - even in the midst of earth-shaking tragedies, because "the God of hosts is with us and the God of Jacob is our refuge."

Any experience of loss sets in motion a whole complex of emotions that psychologists call the "Grief Process " or "Grief Work." As a Christian, I believe, as many of you believe, that faith in Jesus Christ plays a major role in helping us through grief of any kind. We wonder, "How do people who do not have a church family deal with grief?

Some people seem to think a person of strong faith should be above grieving. They even quote from the Bible, "Grieve not" and forget to quote the rest of the passage which tell us, "Grieve not as those who have no hope."[53]

On the first day of our United Methodist Church's annual conference each year there is a memorial service for all the ministers who have died during the year. The bereaved families sit in specially marked places. There is a roll call of the honored dead and a memorial sermon. In 1987, I sat there with several of my children and grandchildren as my husband, who was a pastor for 37 years, was remembered.

After the service people greeted one another with hugs and expressions of sympathy. One lady whose husband had also died in 1986 greeted me with a bright smile saying, "We are not grieving, we know where they are. God is sustaining us."

It is so wonderfully true; we do know where they are. It is gloriously true - amazingly true. God is sustaining us. But she was wrong to deny the reality of grief. We are grieving, but we grieve not as those without hope. We know that we should be "still and know God." (Psalm 46:10)

---

[53] 1 Thessalonians 4:13

A young woman wrote to Dear Abby some time ago, grieving to the point of considering breaking off her engagement to a young man whose job meant they would move to California. If she married him she would have to leave her native West Virginia. She was grieving over a move away from her home State.

Divorce, as a cause of grief, is up next to death of a spouse as a stress level because divorce can create grief in the hearts of those who have lost the love of someone who was once dear to them. Retirement is another form of grief for some. So is a child moving away or leaving to go to school or a new job. The list of losses is endless. We lose health, eyesight, hearing, our mobility.

A woman in her fifties laughed and told me she missed the fact that it had been a long time since any man had turned his head to look at her. Bishop Bevel Jones spoke to us in the Woman's School of Missions I attended a few years ago. He told us that when he looked in the mirror to shave that morning, he kept trying to change the channel. Thus, some of us grieve when we look in a mirror.

Jesus wept at the tomb of Lazarus. So we weep and grieve and mourn, but there is no question mark about who we are. We grieve, but not as non-believers who have no hope. We grieve as Easter people. Easter is not just one Sunday but six Sundays. In fact every Sunday, and every day we celebrate Easter! Amen.

Christ the King

Colossians 1:13-20

*For he has rescued us from the domination of darkness and brought us into the
kingdom of the Son he loves.*
~Colossians 1: 13 (NIV)~

I heard a story about a preacher who went to bed one night after
working on a sermon that was not going very well. He had a dream
that was more like a nightmare. It started with a telephone call
from Heaven. The Lord's secretary called him to tell him that he
had been selected to preach the last sermon on earth. This would
not just be the last sermon he would preach but the last sermon
anyone would ever preach before the end of the world.

Preachers take their preaching very seriously, and this preacher was
horrified, especially knowing that he had been unable to prepare a
very good sermon that week. So he tried to explain all this to the
Lord's secretary, telling about the busy week he had had with
counseling, telephone calls, constant hospital and bedside visits,
funerals, marriages, and meetings. He ended up saying, "You had
better get someone else; I'm not the one for the job." This pastor
was told that someone had to preach the last sermon ever preached
on earth, and he had been chosen as that someone; but the preacher
kept protesting. "I'm really not that good a preacher. You should
get someone more worthy. How about Billy Graham? Isn't he
available? If anyone deserves to preach the last sermon, it should
be Billy Graham who has preached to millions. If he can't do it,
how about asking some bishop, former bishop, or the Pope?"
Again the pastor was told that it was not a matter of being worthy
or unworthy. He had no choice in the matter. He was selected to
preach the last sermon on earth, and that was the final word.
Period. End of conversation.

The preacher woke in a cold sweat, glad that the nightmare was
over and remembering the phrase we have all heard about
preaching, "Preach as never sure to preach again – and as a dying

man to dying men." Or as another preacher said, "When I am pointing one finger at you, I have three others pointing back at myself."

Today is called Christ the King Sunday.[54] Next Sunday will be the first Sunday of Advent when we begin looking at scripture about the advent of the birth of Jesus onto planet Earth. Advent is the looking forward to the birth of our Savior. Then, in the Christian year, we celebrate the Christmas season with Mary's Magnificat, the birth of Jesus, of what it all means, the angels' and the shepherds' songs of praise. Then Luke tells us Jesus was presented in the temple and the prophecies of Simeon, a righteous and devout man who took the infant Jesus in his arms and praised God for Jesus as the "light for revelation to the Gentiles and for glory to the people of Israel." Then we have the prophetess Anna, who "gave thanks to God and spoke about the child to all who were looking for the redemption of Jerusalem." (Luke 2:25-38) Next in the Bible, we have the visit of the wise men and the Epiphany season, the Lenten season with the cross, the Pentecost season and today Christ the King Sunday. These seasons of the church year are designed to help the congregation and the preacher to go through the whole Bible in teaching and preaching rather than just a few favorite Bible passages.

The last sermon Charles Shaw preached was the Sunday after Thanksgiving in 1986. I am not going to do a lot of reminiscing, but that year, as I have said before, all I wanted for Christmas was to hear Handel's *Messiah* sung by a great choir.

I did not know of any church choir in our area planning to sing *Messiah* and I did not feel like driving across Atlanta. Then one night I turned on the TV, and Robert Shaw was conducting the Atlanta Symphony as they were beginning to sing the *Messiah*. I

---

[54] Many Christians celebrate the Feast of Christ the King on the Sunday before the first Sunday of Advent (the Sunday that falls between November 20th and 26th, inclusive).

stood with the wonderful singers when they got to "The Hallelujah Chorus" and sang with them that wonderful piece of music and lyrics with as good a soprano voice as I've ever sang, "King of Kings and Lord of Lords. Forever and ever. Hallelujah, Hallelujah."

Jesus Christ as King is so well put in our Bible lesson today from Colossians, as well as in all four Gospels and in the book of *Revelation*. It has been set to music beautifully in the Christ-inspired Handel's *Messiah* and especially in "The Hallelujah Chorus."

One of the first passages of scripture I memorized as a child was from Matthew 2: "Now when Jesus was born in Bethlehem of Judea in the days of Herod the king, behold wise men from the East came to Jerusalem saying, 'Where is He who was born King of the Jews for we have seen His star in the East and are come to worship Him.'"

We all know that if there had been TV in that time, reporters would have run over Mary and Joseph to put their microphones in the face of Herod. This passage in the New Testament mentions Herod as the king. Jesus was born when Herod was king, and Herod's only claim to fame is one small paragraph in history only because he happened to be king in the life and times of Jesus.

King Herod is quickly dispensed with as history goes on to tell about Christ the King! People of that day thought Herod was the "historic one" but, in the many years since, most of the schools of Western civilization have been built to study every single word that fell from the lips of Jesus.

In our scripture lesson today in Colossians 1, Paul describes the role of Jesus in our lives as "the image of the invisible God, the firstborn of all creation." It is hard to get our minds around this powerful truth, revolving around the word "image." The Greek word of image is "Eikon." John, in his gospel, tells us the "logos," the word, became flesh.

The portrait of a person's likeness, as in the "image of a king" on a coin, was an Eikon. So Paul would have us know that Jesus Christ is the Eikon, the image of God – a representative of the Creator. The word also means manifestation, focusing on how the Creator God manifested Himself through Jesus Christ. Jesus was God in human incarnation, John tells us. Jesus is the only begotten son of God, the Eikon, the image of God himself. He is the manifestation of what we were meant to be before sin entered the world and what, through Christ, we seek to be.

Stephen Hawkins, a professor of mathematics at Cambridge, is considered by some as one of the most brilliant people in the world. Hawkins has come up with a concept for "The Theory of Everything," called TOE for short. His proposal is that the universe is a closed system and that the laws of science are sufficient to explain the universe. But Hawkins admits that even if we had a theory of everything, we would still be left with one final question, "What is it that breathes fire into the equation and makes a universe for them to describe?" And to that Dr. Hawkins admits, "If I knew that, then I would know everything important."

So we are back to the possibility of a God who put fire, not only into the equation, but also in human hearts and souls. I say we are back, not just to the *possibility* but to the *probability*, indeed the assurance, and the personal testimony of a God, Christ the King, who has indeed put fire into the human heart and soul. The King of Kings and the Lord of Lords, forever and ever. Hallelujah!

For Paul, in our lesson today, for millions of others, for me, Jesus Christ is the TOE, the Theory of Everything. His birth, His life, His death, resurrection, ascension, and His ministry give meaning, purpose, life, spirit, and energy to this chaotic world. Without Christ, the world is a jungle of relative laws and incoherent principles that change with every whim. We are seeing this as our nation is drifting further and further away from our Christian roots.

Several public school teachers were at my house for Thanksgiving. Those of us with children now in school find it hard to believe how many children today are being raised without parents or caring adults in their lives and without Christ or the church. Many children have little respect for authority. Their disrespect and vulgar behavior cause many problems in the classrooms at school.

My daughter Beth is a social worker and director of a home for neglected or abused children. Many of these children have been taken out of their homes because they had been sexually abused by parents or by their mother's boyfriends, sometimes with the cooperation and assistance of their drug and alcohol-addicted mothers. My daughter told me that at Christmas, a loving community gives them gifts for the children, and she and all the house parents are so thankful for the many nice gifts for the children. But in spite of all the material gifts they receive, the one thing the children want most of all is the love of a family.

The only thing that can take the place of a family is Christ. The Bible tells us in Psalms that "even if our mother and father forsake us, the Lord will take us in."[55] I have lived long enough to see this happen. I have known people who came to Christ, and Christ Jesus was able to fill the void left by absent or neglectful parents.

But too often these neglected children do not get the opportunity to hear the good news and see it in the lives of others.

Christ and Christian values are the only things that will make us and keep us "one nation under God, indivisible, with liberty and justice for all." It was what created our nation – a nation that everyone wants to come to, even when they hate the God and the people who make it possible.

In our Bible lesson today, Paul tells us that Christ is the image of the invisible God. And thus it is that Jesus Christ has given meaning to all creation. In verse 18, Christ is the head of the church in order that he may become the head of everything else – that in all things Christ Jesus may have preeminence. Verses 19 and 20 tell us that "the purpose of God is to reconcile all things on earth and in heaven." Verse 21 says that we, who were sometimes alienated and enemies, have been reconciled.

---

[55] Psalm 27:10

You may have heard the story of the little boy who wanted a horse. His parents got him a rocking horse, a little model horse, and finally a picture of a horse for his bedroom wall. But one day the boy told his dad he did not want a rocking horse, a model horse, or a picture of a horse. When his dad asked what kind of horse the child wanted, he replied, "Daddy, I want a horse made out of horse!" In other words, a real horse!

> *That is what we all want and need – reality, truth and presence.*

That is what we all want and need – reality, truth and presence. Like the child whose dad was overseas and he was looking at a picture of his dad and said, "I wish Daddy could step out of that frame and be here with me."

Paul tells us that in Jesus Christ, God has stepped out of the frame of the universe and is God-with-us. God has become visible. John, in the first chapter, tells us, "God became flesh and dwells among us, full of grace and truth, and we beheld his glory."

In the Old Testament, God sent prophets with truth about God and brought laws and civilization and structure and worship and many words about God. But one day God stepped out, not just with words about God, but as the Word Himself. The Word became flesh, and we beheld His glory as the only begotten of the Father, full of grace and truth.

In Birmingham, England, there is a great business – a store named Lewis's. They wanted to expand, but one of their stores was next door to a small Quaker church meeting house. So Lewis's sent the little church a letter, "Dear Sirs, we wish to extend our premises. We see that your building is right in the way. Therefore we wish to buy your building and demolish it so that we might expand our store. We will pay you any price you name. If you will set a price, we will settle the matter as quickly as possible. Yours truly, Lewis's."

The great store got this reply from the tiny Quaker meeting house, "Dear Sirs, we in the Friends meeting house note the desire of Lewis's to expand. We observe that our building is right in your way. We would like to point out that we have been here longer than you. If therefore you would like to name a price, we will settle the matter as quickly as possible. Signed, Cadbury."

Cadbury is the enormous chocolate-making people in England and could indeed buy Lewis's several times over, and they happened to be members of the little church. They signed the letter.

Paul's word to us in today's Bible lesson is that the church - regardless of how large or how small - is never in a defenseless position as long as we know and remember who we are and whose we are. We must remember the power available to us through Christ our King who has signed on to be our Savior.

He has signed on not just in ink but in the red blood of Jesus when we invite Him into our hearts and lives as Savior and Christ the King. Amen.

Mary's Song

Luke 1:26-55

And Mary said, "My soul magnifies the Lord. And my spirit has rejoiced in God my Savior.
~Luke 1: 46-47(NKJV)~

The child of Bethlehem was no ordinary baby. Jesus changed world history, and He can change our history also. Year after year our Christmas celebration reminds us that God does not stand at a distance but has come all the way - every step of the way - to us!

In *The Magnificat,* the scripture lesson today, Mary is expressing her joy in the first Christmas carol ever sung. It is one of the noblest songs in any language. The subject is the Savior - Mary's Savior and ours. What a moment! The angel Gabriel appearing in person was not an everyday happening. It was not a daily event! The angel Gabriel was announcing the coming birth of a baby to a girl named Mary.

News of an impending birth spoken to any woman is not an everyday event. The birth of a baby, whether it is a first baby or a seventh baby, is a unique and exciting event.

I was at a hospital nursery window recently and a new father was standing there talking to friends. He was telling his friends how helpless he felt when his wife was in labor, and he kept saying in awesome excitement, "It's a miracle! It's a miracle!"

The news of the coming birth to Mary, a baby whose name was to be called "Wonderful, Counselor, The Mighty God, The Everlasting Father, The Prince of Peace"[56] would have left any of us speechless. Mary was speechless!

In moments when a lot is at stake, we all tend to feel vulnerable and may find ourselves stuttering. When the angel of the Lord appeared

---

[56] From the song "Emmanuel" by Craig Smith

to a young girl named Mary and told her she had been chosen of God to bear a son, a virgin-born son, Mary was speechless!

Many people seem to think that it was easier to believe in miracles in those days because people were not so well informed then as now. Well, Mary seems to have known all she needed to know about procreation then as we know now. She knew how babies came about, just like we know. Mary knew that, in her case, this was not a possibility. "How can these things be," Mary said, "seeing I have had no intimate relations with a man."

I think some of us, perhaps most of us would have said "no" to the angel. At least many of us are saying "no" to God today. It is even possible that other young women may have turned down the offer to be the mother of Jesus. We don't know.

I think I might have said, "Please God...not me. I don't know how to raise such a child, a child that is to be called Wonderful, Counselor, The Mighty God, The Prince of Peace."

No God...not me. Don't you think it would be better to get an older woman - one with more experience or at least one who has completed a few child guidance courses? Or, I might have had a better idea. Many of us can be full of "better ideas."

If I could have recovered from the shock and gotten my tongue, I might have said, "Surely, Gabriel, God does not mean to go with this ridiculous idea of sending His only begotten Son to be a human being. People do not like to see too much of God in another human being. We would like to have just enough to make us kind and cooperative, but not enough to make us oppose sin. If he is fully human and fully God, they'll crucify him."

I might have reminded God how the prophets had been persecuted, and they were just reflecting the light. They were not "the Light."

Mary also had some problems with what the angel told her. We are told she cast about in her mind "what manner of salutation this should be." And finally, nine verses later, in verse 38, Mary made her decision to believe God and to trust Him. Mary said, "Behold the handmaiden of the Lord. Be it according to Thy word."

When we get down to where Mary sings her song, in verse 46, eight verses later, there is still some waiting and still some wondering. To be chosen of God does not mean that everything is going to be perfect - at least from our definition of perfection.

Sometimes there is waiting, tedious waiting. When Mary sings her song, she is waiting for the son that she is told will be born.

In our day, even if we know the gender of the unborn baby, as many today know, most expectant mothers do not know exactly what they are expecting: Will he/she be healthy? Who will the baby look like?

Waiting…Tedious waiting…uncomfortable and anxious waiting. Even as Mary sings her song, she is waiting.

As the mother of seven babies, I know a little about tedious, uncomfortable, and anxious waiting. Even fathers who love their children and the mother of their children know about tedious and anxious waiting for the birth of a baby. Many of us would say the most difficult part of becoming a mother is the last uncomfortable weeks of waiting. Waiting for anything or anyone can become tedious.

We all know something about waiting for Christmas. I remember, as a child, lying in bed on Christmas Eve trying to go to sleep so when I woke up it would finally be Christmas. (I did not have as much reason to be excited about Christmas presents as children today. When I woke up on Christmas morning in the 1920s, there would be a stocking with candy peppermint sticks, little cones of candy called "chocolate drops," raisins dried on the stem and several kinds of nuts - walnuts, pecans and Brazil nuts - perhaps warm gloves, a cap and a scarf or a pair of roller skates.) And the more I tried to go to sleep, the wider awake I became, waiting for Christmas to come!

Mary, the mother of Jesus, on the first Christmas, was a champion waiter. She was waiting for something that had never happened before. This was a never-to-be repeated experience. This was an event that would change history.

Mary was a young girl, not more than eighteen. She may possibly have been as young as fourteen, and she was betrothed to a man she hardly knew, as was the custom in those days. When the angel of the Lord spoke to Mary, she was afraid. She was troubled, and the Bible tells us she cast in her mind for the meaning of all that the angel told her. And finally Mary made a decision, just like you and I have to make a decision if we ever come to God.

When the teen-aged Mary made a decision to believe the words of the Angel of the Lord, she made the longest speech she had ever made in her life. It is known as *The Magnificat*, a Latin word for the first words of the song. "My soul does magnify the Lord." The song is Mary's dawning understanding of what her son will mean to the world and what he still means to the world over 2000 years later and throughout eternity. It was a dawning understanding. She did not understand fully. She was taking it a prayerful step at a time and acting on what she did understand.

Mary's Song is a hymn of faith for her day and ours: "For He who is mighty has done great things for me and Holy is His name." Like the Beatitudes in the Gospel of Matthew, the blessedness of Mary has two parts: past humbleness and future glory. "All generations shall call me blessed."

Everything is upside down in Mary's Song. "God has put down the proud and exalted those of low degree." Mary is prophesying something that is terrifying to the establishment. It is great news for the "down and out," but it is frightening news for the powerful! Mary sings, "God has filled the hungry with good things and the rich (those who are self-righteous and self-sufficient) He has sent away empty."

Mary's Song, that is literally singing her, continues: "God's mercy is on those who fear him from generation to generation." Fearing

God is realizing that there is a higher knowledge and a higher power than human knowledge and human power. It is arrogant for us as human beings to think the latest fad in knowledge is truer than the Holy Bible which has stood the test of time.

> *Fearing God is realizing that there is a higher knowledge and a higher power than human knowledge and human power.*

So Mary sings a song we do not understand. We have a better idea, God. And Your idea and our idea of blessedness are two different things. But Mary did not say that. She said, "Not my will but your will, God." Mary said that she wants us to know that we can trust God to be God and run the universe. God sees the whole, while we see through "a glass darkly."[57]

Mary continues her song. She says she had been afraid but "God has blessed her in her low estate." And God's mercy is on those who fear (are in awe of) God from generation to generation."

It seems we have taught this generation not to "fear God" (revere - stand in awe). We have made God just a little more than Santa Claus. And we have the phenomena of kids turning away from a Santa Claus like God and worshiping the Devil.

Listen to this: God's mercy is on those who stand in awe and who fear the eternal God. God's mercy is on those who have the humility and the intelligence to know that we are not always in charge of our own bodies, our own Merry Christmases and even less of our Happy New Year or our eternal destinies.

Mary is singing, "God has put down the proud from their throne of self-sufficiency and has exalted those of low degree." Imagine that!

The good news is that God came out of eternity into time and lived as a man, sinless, so that we who are sinners can be saved for all eternity.

---

[57] 1 Corinthians 13

Stand in awe, dear ones. This church of Jesus Christ is holy ground. We are on holy ground. The Eternal God is here - Wonderful, Counselor, The Mighty God, The Everlasting Father, the Prince of Peace. Amen.

We are All in This Together

Proverbs 22:1-2   James 2: 1-4, 8-10

The rich and the poor have this in common: The Lord is the maker of them all.
~Proverbs 22:2 (NRSV)~

I remember reading an article in which a woman related an experience she had with cooking a frozen pizza. She happened to be home alone for supper, was hungry, and decided to bake one of those small frozen pizzas. She read the directions on the back of the box that instructed her to take it out of the package and place it on the rack in the oven. Well, she, like many of us, had usually put the pizza in a pan rather than on the oven rack, and the pizza usually turned out okay for her as it did for me when I tried it.

Well, that night she decided to follow the directions and put the pizza on the rack. When this lady took the pizza out of the oven after the allotted time, she was amazed at how much better this pizza tasted than it tasted when she had not followed the printed directions.

God has given us directions for living life. Some of us ignore the directions and do our own thing. The book of Proverbs, as well as James in the New Testament, gives us directions (in the form of proverbs) for living life.

All of us have to deal sometimes with a feeling of insignificance and sometimes we feel like we are only a very small drop in a very large bucket. These proverbs for living in the book of James and the book of Proverbs are given to help us see our place in God's world. The risk of the five-talent person is pride and self-sufficiency. The risk of the one-talent person is hopelessness, inadequacy, and being only a tiny drop in a big bucket.

Actually the scripture teaches that we are all in this life together; we're all in the same boat. None of us has any reason to boast or to expect the best places. We are all guilty; none of us has a right to condemn anyone else. These very wise proverbs lift us all up to very great possibilities, yet they tell us emphatically that we are interdependent. We need each other.

One Sunday Morning when we lived in Ellijay, Georgia - my husband's first appointment out of seminary – and I was rushing around trying to get breakfast for the family and get five children ready for Sunday school and church, someone knocked on the door asking for food. People passing through town had learned where the parsonage was, and so we spent a great deal of time with people needing financial help. However, it had never before happened on a Sunday morning.

My first thought was to say, "We don't have time to help you this morning; we are trying to get ready for church." But before I could get the words out of my mouth, I realized the inconsistency in not having time for a person because of going to church. At least, I thought the Lord might have a problem with me turning them away because it was Sunday morning?

So I added more eggs and grits to the menu (Remember, although this was North Georgia, it was still the South - so the menu included grits). I invited them in to breakfast. The group included two men, one woman and three children. There was a big dog in the panel truck they were in. They later asked for dog food, and since we had a little dog named Hercules that Charles's brother had given the children, we had dog food to share with their big dog.

The people who came that Sunday morning may have been what we call now professional beggars. But they were also children of God – even when we thought the image of God in them was somewhat defaced at that point.

The scripture in our lesson today says, "The rich and the poor meet together. The Lord is the maker of all." The scriptures tell us to show no partiality. We are all in the world together, and we are all blessed to some extent by the goodness of others, and likewise we are diminished to some point by the failure and sins of others. In other words we are not to be in the business of judging one another.

Sometimes we are not sure of the best way to handle things. We need to use common sense as well as love and compassion. Sometimes it seems best to err on the side of kindness. This passage in James tells us, yes, we do have responsibility for one another, and it is to be a blessing, not a burden.

Taken in context, it is even more difficult for us to understand that God is not partial. God sends the rain on the just and the unjust, or he withholds the rain from the just and the unjust, or maybe just the unjust since we are all unjust. We are all sinners. But God is not partial. God has no favorites.

James 2:1-4 tells us: "My brothers and sisters, believers in our glorious Lord Jesus Christ must not show favoritism. Suppose a man comes into your meeting wearing a gold ring and fine clothes, and a poor man in filthy old clothes also comes in. If you show special attention to the man wearing fine clothes and say, 'Here's a good seat for you,' but say to the poor man, 'You stand there' or 'Sit on the floor by my feet,' have you not discriminated among yourselves and become judges with evil thoughts?"

Simply, what we believe is expressed by what we do.

The book of James has been the subject of controversy because of its emphasis on good works; and it is best understood through an analogy of motion. Simply, what we believe is expressed by what we do. When a person becomes a Christian, new life begins, and inevitably that new life is expressed through spiritual motion. He says, "What good is it to claim faith but have no deeds? Movement does not cause life, but it does invariably follow life."

I remember a few years ago my brother, Charlie, told me about his new great-grand baby. He said, "We got to see her just a few minutes after she was born, and she is the most beautiful little thing. I was just fascinated to see her." Then I saw him on Labor Day and asked about the baby, and he said, "We stopped by and I got to hold her. She is only two weeks old, but she kept moving around and looking at me." He was a proud great-grandfather and was just delighted with this new baby – seeing her look at him and seeing her move around.

Similarly, new life in Christ is expressed through spiritual motion. We keep looking at Jesus. We keep moving toward Christ, trying to follow Him with our words and actions and seeking to please Him with what we do.

> *If my words say I'm a Christian and my actions say I am not a Christian, what are you to believe - my words or my actions?*

Genuine faith in Christ always results in action. James tells us that faith without works is dead. We are saved by faith alone, but if faith is alone, it is not faith. If my words say that I'm a Christian and my actions say I am not a Christian, what are you to believe - my words or my actions?

James wants us to know that our acts, our works, are what we are known by. Most of us have heard the axiom, "What you are speaks so loudly I cannot hear what you are saying." The Proverbs tell us that "A good name is rather to be chosen than great riches, and favor is better than silver and gold."

One of the little daughters of William Howard Taft III was asked who she was. She said, "My great-grandfather was President of the United States, my grandfather was senator from Ohio, my father was ambassador to Ireland, and I am a Brownie." She took pride in her ancestors, but she also valued her own integrity and simple identity as a Brownie.

These proverbs in the Book of James in the New Testament as well as the Proverbs in the Old Testament are directions for a fulfilling life. We are to value ourselves and others. We are all in this together. Our common origin is in God!

The ground is level at the foot of the cross. Not one of us stands taller than another at the foot of the cross. We are all sinners in need of forgiveness. So we are told in verse 13 "to speak and act as those who are going to be judged by the law." The rich and the poor meet together; the Lord is the Maker of all.

> *The ground is level at the foot of the cross.*

The most difficult problem of modern labor is to find a meeting place where labor can meet together on some level and settle differences in a spirit of brotherhood and sisterhood and love. The scripture points to the answer. Christ is the answer. The rich and the poor do meet together on the level of common humanity. In our human nature we are all alike. Birth and motherhood are the same whether we are a common worker or the Queen of England. Hunger and thirst know no social distinctions. We all have to eat to live. Pain and sorrow, suffering, and death come to all of us. Therefore, the rich and the poor must meet together on the same footing at the judgment seat of God.

I grew up hearing the story of Bud Robinson. He came from a deprived background in the backwoods of Kentucky. One day as a young teenager, he spent the night with a classmate. The family he visited happened to be a Christian family. Bud noticed that they had a tablecloth on their table and they prayed before they ate supper. This made a profound impression on Bud. He thought, "When I grow up, I want to have a tablecloth on my table and say a prayer before we eat." He went to church with that family that night, went to the altar and found Christ. He became a great Christian and a noted preacher in spite of a deprived background and a serious speech impediment.

There is no physical or material blessing we can hand out to the needy as valuable as leading them to the Lord. In other words, it is even more valuable than "not just giving them fish for a day, but teaching them how to fish for a lifetime."

Our task as Christians is to feed and minister to the hungry and to lead others to the knowledge of Christ as Savior and involve them in fellowship with other believers in the church.

We, as Christians, seek to do both. Much of our money in the Church goes to mission work and social service. The rich and the poor meet on perfect equality in the church of Jesus Christ. There is a great democracy in the things we all inherit - the possibility of knowing God.

Along with directions, whether it is for cooking a frozen dinner or putting together a toy on Christmas Eve, there is sometimes a diagram of the finished product and sketches for each step. We can copy the model. Any of us who have tried to assemble something, whether it is a pattern for a dress, a recipe or putting together a piece of equipment, if we have a picture of the finished product, it makes all the difference. In Jesus Christ, we have the pattern - the directions - the model of what God intended life to be.

God plays no favorites with either the rich or the poor. This is symbolized by the cross. The arms of the cross are of equal length - the rich and the poor, the strong and the weak, the educated and the uneducated, black and white, men and women.

We live in a world of inequities; but in the final analysis, God plays no favorites. In our courts today, we may stand before lawyers and judges who are not as interested in guilt or innocence but in finding a technicality or loophole to acquit or convict; but when we stand before the judgment seat of God, our judge, will not be bribed, and he is not guilty of anything for which he judges us. And, of course, this puts us all at risk.

James tells us that "whosoever keeps the whole law but fails at one point has become guilty of all." None of us is perfect. We all fail on at least one point of the law. But this is where the gospel comes in. The death of Jesus Christ spared us from our spiritual and eternal death.

A gunman came into a school cafeteria a few years ago in South Carolina and opened fire on 100 students. A teacher named Kate Finkbeiner threw her body over one child to protect her and followed the man into a third grade classroom and tried to pull the gun away from the throat of a little boy. The man turned and fired at the teacher, striking her in the mouth, shattering her jaw. On the cross, Jesus Christ literally threw his body over us to protect us from certain destruction.

I was unworthy to sit at the table of life, but love made provision for me! None of us can put our lives together rightly, correctly, without the saving grace of Jesus, available to us all, every one of us equally, through repentance and faith. We need to read the directions from God's Word, assemble the parts of Christian character, copy the model of Christ and then use the vast resources available through the Holy Spirit of God. Amen.

The "Going Away" Shower

John 14:15-27

And I will pray the Father, and he will give you another Helper, that He may abide with you forever.
~John 14:16 (NKJV)~

John 14 is a familiar passage to many. It is also a Scripture passage in which we find new and awesome thoughts every time we read it. Jesus and the disciples were gathered in the upper room and it was a time of parting. Jesus knew he was headed toward the cross to give his life for the salvation of the world.

The disciples were troubled. Jesus was saying goodbye, and it was a three-chapters-long goodbye, beginning with the famous first verse, "Let not your hearts be troubled" - verses often read at funerals where hearts are troubled. At funerals we face one of the most traumatic and saddest of all goodbyes. I don't like goodbyes. Leaving is change, and change is difficult.

The last time my mother saw her own mother was an unforgettable memory for her. Mama told me how she had stood in the country road in front of their farm house. She had waved and watched her mother's horse-drawn carriage until she could see just a puff of dust down the long country road. A few months later Mama got word that her mother was dying, and she took a train to go to Griffin, Georgia from their farm near Covington, Georgia. When she got there, her mother had already died.

This experience was so traumatic for my mother that she would never again watch anyone out of sight. Even when she was old and we would visit, my dear mother would kiss us goodbye in the house and sometimes on the porch, but she would always turn back inside before we started our car to leave.

"Goodbyes" can be painful! Many of us, when our loved ones are going away, say, "I'll see you again" or "you all come" or something besides "goodbye." Actually the word "goodbye" is a comforting thought. In most languages, "Goodbye" is a blessing, a shortened form of "God be with you."

I could go on with many accounts of goodbyes and going-away-times because my husband and I were in the itinerant ministry for thirty-seven years, and I have continued alone since my husband's death in December of 1986. We never said goodbye from any pastorate without tears and prayers.

When my husband and I and our family were moving from Rome in 1968, after nearly six years at Trinity, the ladies of the church gave me (as their pastor's wife) a surprise "Going Away Shower" of personal gifts like gowns, housecoats, jewelry and hosiery.

Today, I want us to look at this Scripture in the Gospel of John about Jesus "going away" from his disciples. The disciples did not give Jesus a goodbye gift, but Jesus gave them and all of us a going away gift. It occurs to me it was not just a gift. The gift that Jesus gave was truly a "going away shower" of gifts that keep on giving!

Jesus had deep concern for these frightened, grieving disciples. In this Scripture, Jesus tells them he is not leaving them comfortless. Jesus assures them, and assures us, that he is sending a "helper."

Have you ever wished for a helper? Husbands and wives are often helpers to one another. For example, I think of all the things I used to do for my husband in the early days when I was a stay-at-home wife and mother and he was to conduct a funeral. A funeral is so very important to most people. The pastor often doesn't have much notice, there are all kinds of emotions, and there are many things a pastor has to do at the same time. And his or her other work goes on. I used to check and lay out my husband's clothes to wear.

Sometimes I would type up a poem or an order of worship when he needed copies for the organist, the soloist and the funeral director. I have cleaned out and sometimes washed his car so it would not be the dirtiest car in the funeral procession. Much of this, people can hire someone to do, but to have someone at our fingertips to anticipate the need and do whatever needs to be done is what many loving wives and husbands do for each other.

> *So Jesus anticipated our greatest need and sent us a "helper." He sent the Holy Spirit, closer than breathing and nearer than hands and feet!*

There are times when all of us need help beyond just a physical helper. So Jesus anticipated our greatest need and sent us a "helper." He sent the Holy Spirit, closer than breathing and nearer than hands and feet! This "helper" is God's gift to us - a going away gift from Jesus to His disciples and to us who have come after them.

"Paraclete" is the English translation for the title John uses for the Holy Spirit or "Holy Companion." Paraclete is a wonderful word. There is no single word in our English that can express the rich and powerful meaning of "paraclete." The Greek word "Para" means "alongside" and the root of "kletos" is "to call." So this Paraclete, the Holy Spirit, is a helper that is "called to go alongside."

When we try to describe the Holy Spirit, the Paraclete, the Helper, we need many words, not just one word: Encourager, Counselor, Advocate, and Witness - truly a "shower of gifts!" In verses 18 and 19 Jesus says, "My peace I leave with you, my peace I give unto you, not as the world gives. Let not your hearts be troubled, neither let them be afraid."

This peace that Jesus gives is not always a force to protect us from the wounds of life, but a force inside to empower us for living. Jesus said, "You shall receive power after the Holy Spirit has come." This "going away" gift of the Holy Spirit is not only for the Disciples but for all believers.

As some of us have been blind to Jesus, so we are blind to the Holy Spirit, the Helper! Many of us see peace as an end in itself and search like orphaned street children searching for food in garbage cans. We struggle to find peace by taking pills and/or alcohol and in all kinds of entertainment and activities - new wives, new husbands, or affairs. We frantically drive seventy miles an hour for hundreds of miles to get to a vacation spot and grit our teeth and say, "I'm going to have a good time if it kills me!"

I read this week that college students were interviewed about what they most wanted in life. Many of them stated, "The three things I want most in life are love, happiness and peace."

> *This peace that Jesus gives is not always a force to protect us from the wounds of life, but a force inside to empower us for living.*

I have wonderful news! The three most prized possessions students are seeking in life - love, happiness and peace - are the first three of the fruits of the Holy Spirit as listed in Paul's letter to the Galatians. They are listed as love, joy, peace, longsuffering, kindness, goodness, faithfulness, gentleness and self-control.[58]

While America has never been "a Christian nation," this basket full of fruits of the Spirit of God has been received by enough Americans to build the greatest nation the world has ever seen. The gifts of love, joy and peace and other spiritual gifts that God offers to us do not provide the absence of all conflict, not the absence of all sorrow, not an escape from worry, but they provide the power to overcome.

The Helper that Christ gives us - the peace that the Lord showers upon us in the power of the Holy Spirit - is something that the world cannot give and the world cannot take away, even in the midst of an uncivil world of terror and suicide bombers and fanatic enemies.

---

[58] Galatians 5:22

When Cardinal O'Connor[59] died in 2000, a reporter reviewed his life, and they showed a clip where someone said to O'Connor, "You are so gifted, intelligent, talented. Have you ever thought what you might have been if you had not gone into the ministry?" The brilliant O'Connor looked incredulous. He said, "I was one of five children born in a row house in Philadelphia. I might have been a truck driver if I could have learned to drive one."

O'Connor knew about our Lord's "Going Away" gift of power and grace, offered to all of us regardless of our birth. It opens our minds as well as our hearts to the possibility of the impossible.

In another clip, O'Connor said the best advice he had ever received was when Mother Teresa told him, "Give God permission."

On May 24, 1738, John Wesley was a highly educated Oxford don. He went "quite unwillingly" to a church meeting in Aldersgate. Someone was reading Luther's preface to the book of Romans. Wesley tells us he felt his heart strangely warmed, and he knew that Christ has died for the world and also had died for him. He said he knew God had forgiven his sins and had saved him from the power of sin and death. Wesley went out from this personal encounter with the Living Lord to change the world.

Into our burdened world of troubled youth and frightened elders, of war and terror, of "dog eat dog" work places, of hospitals and nursing homes and funeral parlors and war, Jesus offers the Paraclete - the Helper - alongside us with a shower of gifts like love, joy and peace.

It is more than a Beautyrest mattress or a Lazy Boy recliner at the end of a long and tiring day. It is more than a devoted spouse, a cleaning lady, a gardener or a secretary (all of which I sometimes wish for). Those helpers are valuable but transient. God is the Helper always present. He abides!

I love the old camp meeting hymn, "He Abides:"

---

[59] John Joseph O'Connor was an American prelate of the Catholic Church. He served as Archbishop of New York,, and was created a cardinal in 1985.

I'm rejoicing night and day
As I walk this Pilgrim way
For the hand of God in all my life I see
And the reason for my bliss
Yes, the secret all is this
The Comforter abides with me
He abides, He abides
Halleluiah! He abides with me.

Paul tells it like it is in Romans 8: "Nothing, neither life (with all its problems and pains), nor death (with all its fear and uncertainty), nor angels, nor principalities, nor powers, nor things present, nor things to come, nor height, nor depth, nor any other created thing, nothing can separate us from the Love of God which is in Christ Jesus."

I don't know about you, but I say again, "O God, shower my life with the gift of the Comforter, the Advocate, the Helper to walk with me every day of my life, to fill my heart and my life with Your love, joy and peace (Your shalom)."

As we surrender our burdens to God, they are replaced with the going away gift that Jesus left for us: a shower of gifts that keeps on giving every day of our lives and on into eternity with Him in heaven. Amen.

Grace and Peace

1 Corinthians 1:1-9

Grace to you and peace from God our Father and the Lord Jesus Christ.
~1 Corinthians 1: 3 (NKJV)~

There are some places that you and I avoid, especially after dark! When I was serving as pastor of the East Point Avenue United Methodist Church, one of the older women called me near dinner time one night and invited me to have dinner with her. This dear lady had prepared dinner for the mother-in-law of her son, who was driving through Atlanta on her way to her home in Florida and was to stop and have dinner and spend the night with Lou. But the lady called Lou from a service station on Stewart Avenue in Atlanta, where she had stopped for gasoline, just before dinner time saying she has been delayed by heavy traffic and was exhausted so just wanted to stop at a motel and would go on home from there early in the morning.

When Lou heard this friend was on Stewart Avenue, she tried to encourage her to continue to Lou's home in East Point. Lou did not want to frighten the lady about her surroundings but was concerned, if not frightened, for her. Lou ended up just telling her to be careful. Then Lou called me and invited me to come over and share the wonderful meal this lady had passed up. It so happened I had not eaten, and so I accepted Lou's invitation. Lou and I had a wonderful dinner and visit together.

Atlanta, like every other large city, I am told, has pockets where Mafia types cruise around - a place where strippers are evident and drug dealers, prostitutes and worse seem to congregate. Stewart Avenue (only a few miles from East Point) had that reputation at that time. It was the kind of place we try to avoid, especially at night.

Bible historians tell us ancient Corinth was that kind of city and not just pockets of the city. All over the Roman Empire, the Corinthian people were known for this kind of lifestyle.

Corinth was on a vital trade route which made her quick profits. But Corinth was also near enough to Athens to give it a layer of sophistication.[60] So Corinth was not the type of city where people would expect to find converts to the Gospel of Jesus Christ.

Yet the great Apostle Paul came to Corinth, as the Scripture tells us in the second chapter of Corinthians, "with weakness and much fear and trembling." Paul spent eighteen months in Corinth and there established a church that became the largest church of the first century.

Our environment and the people with whom we associate do make a difference in the way we live. Several years later Paul heard sad reports from Corinth. He was told that some of the church people there, true to the city's heritage, had gotten into problems and sins.

> *Our environment and the people with whom we associate do make a difference in the way we live.*

These wonderful letters from Paul to the Corinthians were addressed to specific people regarding specific problems. Paul begins his letter with the usual salutation of the day, "Grace and Peace," which was as common a greeting then as our "Hi" or "Hello" is today. But Paul gave a whole new dimension to it by adding "from God through our Lord Jesus Christ." This greeting reminded them of God's unmerited favor which is "Grace." And it reminded them of the wholeness and unity of the gospel which is "Peace." Shalom! Paul wanted the Corinthians and all of us to know this unmerited favor and unity that God brings into our lives through Jesus Christ.

So in verse 3, we read, "Grace to you and peace from our Father and the Lord Jesus Christ." Then Paul uses the word "called" in relationship to himself and also in relation to them. Paul reminds

---

[60] When Charles and I visited the Holy Land in 1979, we visited both Athens and Corinth the same day.

the people that he was called to be an apostle of Jesus Christ. He reminds the church at Corinth that they also have a calling. Paul wants them to know in verse 2, "the same God who called Paul to be an apostle had called them to be "sanctified in Christ Jesus." The Greek word for "sanctified" means "set apart for God - separated." The Christian is to be different - set apart from the crowd.

One of the old stories I remember is of a teenager who became a Christian soon before he left for college. He and his family and Christian friends in his home town were concerned that his fellow college students might be intolerant of his Christian lifestyle. When he came home for a break, his Christian friends asked if his Christian faith had caused any problems. He replied, "No, they have not found out about it yet."

Paul would have us know that even though we are living on Stewart Avenue or Bourbon Street or in Corinth, we are "called," we are "chosen," and we are set aside to be different, even in an evil environment.

I watched a talk show once that had interviews with several celebrities who had been adopted as infants. Most adoptive parents tell their children from the beginning that they are adopted because they are special and because they were not born to their parents but were chosen by their parents!

One of the successful persons on the panel was the man who founded Wendy's Hamburger Chain. He said he had such an unhappy childhood that he left home and was on his own at age 15. The others on the panel said they had relatively happy childhoods.

I became interested in Faith Daniel's Story. Faith was a beautiful young news anchor for a time back in the seventies. Faith said one day when she was about four years old, a man had stopped by their home and said, "You are so cute, I think I will adopt you." She replied, "You can't, I am already adopted."

Faith Daniel had been told from the beginning that she was so very special and was chosen by her parents. So she grew up with loving parents. At the time of the talk show interview, Faith's mother had died recently. Faith said when she looked down at her mother in death - the mother who had always told her they had chosen her because she was so special - she looked at her mother and said, "No, Mama, it is not me that's special. I am an orphan. It is you and Daddy who are special."

When we read Paul's writings here in First Corinthians and elsewhere, sometimes we get the feeling that Paul is special, and he is. The great Apostle Paul's qualifications and accomplishments are a matter of record. Paul was probably the greatest man who ever lived except for Jesus Christ, who was more than a man.

But Paul knew who he was; Paul knew he was only a poor sinner. But Paul would tell us that God, in Jesus Christ, had chosen him. Paul talked about "being apprehended by Christ" to be a special messenger to the Gentiles. I understand a little of what Paul meant when he talked about "being apprehended by Christ."

I read a story just this week about Elizabeth Sherrill.[61] She told about the time she spent with her husband on a missionary trip to Uganda. They met a missionary named Marilyn who never called God, "Father." One night they asked Marilyn about her childhood, and for about five minutes Marilyn just sobbed. Then in the following weeks she told about the emotional and physical abuse from her Dad toward her and her mother. So they realized that with such a history Marilyn could not see a loving God as a father.

Then one night a member of their prayer group began describing his very good father - a dad who had time to listen and play a game of catch with his child. Then a friend witnessed to Marilyn. He told her he did not know his biological father, but he knew that neither his father nor his mother wanted him. But one night late, he went forward at a church service and was adopted by the "true Father."

---

[61] Elizabeth Sherrill is the author of over 30 books – many co-authored with her husband, John. Among them are *The Hiding Place*, *God's Smuggler*, and *The Cross and the Switchblade*.

He was adopted by God, our heavenly father. He told Marilyn that the same father wanted to adopt her. Later they held an adoption service for Marilyn to be adopted by her Father God!

Paul, in Romans 8:15, tells us that regardless of our past, we can "receive the spirit of adoption" whereby we can cry "Abba Father," literally meaning "Daddy" or "personal father."

The central theme of today's passage in I Corinthians 1:1-9 is the nature of the church whose members are called, adopted, chosen and set apart by God for God's unmerited favor. His grace and his peace are given to us. It is our inheritance as children of God. Amen.

Come into His Presence with Singing

Psalm 100

Make a joyful noise unto the Lord, all ye lands. Serve the Lord with gladness;
come before his presence with singing.
~Psalm 100:1 (KJV)~

In Psalm 100, one of numerous Psalms I memorized as a child, we are told to "Make a joyful noise unto the Lord, all ye lands. Serve the Lord with gladness: come into his presence with singing."[62]

Hymn singing in church has been and still is a vital part of our worship and our discipleship. Our hymnals, next to the Bible, have been our most formative resources. Christians have been singing as long as there have been Christians. After finishing his last supper with his disciples, Jesus, on the very night when he was betrayed, sang a hymn with his disciples before they all went out to Gethsemane.

Our Jewish spiritual ancestors sang. The 150 Psalms in the Old Testament comprise the Jewish "book of hymns."

John Wesley in 1761 wrote "The 7 directions for singing" and they continue in our Methodist hymnals. In our *United Methodist Hymnal*, Wesley directed us to "have an eye to every word" and "above all to sing spiritually with an eye to pleasing God" more than ourselves or anyone else. We are to direct our singing to the Lord. So our hymn singing is "to the Lord."[63]

---

[62]When I was a child (born in 1923), we memorized Scripture, not only in Sunday school but in public school as well, in the King James Version which was the available text. So in my Sunday school and mission teaching and later as a pastor, I often used the familiar KJV and the NKJV, even though the KJV is more difficult to understand.   I bought the Revised Standard Version in seminary and used it in many public readings. In retirement, I have read through *The Message* by Peterson and the New International Version. They are all valid versions.
[63] *United Methodist Hymnal*, p. VII

I am not a musician, but I keep singing anyway. I enjoy singing and was allowed to sing in the Candler Chorale in Seminary at Emory University. I love to sing and I love to cook. So I sing around the house, especially in the kitchen. My daughter Beth likes to laugh and tell that every time she brought a boy into the house after a date, I would be in the kitchen banging pots and pans around and singing, "His Eye is on the Sparrow and I know He watches me." Parents learn more than they want to know about themselves when they have grown children.

My parents loved to sing. My mother sang solos in church as a young woman. She was 38 when I was born, and I never heard her sing in church. However, I learned every hymn in the hymnal from hearing my mother sing them as she did household chores. As a teen, it embarrassed me to bring friends home when Mama was in the kitchen loudly singing hymns. Today my dear mother's singing is one of my happiest memories.

I do not have many memories of my father since I was only nine when he died after being bed ridden for over a year. But his witness in life and song had a profound influence on me and some of it was tied up with his gospel singing.

I remember hearing Papa sing several hymns that are still in our United Methodist Hymnal. Also he sang other hymns like, "I'm a Child of The King." My sister, Louise, told me that on his deathbed, Papa sang all the verses of "Palms of Victory," an old hymn about the first Palm Sunday.

G.K Chesterton wrote a few lines of poetry about the lowly donkey that Jesus rode that first Palm Sunday.[64] Chesterton has the donkey to say:

> *Fools! For I also had my hour;*
> *One far fierce hour and sweet:*
> *There was a shout about my ears,*
> *And palms before my feet.*

---

[64] From the poem "The Donkey" by G. K. Chesterton

The donkey was telling us that whatever or whomever Christ touches he dignifies, whether a lowly donkey or a lowly person.

In the devastated South still struggling to recover from the Civil War, I did not need lessons in "self-esteem." We were taught in church that we were so loved and important that Jesus died to save us. My dying father was as sure that heaven was his destination as if his ticket was already in his hand. And I was a witness as I learned the lyrics and tune to "Never Grow Old"[65] by hearing papa sing:

> *I have heard of a land*
> *In the far away strand*
> *Tis a beautiful home of the soul*
> *Built by Jesus on high*
> *There we never shall die*
> *Tis a land where we'll never grow old*

Charles Wesley, the Bard of Methodism, wrote over sixty-five hundred hymns. When we learn the words of Wesley hymns we are also learning Bible truth. For example, "Love Divine, All Loves Excelling" is truly a message of the Holy Spirit in song. It contains fourteen references or allusions to scripture passages.

> *Breathe, O breathe thy loving spirit*
> *into every troubled breast!*
> *Let us all in thee inherit,*
> *let us find that second rest.*
> *Take away our bent to sinning;*
> *Alpha and Omega be;*
> *end of faith as its beginning,*
> *set our hearts at Liberty.*
> *Finish then thy new creation*
> *Pure and spotless let us be*
> *Let us see thy great salvation,*
> *Perfectly restored in thee*
> *Changed from glory into glory*
> *Till in heaven we take our place*
> *Till we cast our crowns before thee*

---

[65] From the song "Never Grow Old," written by James C. Moore

Lost in wonder, love and praise.

Bishop Arthur Moore, A South Georgia native and one of our greatest bishops, used say about Charles Wesley's "O For A Thousand Tongues to Sing," "We sing *O for a thousand tongues to sing* and do not use the one tongue we have."

Wesley's "A Charge to Keep I Have*"* reminds us that as Christians we've been given a "charge to keep and a God to glorify." We have also been given a particular charge or calling that is unique.

When we sing "When I Survey the Wondrous Cross," written by Isaac Watts, we are also hearing a good sermon about the cross and the doctrine of the atonement:

> *When I survey the wondrous cross*
> *On which the Prince of glory died,*
> *My richest gains I count but loss,*
> *And pour contempt on all my pride.*
>
> *See from His head, His hands, His feet,*
> *Sorrow and love flow mingled down.*
> *Did e'er such love and sorrow meet,*
> *Or thorns compose so rich a crown.*

One of the hymns I connect with my parents' singing is "He Keeps me Singing." The hymn is still on page 110 in the Cokesbury hymnal. The words and music were written by Luther Bridgers (1884-1948), a Methodist pastor and evangelist from Georgia. He was away in a revival meeting in Kentucky when his wife and three children were burned to death in a house fire. Bridgers was so devastated and dismayed he stayed to himself for many months.

My mother told me about meeting Bridgers and hearing him preach and tell the sad story about how he came to write "He Keeps Me Singing" in the midst of this great sorrow. The words are:

> *There's within my heart a melody*

Jesus whispers sweet and low
Fear not I am with you
Peace be still
In all of life's ebb and flow,
Jesus, Jesus , Jesus,
Sweetest name I know.
Fills my every longing.
Keeps me singing as I go.

Many of our most beautiful and effective hymns were written and sung in the midst of tragedy.

Many of our most beautiful and effective hymns were written and sung in the midst of tragedy. It is in crisis times that we are stopped in our tracks and say, "Where is God when bad things happen?" Strangely, we do not stop often and think to say, "Where is God when good things happen?"

When things are going smoothly, we tend to focus on other things - our work, our vacation, holidays or the latest movie or ball game.

But let sometime happen - losing a spouse, a job, or discovering you or a loved one may have heart failure or cancer - and suddenly life changes and God is back in the picture. Crisis and tragedy serve the function of bringing us back to the recognition of our limits and our mortality.

My brother Tom dropped out of church for a few Sundays as an older teen. One day he ran into our town's mayor who told Tom he had been missing him at church. Then he said, half in fun, "One day you are going to die and I will say, "Poor Tom, he had to die before we could get him back in church." Tom came home, told Mama about the conversation and asked her to wake him up in time for church the next day.

Some of our favorite hymns were written in times of distress. The hymn, "What a Friend we have in Jesus," was written by Joseph

Striven after his fiancée was drowned the night before their scheduled wedding.

It is said that George Matheson wrote "O Love That will Not Let Me Go" after his fiancée broke her engagement to him when she learned of his impending blindness.

In reflecting on my spiritual journey, I was influenced by hymn singing. As a child of eleven, I was sitting in the Methodist church where I had been baptized as an infant, listening to the words of a hymn we were singing and pondering the first Biblical question I ever remember considering. We were singing:

> *Alas! and did my Savior bleed*
> *And did my Sovereign die?*
> *Would He devote that sacred head*
> *for such a worm as I?*

Years later some of our church musicians, contrary to Wesley's advice, took liberties with Isaac Watts's hymn and replaced "such a worm as I" with the more palatable "sinners such as I."

We might debate the question of whether or not someone should change the lyrics in a hymn after the poet has died. But most of us think it is a nice change. We do not mind being "a sinner." We may even brag about being a sinner, but none of us relishes the idea of being called a "worm."

This was before World War II, a time when we believed that human beings were getting better and better. All we needed was better education and more bathtubs. Then we learned about the Holocaust in Germany, where one of the most enlightened and educated nations in Europe killed 6 million Jews. We learned about the atrocities of Japan, another educated and prosperous nation, and on and on. Worms?

The evidence is in. Education and prosperity and social action are all good things - all much needed things - but they cannot save us. They sometimes only increase our capacity and opportunity for evil.

That day at age 11, sitting in church, I was paying attention to all the words of this old Isaac Watts hymn and especially the words, "Was it for crimes that I have done, Christ died upon the tree? Amazing pity, grace unknown and love beyond degree."

I was thinking, "How in the world could the sins I commit today have anything to do with Jesus dying on a bloody cross 2000 years ago?" I was then a thoughtful and obedient child. More serious than many, I think, because of the illness and death of my beloved Papa two years earlier. I suppose I was somewhat like the little 8-year old girl who wrote her pastor one Monday morning. "Dear Pastor. Yesterday you preached about loving our enemies. I do not have any enemies yet. But I hope to have some by the time I am nine. Love, Mary."

I could not think of specific sins I had committed, but somehow I grasped a profound truth. I accepted the mystery that God could see into the future as well as the past, and Jesus had shed his blood on the cross for me and my generation as well as those of his generation. I did not "go forward," quiet child that I was, but I accepted the truth of God that day.

I have not mentioned most everyone's favorite hymn, "Amazing Grace," by John Newton who had been a slave trader and became a Christian and an Abolitionist.

I have not mentioned two of my favorite hymns, "Great is Thy Faithfulness"[66] and "All Hail the Power of Jesus Name."[67] We must also include the greatest of all, Handel's *Messiah* and the "Hallelujah Chorus" that lifts us to our feet in awe and praise!

And let me mention Fanny J. Crosby (1820-1915), the blind poet, who wrote the lyrics and music to over eight thousand hymns - many of your favorites and mine. One of the Crosby hymns still in our Cokesbury and United Methodist Hymnals, is "To God be the Glory:"

---

[66] Written by Thomas Chisholm in 1925
[67] Written by Edward Perronet in 1779

Praise the Lord, Praise the Lord,
Let the earth hear His voice.
Praise the Lord, Praise the Lord,
Let the people rejoice.
Come to the Father
Through Jesus the Son
And give him the glory
Great things he has done.

Crosby also wrote the words and music to "Blessed Assurance:"

This is my story.
This is my song.
Praising my Savior
All the day long.

Thank God, we can come into God's awesome presence with singing and say with the Psalmist, "Let everything that hath breath praise the Lord." May we say with our lives and with our words, "This is my story, this is my song, praising my Savior all the day long." Amen.

Sand in the Crankshaft

Romans 14:5-12

Some judge one day to be better than another, while others judge all days to be alike. Let all be fully convinced in their own minds. Those who observe the day, observe it in honor of the Lord. Also those who eat, eat in honor of the Lord, since they give thanks to God; while those who abstain, abstain in honor of the Lord and give thanks to God. We do not live to ourselves, and we do not die to ourselves. If we live, we live to the Lord, and if we die, we die to the Lord; so then, whether we live or whether we die, we are the Lord's. For to this end Christ died and lived again, so that he might be Lord of both the dead and the living. Why do you pass judgment on your brother or sister? Or you, why do you despise your brother or sister? For we will all stand before the judgment seat of God. For it is written,
"As I live, says the Lord, every knee shall bow to me,
and every tongue shall give praise to God."
So then, each of us will be accountable to God.

~Romans 14:5-12 (NRSV)~

Today's Bible lesson has to do with different understandings about the correct way to practice faith, such as whether to eat meat or abstain from meat on certain days and whether or not to observe certain holy days. (Verses 5 & 6)

Christians have disagreed for centuries over issues such as these. They are the sand in the crankshafts of church life for some Christians. These are some of the things that keep Baptists, Methodists, Presbyterians, Catholics and the non-denominational churches uncomfortable with one another or fighting each other. These are the issues that keep people within the same church fighting one another, while the Devil and our common enemies are leading multitudes away from Christ and the church.

The church of the Romans was made up of Jews and Greeks. This is significant to Paul because he believed one of the greatest values of Christianity was its ability to bring together people from segments of society that would normally be estranged from one another. He believed, as written in Galatians 3:27-28, "There is neither Jew nor Greek. There is neither bond nor free. There is neither male nor female. For you are all one in Christ Jesus. "

Paul insisted that, in Christ, societal, cultural, economic, and gender barriers were broken down.

> *In Christ there is no East or West.*
> *In Him no North or South,*
> *But one great fellowship of love*
> *Throughout the whole wide Earth.* "[68]

The one common denominator through the years has been our love for Christ and our relationship to Jesus as Savior and Lord. The walls and partitions are broken down in our love and faithfulness to Jesus Christ. But sometimes these walls have put themselves back up. Those walls are the sand in the crankshaft. They keep the machinery of the church from running smoothly.

The points that the Roman Christians argued about - their sore points - were food and holy days. The Jews had numerous dietary rules that they wanted to continue and that they wanted other Christians to observe. They also had many rules about the observance of their holy days.

We see the same things today. Shortly after my husband died, a long-time school friend of mine invited me to go with her out of state to visit her son and his wife. Her son was a witnessing Christian and a member of a Baptist church. He was a kind and considerate person and was also a chain smoker. He told me that they had moved their membership from another Baptist church because one of the deacons had been divorced and yet was allowed to keep his leadership role in the church.

I was interested in this because I had a Christian divorced friend who was vocally intolerant of Christians who continued as cigarette smokers.

---

[68] Hymn "In Christ There Is No East or West" by John Oxenham. *The United Methodist Hymnal,* Page 548

> *The point Paul was making is that we are not
> to judge one another.*

Paul tells the Romans in verses 4 and 5, "Who are you to judge another?" Of course, Paul was not talking about the more serious issues of divorce or cigarette smoking but about dietary rules and Holy days. He told them they were to "Let each person be fully persuaded in his/her own mind." The point Paul was making is that we are not to judge one another.

Paul was committed to a nobler, and a definitely more difficult solution. He did not care whether they ate meat or not. Actually, in this case, it was meat that had been offered to idols. Paul believed that meat offered to idols in some pagan temple and later sold was still the same meat as before because idols were nothing, So the people had to decide on the basis of what they understood the Lord's will to be.

In some areas of spiritual experience there are no hard and fast rules. This does not mean that it does not matter what Christians believe or how they behave. Paul was, on occasion, very explicit and emphatic about the behavior of Christians. We do have the Ten Commandments which are our directions for a good life.

The Old Testament reading for today is the Decalogue, the Ten Commandments. In Psalm 19 there is lyrical praise of the law of the Lord. The Psalmist would have us to know that "The law of the Lord is more desirable than gold. Yea, than much fine gold. Sweeter also than honey in the honeycomb."

When we come to realize this truth and respect the laws of God - that the laws of God are indeed written in our bodies and in our psyches - our lives are forever changed.

The laws of God were written inside us - as humans made in the image of God - before these laws were written in the Bible. The loving creator who made us is also our Father, who gave the laws for our benefit and protection.

It is not a sin (sin being anything that hurts or damages) to commit adultery because it is written in the Bible. It is written in the Bible because adultery damages and hurts and kills vital relationships. It is not a sin to get drunk because it is written in the Bible. It is written in the Bible that "wine is a mockery; strong drink is raging, and whoever is deceived thereby is not wise" because mind-altering drugs are damaging, unhealthy, addictive and dangerous to our bodies and our minds.

From the point of view of our text in Romans 14, the first fact that we face in the context of this scripture lesson is that each of us is responsible for a cultivated conscience.

You may have heard the story of the little boy who had failed to do some of his chores. He knew he should have done them, so he finally started out after dark to do them. His dog followed him out, and he was heard to say to the dog, "Wag, go on back to the house. Isn't it enough to have Jesus tagging after me all the time?" Everyone does not cultivate the kind of conscience that this little boy still had.

One man was asked if he had a good conscience, and he replied, "I should say so! It's as good as new; it has never been used." It was only a quip, but it points up a serious aspect of our living: our conscience as such is not to be trusted – unless it is a healthy and informed conscience.

Paul deals with this question. In the Christian community in Rome there were those who had been converted out of paganism and those who had been converted out of Judaism. Those of Jewish background were accustomed to an elaborate system of regulations and laws that went far beyond the Ten Commandments. The converts out of paganism placed no such dependence on ritual or form.

These two groups from different backgrounds were together in the church. Consequently, there was a clash that threatened the well-being of the church as a whole.

So our text, Romans 14, deals with the concepts treated in the second part of the Decalogue – that of human beings getting along with one another. Christian communities are like other social groups in at least one respect. Our members are not all alike. We disagree with one another. The solution that Paul recommended was a more enlightened conscience on both sides. And the Christian principle was to take two forms: (1) the Christian principle of liberty in Christ, and (2) the recognition of the Christian principle of responsibility. The principles of LIBERTY and RESPONSIBILITY.

What about liberty in Christ? Verse 5: "Let everyone be persuaded in his own mind." Does this mean that everyone just does what seems like the right thing to do? No! This same Paul, in speaking to the Galatians (1:8), says, "Though we or an angel from heaven preach any other gospel, let him be accursed."

In the overall writings of the New Testament there are distinctions between convictions and opinions. When it is a matter of opinion, let every man be persuaded in his own mind. When it is a matter of conviction, (e.g. "Jesus Christ is the way, the truth and the life and no one comes to God except by Him"), the words of scripture are our guide.

In today's text, the differences are not necessarily ultimate. It has to do with everyday religious practices and not, as John Wesley said, things that cut at the heart of the Christian doctrine.

Paul says that to eat or not to eat meat is not a matter of eternal importance. But when it gets down to the question of Christ as the Son of God and the Savior of the world, and the cross of Christ as essential to salvation, a person has no liberty to deny that and still call himself or herself a Christian.

But in the Roman church, the problems that were straining the fellowship and putting sand in the crankshaft, that were hindering the running of the church, had nothing to do with the basic doctrines of the faith or Christian morals. They were external questions of form and custom. This is where we have the liberty to decide.

I have often wished that the Bible was a little clearer on things that people argue about today. But we are given a great deal of liberty of interpretation in some things – in the concept of the priesthood of all believers.

So we have liberty. We hear Paul say, "Let us therefore not judge anyone anymore." And the bottom line is love for God and others.

But just when we are relaxing and thinking He'll understand and say "well-done" regardless of how we behave (because we are not to be judged or misjudged by one another), Paul continues by saying, "But judge this rather, that no man put a stumbling block or an occasion to fall in his brother's way."

Then we realize that this is the limitation that we are willing and obligated to put on our liberty! God will hold us responsible for harsh and condemning criticism of those with whom we disagree. Each of us is personally responsible for a careful and constructive use of our opportunities.

> *So when we stand before the tribunal of God,*
> *He is not going to ask us what church we*
> *joined or by what mode we were baptized, or*
> *many other things that the body of Christ*
> *finds to disagree about.*

So when we stand before the tribunal of God, He is not going to ask us what church we joined, or by what mode we were baptized, or many other things that the body of Christ finds to disagree about. He will ask about our relationship with Jesus Christ and what we did about His commission to go and tell the good news of salvation!

John Wesley said, "We live and let live, agree and disagree, except in matters that cut at the heart of the gospel. If your heart is right as my heart is right, give me your hand." In John Wesley's day, in Paul's day, and in our day, it is so much easier to sit in judgment on other people than on ourselves. When we possess no vision beyond the confines of the identity with which we were born, suddenly gender issues, white issues, black issues, Baptist issues, Methodist issues and male and female issues become something about which to contend.

By the time I became a pastor, I had never found time to raise much enthusiasm for "woman's rights" or "inclusive language," and yet I am indebted to people who have paved such roads over which I was also called to walk. And sometimes it gets a little tiresome, for example, to have some dogmatic quoting of texts out of context by some who have never read the complete Bible. But we are to remember, we are called to love and to forgive one another.

A major claim of Paul in Romans is that Jesus Christ means to dispense with the superficial, culturally-bound labels by which we identify ourselves and wall others out. How can Paul mean otherwise when in Galatians 3:27-28 he writes, "For as many of you as were baptized into Christ, have put on Christ, there is neither Jew nor Greek; there is neither slave nor free; there is neither male nor female, for you are all one in Christ Jesus."

This community (this church) now calls us by an inclusive, infinitely more interesting name: CHRISTIAN. This name has been borne by woman and man, Gentile and Jew, "red and yellow, black and white." As Paul further says, "With God there is no distinction."

Yet, with all this scripture and all the admonitions - "Love one another." "God is love." "Little children, love one another." - we still run around throwing sand and sometimes, sneaking sand in the crankshaft of the church because we are more interested in carrying the identity of Methodist, Baptist, women, men, white, black, rich, poor, liberal, conservative, Democratic, Republican, young, old than we are in identifying ourselves as Christian!.

In Paul's day, the Roman Empire was the center of the world in culture, law, power and learning. The study of this book of Romans has been the source of renewal by famous Christian leaders such as Augustine, Martin Luther and John Wesley and unknown persons such as Sarah Ruth Baird Shaw.

I remember, at a difficult time in my life, reading Romans 12 and knowing one does not have to be conformed to the world but can be transformed. We can even have a new mind and be able to test and approve what God's will is. We will learn his good, pleasing and perfect will. (Romans 12:2 NIV)

It is easy for us to forget that each of us must give account of ourselves to God (Romans 14:12), or as the Moffat's translation tells us, "Each of us must stand before the tribunal of God." So in this scripture lesson, Paul has "stopped preaching and started meddling." He tells us in this passage that we have more to do than confess other people's sins. We confess our own! Paul would have us understand that we need to get our own case ready because each one of us must stand at the tribunal of God.

The thing I need to know – and you need to know – is that, regardless of who is responsible for my problems and my faults and sins, each one of us must eventually stand or fall before a higher court than a human one. Paul would have us to know the truth: that each of us must answer for him or herself.

What is different is that we disagree on matters of ultimate importance. To disagree in the garden club about whether to plant roses or azaleas, or in the Lion's club about whether to focus on one project or another, or in the writers' club whether or not to invite a well-known or an unknown poet is not quite the same as to disagree on matters of ultimate importance.

The book of Romans is Paul's message that none of us are righteous (Romans 3:10), but the great news is that God's amazing grace is available to all through Jesus Christ our Savior and Lord.

When Paul gets down to chapter fourteen, he wants us to know that to disagree on wages and benefits is one thing, but to disagree on our final salvation is quite another. Paul tells us that it is the difference between welfare here and welfare hereafter. Amen.

The Baptism of Jesus

Matthew 3: 13-17

Then Jesus came from Galilee to John at the Jordan to be baptized by him. And John tried to prevent Jesus saying, "I need to be baptized by You and are You coming to me?" But Jesus answered and said to him, "Permit to be so now, for this is fitting for us to fulfill all righteousness."
~Matthew 3:13-15 (NKJV)~

I read a "Humor in Uniform" story in *Readers Digest* a few years ago. A woman wrote about her daughter, an army sergeant, stationed at Fort Stewart for a forest encampment under primitive conditions. In a telephone conversation the soldier told her mother she had met a young man she liked very much and would like to get to know him better. "But there are problems," she said. She told her mother, "We are not allowed to wear any makeup out here and he has no idea what I really look like."

We laugh when we read that, but the truth is that we often wear, not just makeup, but also masks that hide our real selves not only from others but also from ourselves. We even began to see the "real me" as the person behind the mask; the person who comes to church on Sunday not to get right with God but to carry on the pretense that everything is all right.

> *We would revolutionize our world if the church became a supportive, loving fellowship where we could . . . really share our burdens, our failures, our sins and our addictions.*

We would revolutionize our world if the church became a supportive, loving fellowship where we could come to church and really share our burdens, our failures, our sins and our addictions. We need to share our deepest selves, truly pray for one another, and help one another as they do in Alcoholics Anonymous.

One church member told me, "If I really had a serious problem, I would not feel free to come to church and talk about it. In fact," she added, "the church would probably be the last place in the world I would tell it."

So we keep on our masks, even in church, and refuse to "get real" enough to confess our sins even to the Lord and hesitate to call on one another for help. We cannot "get real" until we stop making excuses and seriously confess like the members of AA do: "My name is Ruth Shaw, and I am a sinner."

We had an Alcoholics Anonymous group that met at our church when we served in Ellijay, Georgia. Charles and I got to know many of those who were struggling with addiction to alcohol. One of the young women in the group said, "People ask me how I can stand up there and admit I am an alcoholic. People have seen me drunk; I might as well admit it and take steps to get well."

Most of us have a hard time admitting our need. You may have heard the story of two men out fishing on Wednesday night, and one of the men said, "I feel guilty about us being out fishing on Prayer Meeting night. The pastor is working hard to build up attendance." The other man said, "Well I couldn't be at church tonight anyway - my wife is sick."

In this scripture lesson today in Matthew 3, Jesus is at a point of a new beginning. He has ended his years of obscurity in Nazareth and intentionally comes to John for baptism. We might ask why Jesus chose to submit to baptism. Jesus, who did not have anything to repent of, chose to submit to baptism to identify with sinning humanity. Jesus was thus saying, concerning his life and ours, "Whatever the cost, we should do the things that are right. We should get honest. We need to 'get real.'"

For Jesus in Matthew 3, it meant public baptism. Later it would mean resisting temptation. Still later it would mean teaching and preaching. Even later it meant going to the cross and dying for the sins of the world. For the whole of life, it would mean at every time and in every place being committed to being and doing the thing that is right.

The Gospel passages make it clear that Jesus was the Messiah from the moment of his miraculous conception, but His baptism became the occasion when the Holy Spirit came upon Him in a new and dynamic outpouring of power. His identity was affirmed by God who said, "You are my beloved Son."

Carlyle Marney[69] tells us we are all shaped by the people in our cellar and the people in our balcony. We learned about those cellar influences primarily from the Psychiatrist Sigmund Freud, who taught that we are shaped by the negative influences of early childhood. Freud believed these early experiences erode our self-confidence by reminding us of our weaknesses and failures.

In recent years, thoughtful scholars have taken a second look at Freud's concepts of psychoanalysis that were previously taken so seriously by educators. Today they have not only questioned them but have dismissed much of Freud's research. But Freud and generations of psychologists after him taught that only lengthy psychoanalysis can help us to come to terms with the negative forces of our childhood.

But Carlyle Marney's message was that in addition to these negative cellar influences from our childhood, all of us also have people in our balcony. In our balcony are special people, living and dead, who are yelling down to encourage us and to tell us who we really are. It might be a parent, a scout leader, a teacher, a pastor, a friend. It is someone who believed in us before we dared to believe in ourselves. It is someone who kept saying "You can do it. You are somebody. You are loved."

My father died when I was nine and I was raised during the Great Depression in a small village. My mother used to tell me, "You have a good inheritance. We came from good stock. Your name is important." In our balconies, there are people who have gone

---

[69] Carlyle Marney (1916-1978) was a Baptist minister, speaker, writer and professor.

before us - not just a parent or grandparent – who allow us to rest on their laurels.

Paul put it this way in Hebrews 12: "Seeing we are surrounded by such a great cloud of witnesses, let us throw off everything that hinders us and the sin that so easily entangles us. Let us run with patience and perseverance the race that is set before us."

How can we run this race? Paul tells us, "Looking unto Jesus!" Let us fix our eyes on Jesus, the author and perfecter of our faith. The King James Version translation tells us that Jesus is "the author and finisher of our faith." Jesus is the "finish line" of our faith. Jesus, who for the joy set before Him, endured the cross, despising its shame and has sat down at the right hand of the throne of God.[70]

Paul goes on to tell us: Do not grow weary! Do not lose heart! Do consider Jesus who endured much opposition from sinning humanity.

This great cloud of witnesses that Paul describes in Hebrews 11 is in our balconies to help us to make new beginnings and new resolves as we struggle with the questions of "Who am I?" and "How important am I?"

In our balconies, there are people who have gone before us. And even more important, there is Jesus who loved us and who, even while we were yet sinners, died to save us. I love the Psalm that tells us "Even though our mother and our father forsake us, the Lord will lift us up."[71]

On Christmas 1985, the secretary at Rico United Methodist Church gave Charles and me a little desk calendar with a scripture verse for every day. The verse for Dec 3, 1986, the day Charles left this earth, was I Kings 8:56. I kept this verse on my kitchen bulletin board until I moved to Rome 12 years later. It is a part of Solomon's message to the people of Israel after David's death: "Blessed be the

---

[70] Hebrews 12:2
[71] Psalm 27:10

Lord who has given rest to His people. There has not failed one word of His good promise."[72]

Beginnings and endings are always emotional - always poignant. Our lives are marked by those times when we move from one phase of life to another. On December 3 1986, I, who had been a wife since I was a teen, became a widow - a word I avoided using for a long time.

I remember the first time I had to check the box labeled "widow" on a form. I sat at my desk looking at the form for a long time before I could put the x in the correct box. Birth and death are the ultimate passages, but in between are baptisms, graduations, marriages, job changes, parenthood, widowhood, divorce. At these passages, we sometimes stop and reflect on who we are. Each year is also a new beginning. Each day is indeed the first day of the rest of our lives.

Bruce Larson tells the story of his mother who made a new beginning at age 14. Her mother had died when she was born. Her father remarried and had 11 more children by his second wife. So this child was the only stepchild. She said she made life difficult for her stepmother, and they sent her off to a relative in America against her will. She arrived in America from her native Sweden without money and unable to speak English. But her father gave her a Bible that she treasured all her life and passed on to her son. In the Bible her father had written two verses.

> I have no greater joy than to hear my children are walking in the truth. ~III John 4~
>
> and
>
> I am the way, the truth and the Life. ~John 14:6~

---

[72] I Kings 8:56

Bruce said apparently his grandfather wanted to give his daughter something tangible at this new beginning in her life to let her know she was loved by her dad and also by her Heavenly Father.

I visited a woman in a nursing home a few years ago, and she introduced me to another woman as a Methodist preacher. The woman was a Baptist and she said she did not suppose there was much difference in the Baptist and the Methodist churches, and I agreed. Then she said, of course, the Baptist baptized and we did something else - she wasn't quite sure what. I told her we baptized too and that Baptism and Holy Communion were the only two sacraments in both the Methodist Church and the Baptist Church.

We often emphasize Holy Spirit baptism as well as water baptism. On the day of Pentecost when the Holy Spirit descended on the people, "tongues of fire" sat on the heads of the people who were baptized in the Holy Spirit. So the word "baptize" does not always mean "immersion." We read that three thousand people were baptized on the day of Pentecost. If 3000 were all immersed in the sea, one would think something would have been said in the Bible about wet clothes.

However, many New Testament passages sound more like "immersion" than "sprinkling." And John did baptize Jesus in the Jordan River. The Bible does not go into detail but most assume it was immersion. So Methodists have always baptized by immersion or sprinkling. The water touches the top of the head in both instances.

But regardless of the different understandings concerning water baptism, one thing is evident. Baptism is a public confession and commitment to Christ, and Christians are to openly confess their faith in Jesus Christ and be baptized. It is a starting point in getting real with God.

Am I prepared to repent of my sins and get real with God? When I repent I realize my utter helplessness in saving myself. I know, in the words of John, "I am not worthy to untie His shoelaces."[73]   I

---

[73] John 1:27

need to ask myself, "Have I repented like that? Is there some lingering suggestion of making excuses for myself?"

The reason God cannot change many of us is because we will not repent. We think so highly of ourselves we cannot bend a knee and admit how fragile and helpless we really are.

This amazing scripture today tells us that instead of Jesus taking over the baptizing when He came to John at the Jordan River, the sinless Jesus got in line with sinners and took His turn in the river. Can you imagine that? We preachers and church members may strut around and hold ourselves aloof, but Jesus got in the baptismal line with sinners.

And after Jesus was baptized, the voice from heaven identified Jesus by saying, "This is my beloved son in whom I am well pleased." He was named at his baptism.

We are also named at our baptisms. The pastor calls us by name as we are baptized. You will note that in infant baptism, the pastor asks the parents, "What name shall be given this child?" That is why some people call an infant baptism a "Christening." We are given our "Christian name" at baptism.

I was christened "Sarah Ruth" at my baptism as an infant. However, infant baptism is more than christening. Infant baptism also signifies that the child is "saved" until they reach the age of accountability and can make the decision for themselves. The parents agree to keep the child under the influence of the church until they are old enough to personally accept Jesus as Savior and Lord.

When my husband, Charles Shaw, was a young student pastor, a man called the parsonage just after we had moved in and asked if the pastor would come and baptize their baby who had died at birth. Of course, we all know the baby did not need to be baptized. But the parents may have needed to acknowledge that their baby was "safe in the arms of Jesus."

We might think that Jesus did not need to be baptized. At the baptism of Jesus, the voice from heaven said, "This is my beloved son in whom I am well pleased."

What did Jesus do that was well pleasing? He had not pulled away from sinning humanity but had taken His place in the Jordan River. Why was Jesus baptized when He could have stayed on the bank and supervised? Why was He crucified when He could have saved Himself from the horrible grief and pain? Because He loves us! Because He had come to lead us through the waters of life and death into life everlasting. So Jesus, who was without sin, submitted to baptism for the remission of sins to avoid the sin of standing apart from us.

In John Bunyan's *Pilgrims Progress*, Christian arrived in his journey at the heavily guarded palace. It would be a battle to seek entry. A man sat at the door to take down the names of those who would dare to enter. Many were hanging back, reluctant and afraid - just as many today are hanging back from making a firm decision for Jesus Christ. Many are hanging back wanting to keep one foot in both worlds; reluctant to identify with Jesus Christ in a world that mocks Him. So Christian was standing there at the gate of the palace. He was reluctant and afraid. But then, with a stout countenance, he finally walked up to the guard at the gate and said, "Put my name down, sir." I like that!

In essence, that is what Jesus did when he came to be baptized. He came to identify with us human beings. Jesus did not shout directions from a safe place on the bank of Jordan. He was there with them, and He is here with us.

"Set my name down, sir!" This is what public confession is - setting our names and our lives on the line for the Kingdom of God. It starts with coming forward and taking a stand for Jesus. Amen.

Holy Crumbs
Luke 16:1-31

There was a rich man who was dressed in purple and fine linen and lived in luxury every day. At his gate was laid a beggar named Lazarus, covered with sores and longing to eat what fell from the rich man's table. Even the dogs came and licked his sores.
~Luke 16:19-21 (NIV)~

On World Communion Day each October, we have another opportunity to celebrate the greatest good news human ears have ever heard. Each World Communion Sunday, we take our place with Jesus and our brothers and sisters at the Lord's "dinner table" that is 25,000 miles long! In church we will prayerfully partake of food for the soul in celebration of Jesus, the bread (food) of life. There is an old gospel song that starts "Come and dine, the Master's calling. Come and dine."[74]

On, Saturday at 7 pm the "Lord's dinner table" starts serving in New Zealand
at 8 p.m. in Brisbane
9 p.m. in Tokyo
10 p.m. in Hong Kong
11 p.m. in Malaya
at midnight in Burma

On Sunday,
1 a.m. in Ceylon
2 a.m. in India
3 a.m. in Mombasa, East Africa
4 a.m. in Leningrad
5 a.m. in Rome
6 a.m. in Paris and London
7 a.m. in Portugal

---

[74] "Come and Dine" is a gospel hymn written in 1906 by Charles B. Widmeyer (1884-1974)

8 a.m. in Iceland
9 a.m. in Greenland
10 a.m. in Buenos Aires
11 a.m. in Rome, Georgia and other Georgia churches
12 p.m. in Alabama, Tennessee and Chicago
1 p.m. in Denver
2 p.m. in Los Angeles
3 p.m. in Prince Rupert, Canada
4 p.m. in Anchorage
5 p.m. in Honolulu
6 p.m. in Midway Island

On my way home after a long weary day, I stopped by a grocery store near my home a few years ago. I had hastily torn out a few coupons from the store ad to take advantage of the discount on some food I planned to purchase. As I handed the coupons to the cashier, she gave me a withering look and said, "Someone will sure have a job trimming these up."

I replied, "I'm sorry, I didn't know it mattered." She replied that it most certainly did matter and rudely informed me that for a long time they were not allowed to accept coupons if they were not cut out instead of torn out.

I had torn the coupons rather neatly, I thought. I felt she was being fussy to make such an issue of it. Anyway, when I finally got through the long line and to the door, I realized that after all that fuss and fanfare; she had not subtracted the amount for the coupons! I stepped back over and showed her the mistake. She apologized with her words, handed me the change (about $2.70), but she frowned her displeasure and frustration.

I finally went on my way, frustrated and wishing I had never bothered with the coupons or set foot in the super market. (Something I rarely had time to do at that time, as I was a seminary student and a new pastor.)

A couple of weeks later I went into that market again as I had to drive by it to get home from classes at Emory University. All of the lines were long except this particular woman's. I thought to myself, "I'm probably not the only customer she has told off."

And then I thought, "This is silly." I did not have any coupons and only a few items to purchase. So, very tired after a long day, I took my place in her short line. I paid for my bread and milk, and as she counted out my change, she dropped a hand full of change on the floor. She didn't seem to notice but took more from the cash register and gave me the correct amount.

I timidly said, "You dropped some change."

She snapped, "I know it. I am going to get it."

Then I think she realized that I was not criticizing and she said, "My back hurts so bad I thought I would wait a minute."

I instinctively said, "Let me get it for you," and started to bend over. But she quickly bent down and retrieved the change before I could do so.

She said, "I went to the doctor but all he did was give me some medicine for my heart."

This got my attention. The grey-haired cashier was obviously retirement age. A short time earlier I had buried my husband because of a fatal heart attack. I asked, "Are you on medication for your heart?"

She nodded, and I said, "Maybe you should go back and get the doctor to check it out again."

Then she said something I have not been able to forget. "Well, it don't matter nohow. Sick or not, I've got to work. There ain't nobody but me."

"God forgive me" I thought, "and don't let me ever look at a 'checkout' person, or any person serving me, without really seeing them as persons."

The rich man in the parable Jesus tells[75] was not a cruel man as far as we know. He was just absorbed in his own affairs, his own problems connected with his own house, his own taxes, and his own estate. He was just too absorbed to see a beggar at his gate. He was just going through check-out lines, counting out his money and his coupons - not seeing people.

This Bible lesson seems to be the most inappropriate text in the Bible to use on Communion Sunday. How does it relate to Communion?

In further study, the parable of the rich man and the beggar and the story of Jesus the night before his crucifixion when he instituted the Lord's Supper, have a similar message. The truth that we are to remember!

> *Communion is a time to remember that all of life is a trust, a holy trust.*

Communion is a time to remember that all of life is a trust, a holy trust. Even our bread! Holy Bread! Even our crumbs of bread, holy crumbs. Just a crumb, a taste from the altar of God is a banquet of Holy food for our souls.

Throughout the Gospel of Luke and in Acts, Doctor Luke talks about possessions and about life.

This parable of the rich man gets to the point immediately. First, there is this rich man who is usually called "Dives," which is the Latin word for rich. Every phrase adds something to the luxury in which this rich man lived. He was clothed in purple and fine linen. That is the description of the robes of the high priests. His robes cost many times the amount of a working man's daily wage. He feasted on gourmet food every day. Like many of us today, he had more than enough food to sustain his body, but his soul was starving.

---

[75] Luke 16:19-21

When I heard the story as a child, I pictured the beggar Lazarus sitting against the table, like a family pet, waiting to get the scraps, even the crumbs, that fell from the rich man's table.

Bible scholars tell us that in the time of Jesus, there were neither knives nor forks nor napkins. Food was eaten with the hands and in very wealthy families, the hands were cleansed by wiping them on chunks of bread and then the bread was thrown away.

This was the bread that Lazarus was waiting for, as were the scavenger dogs that were no one's pets. And poor Lazarus was too hungry to refuse the bread Dives used for a napkin and too weak to drive off the scavenger dogs that pestered him and licked his sores. Lazarus was the only character in any of the parables that was given a name. The name Lazarus means "God is My Help."

This parable doesn't tell us everything. We do know that wealth is not necessarily wicked. The rich man did not go to hell because he was wealthy. But wealth does carry with it some responsibilities. Jesus, in another story, reminds us that it is easier for a camel to go through the eye of a needle than for a rich man to enter heaven.[76] "But," he added, "With God, all things are possible."

On the other hand, we know that there is no virtue in poverty. What was Dives' sin? I personally would have had a hard time eating with a beggar and dogs at my gate. But Dives had not ordered Lazarus removed from his gate. He was not deliberately cruel to Lazarus as far as we know. Dives' sin was that he didn't even notice the beggar at his gate. He seems to have accepted Lazarus as part of the landscape. Ouch!

Dives was just going through life counting out his coupons and making sure he got every dollar and dime coming to him. This is a popular attitude in this twenty-first century in our impersonal, lonely society. The popular attitude is that if I don't look out for myself, no one else will.

This story was the spark that touched off the revolution in the life

[76] Luke 18:18-27

of Albert Schweitzer. He concluded that Africa was a beggar lying at the doorstep of Europe. He went to Africa and founded Lambarene Hospital. Schweitzer went as a medical doctor because the Mission Board could not send him at the time. He was told he was not to preach the Gospel, but one day when he did lifesaving surgery on a patient, the man asked, "Why did you come to our country to help us?" Schweitzer replied, "Because the Lord Jesus sent me." The man said, "Who is the Lord Jesus?"

This is the testimony that a hungry world needs to hear. Just who is this Lord Jesus that sent Schweitzer and has sent numerous others away from the comfort of home to faraway lands? Just who is this Lord Jesus whose sacrifice and death we are to celebrate at this World Wide Communion Table? Amen.

Unexpected Bumper Crop

Mark 4:1-20

But other seed fell on good ground and yielded a crop that sprang up, increased and produced: some thirtyfold, some sixty and some a hundred.
~Mark 4:8 (NKJV)~

When I lived in East Point, my dentist had a hygienist who was a very nice and efficient lady, but she was a quite a big talker. She talked the whole time she had my mouth propped open and even asked questions. And I would sit there with her hand in my month and try to squeak out answers to her questions.

I remember the last time I was there she asked if I had a garden. I grunted "no" and she went on to tell me her son had planted a garden - even giving me the measurements – twenty-five feet long but only six rows wide. She said her son was so excited to bring in 4 ripe tomatoes and three small cucumbers the day before and said to her, "Just think, Mama, in spite of the heat and lack of rain, I've already gotten more out of my garden than the seeds cost!" The way she told it, it was like an unexpected bumper crop to this young novice farmer. All of us who like to garden, know it is exciting to put seeds or small plants in the ground and watch them sprout and grow into vegetables.

In our scripture lesson today, Jesus gives us a parable. Jesus was a master of the short story and His parables are amazing exercises in storytelling.

This famous parable of the sower is also told in Matthew 13: 1-9, 18-23, and Luke 8: 5-15. It tells about all the pitfalls of sowing seeds, but the emphasis is on the joy of the unusual and surprising harvest! A hundredfold harvest! A bumper crop!

In spite of all the difficulties - the birds, the rocks, the heat, and the lack of rain - the farmer reaped a bumper crop. The Bible says it was hundredfold! With all the difficulties listed, one would expect little productivity at best. But in the harvest, they not only got more than their seeds back, some of the seeds multiplied a hundred times. A result any farmer would covet.

> *The bottom line for Jesus is people, and Jesus wants us to know that God is going to bless our faithfulness. We are not to worry about results in our works and prayers and efforts.*

Jesus brought the parable down to where we live. He tells his disciples that despite all the difficulties that await them in sowing the seeds of the gospel, God will bless their faithfulness wonderfully and miraculously. I don't know about you but this message is for me. And this message is for all of us in a world where we hear a lot about "bottom lines." The bottom line for Jesus is people, and Jesus wants us to know that God is going to bless our faithfulness. We are not to worry about results in our work and prayers and efforts.

Can this lesson be God's word for us in our troubled world today?

Scott Peck wrote a best seller entitled, *The Road Less Traveled*. The first sentence in the book is "Life is difficult." But long before Scott Peck, Jesus said the same thing. Jesus tells us, "Life has difficulties - rocks, thorns, tribulations, and enemies." But Jesus also tells us over and over, "Be not afraid." In spite of the fact that some seed is eaten by birds, Jesus tells us, "Be not afraid." He told the farmer, "There will be a bumper crop. In spite of the fact that some seed fell on rocky soil and wilted in the scorching sun." Jesus said, "Be not afraid. There will be a bumper crop."

Great confidence is thus given to those who proclaim the good news, because a victorious harvest will be attained if we are faithful. Sometimes we focus on the negative. Yet this parable tells us to expect victory! How often we gather for church meetings and talk about our problems. We are not to focus on our problems but on the power available to us in Jesus Christ.

From this parable Jesus is teaching the truth that from small beginnings we often get big results. Who would have thought that from only 12 disciples would spring forth a worldwide church - a hundredfold spiritual harvest that would encircle the globe?

In an age preoccupied with issues of self-image and self-worth, our self-esteem is assured and our self-respect is anchored in the awareness that God loves us and we are so important to God that Jesus died to save us. Our self-worth is "certified" by the fact that the Creator, mighty and great, dwells in the creature and calls us sons and daughters! Jesus came to earth to reconcile us back to the true understanding of God.

Back centuries earlier, our fore parents, Adam and Eve, had listened to a serpent's word that God was our enemy. Our fore parents believed the snake instead of God and thus became little more than terrified animals.

But Jesus tells us, "Fear not." Jesus tells us, "Fear not" over and over, and he tells us over and over, "I have come to bring you joy and that your joy may be full."

We are certified inheritors of the kingdom, with all its joy and freedom, but we can take ourselves out of the will. Christ invites us to become benefactors of his last will and testament.

Verse 9 tells us, "Who has ears to hear, let him hear," or as in one version, the text tells us, "You have ears. Listen!"

In other words, we do not have to hear this message of Jesus. As human beings, we have been given free will. We can say "no" to God and be lost.

We get the idea from some preaching that everyone is going to be saved, but the Bible teaches that some will be lost. We have been given the right to say, "Leave me out of the inheritance."

For centuries earlier human beings operated out of a totally false perception of God. Many still do. Fear has brought about a world of evil where "fear has cast out love," but Jesus tells us that "Perfect love casts out fear." A sizable number of people believed Jesus, accepted this great truth and became wise and civil enough to build a civilization. In our post Christian America, our cut flower generation is becoming less and less civil.

A few weeks ago a friend emailed me pictures of a smiling Jesus. I am sure Jesus was smiling with joy when he told us there was joy in heaven when just one person repents. There is joy in heaven when just one person decides to believe God instead of the serpent.

We in America, even those of us raised in the church, need to know that we can take ourselves out of the bounty of the will of God! We are free to shake our fist at the eternal God and say, like the little old lady on TV, "I'll do it my way." Then the unexpected bumper crop we get is a garden full of weeds.

When I was the interim pastor at Oostanaula United Methodist Church, a lady, age 47 and a grandmother, found my name in the phone book and called asking if my church could help her with her rent, and if not, did I know of anyone who could. I told her our church was small and our available mission money was already spent and we have more calls for money than we can possibly fill.

People come to the church to ask for help. They do not go to the bank or the liquor store or any store or business. They go to the church or they find out where the pastor lives and go there.

I knew the family of this lady. When my husband was pastor at Trinity Methodist Church in Rome, Georgia (1962-1967), we had helped this family time and time again. The father was then in prison and there was a wife and children. We bought a lot of groceries and paid many utility bills. We made arrangements for the oldest girl to go to summer camp one summer. Some of the help was with the church's local mission money and some was with our money. Of course we also prayed for and spent time with the family.

Now this woman, who was a small child when we first knew them, was now a grandmother on welfare. I was disappointed because this family never got the point of coming to Jesus and getting into partnership with God.

Anyway, after giving some thought and prayer to the situation, I did not ask the church to help but decided to give her the money she needed and a little more. I visited with her, prayed with her and wrote checks paying for her rent and utilities. I was glad to see her again after forty years and hear about the family - even though much of it was bad news.

I learned that two of her siblings were doing well and were off welfare, including the sister we had sent to camp that summer. But in the end, I still felt helpless about the situation.

There are many sermons here, but I struggled with this situation and other situations that many pastors deal with in trying to help those who somehow cannot or will not know the Jesus of the hundredfold harvest.

A neighbor of mine told me they went to church for a long time and would always put a few dollars in the offering. One day, he said, a lay speaker spoke about tithing. My neighbor told me that he had never thought about it before, but he went home and said to his wife, "We are going to start tithing our income." His wife replied, "What with?" He told her it would be with whatever they had. He told me they were living from paycheck to paycheck at the time.

This neighbor friend said he could not believe the hundredfold harvest they realized from tithing to the work of the Lord. He told me that when they bought the nice house they were now living in, they paid cash.

In the year 1215, King John of England and the English Barons signed the Magna Carta - that great charter that marked the beginning of the end of the divine right of kings and the beginning of Western democracy.

It was not much in 1215, but it was seed that fell on good ground and grew in the fertile minds of John Locke, the Dissenters and later such people as John Adams, Thomas Jefferson, James Madison, Alexander Hamilton and George Mason!

And at about the same time this country was getting ready to fight for independence, a man named John Wesley was preaching to the common people in the fields of England. He was telling people about Jesus Christ who loved them and had a wonderful plan for their lives – lives filled with love that frees them from the fear and evil that so cripples them.

No one would have believed that the seeds he was sowing would germinate into the worldwide Methodist church, which has built schools, hospitals, children homes and churches to tell the good news of Jesus to the poor and disenfranchised. There is at least one Methodist Church in every county in our nation, I am told.

Did you know that Christians are the first people to ever build a hospital? The great Roman Empire never built a hospital. As Baron von Hugal said, "Christianity taught the world to care."

The underpinnings of democracy are made up of a theological alloy that blends the metals of biblical understanding and history's experience. One of the ores in that alloy is the belief that all human beings are sacred creations of God. Jesus came to bring us joy and love that casts out fear. We are endowed with inalienable rights that foster a participatory democracy.

Fear not! We are all created by God! Fear not! God loved us enough to die for us.

When the seeds of the Magna Carter were conceived in 1215 and later had blossomed into the Bill of Rights, the voice of government changed from the voice of kings to the voice of the people. America's founders created checks and balances with three branches of government.

But we need to be confronted with the serious warning in our text today - the analogy of the no-growth soil.

C. S. Lewis spoke of being awakened in the middle of the night in his bedroom at Magdalene College, and it was as if he was alone in a vacuous black hole. Suddenly Lewis said he sat bolt upright in bed, for it dawned on him that such isolation was the logical end of a self-centered life. Lewis found himself asking, "What if we get in eternity exactly what we have lived for in time?" This means that if our thoughts and concerns have revolved around ourselves, "Could it be," Lewis wondered, "that in eternity we get only ourselves and nothing more?"

Such a condition would amount to total isolation, solitary confinement! Such a fate cuts across the very heart of what we human beings need and what we are. To be utterly and totally alone makes the image of a burning hell seem mild by comparison.

C.S. Lewis said the scripture teaches that there will come a time when we will say to God, "Thy will be done" and enter into the joy of the Lord. Or God will say to us, with infinite sadness, "Your will be done" and let us go back to the burning hell of solitary confinement.

If we do not receive the gift of God's love, sadly it cannot be injected into us like penicillin.

Thus all the dark sayings about the end times are put there as a monument to our human freedom and our free will. Jesus said, "You have ears. Hear." This is a reminder that you and I get to make the decision. We have been given free will.

We get to decide if we want to be in the Lord's will - the Lord's last will and testament - if we want to claim our certified will of God! Amen.

United We Stand

John 17: 20-26

I do not pray for these alone, but also for those who will believe in Me through their word; that they all will be one, as You, Father, are in Me, and I in You; that they also may be one in Us, that the world may believe that You sent Me.
~John 17: 20-21 (NKJV)~

I remember getting up early on September 12, 2001 and turning on the television immediately to see if there was anything new to report about the horrible September 11, 2001 Islamic terrorist attacks. All the television stations were replaying the shocking scenes of the burning and falling of the twin towers.

Even more shocking were the televised scenes of people in Islamic countries laughing and celebrating in glee that the planned attacks against Americans that cost nearly three thousand lives and countless financial resources had been successfully accomplished.

Scrolling along the bottom of the television screen on 9/12/01 were the words, "AMERICA UNITED."

In September 2001 God made the front page of American newspapers! Democrats and Republicans and Independents sat together in church singing "Amazing Grace" and "God bless America" with television cameras capturing the scene. If anyone was worried that a line had been crossed concerning "separation of church and state," no one reported it. America was united. United we stood![77]

On September 11, 2001, we also saw many heroic acts. As people rushed out of the World Trade Center towers, fireman rushed in, bravely giving their lives as the towers fell on them in their rescue efforts. We saw police on the scene keeping order and risking their

---

[77] Separation of Church and State means simply the United States will not have one denomination to be The Church of the United States as the Episcopal Church is The Church of England. It does not mean there can be no prayer or Bible reading in public places.

lives.

There were the passengers of United Flight 93 who died fighting the terrorists, thus preventing the plane from crashing into the White House or the Capitol Building.

We saw the selfless bravery of doctors, nurses, EMTs, construction workers, ministers, and blood donors who rushed to help. We learned something about heroism that day as the words "America United" scrolled across television screens in our nation.

Now it is more than ten years later. America is not united! Americans, as well as our infiltrated enemies, continue hanging America's dirty propagandized laundry out on our TV and internet clotheslines for all the world to see.

In addition to our divisions, we have allowed our country to be flooded with drugs, gambling, alcohol and pornography to addict our children with dangerous evils to rot us from within and to make many of us drunkenly unaware of the enemy on our doorstep. God help us! Only God can help us and bless our world with the love, joy, and peace we so desperately need.

"United we stand" is a motto for the United States, and it is also the motto of John 17, a passage from the Bible as up-to-date as this morning's newspaper![78] Unity is the theme of our Bible lesson from John 17. Jesus used the term "one" four times in John 17 to describe God's desire for his people.

People looking on the early church said, "See how they love one another." Imagine what a witness we would be to the world if we presented a united front of love and concern for the common good which were the values that built our great nation.

You may have heard the story about a new group of arrivals at the Pearly gates when Saint Peter is showing all the delights of heaven. This story has St Peter pointing out areas of interest as he leads this

---

[78] John 17: 20-23

tour through heaven. Suddenly he stopped short of one building and asked the group to be very, very quiet and not utter a sound as they walked past this particular building. When they tiptoed quietly past the building, they asked St. Peter why they had to be so quiet as they passed that building. St. Peter explained, "They think they are the only ones here."

Many of us can be pretty arrogant about our own beliefs and disbeliefs, our particular likes and dislikes, not only politically but sometimes even in ways of worship. We disagree about the way a preacher presents the sermon or the kinds of music used. I heard a story about the District Superintendent sending one of our older pastors to a church to show a certain pastor how to conduct an eleven o'clock traditional worship service. His people had complained that their pastor only knew how to conduct a contemporary service.

Dr. Richard Wills, a well-known United Methodist pastor and teacher, spoke to a group of pastors a few years ago and told us the story about his church erecting a large modern activities building on their church property. One day a lay leader in his church, a man named Roscoe, asked Dr. Wills if he could put up two large posters about a meeting on the beautiful glass doors of the new building. This was a "no-no" for Richard Wills!

Dr. Wills suggested to Roscoe, "Instead of using the windows of the new building for bulletin boards, why not put the posters on easels going into the building?" Wills pointed out that the easels could actually be seen better and Wills offered to help Roscoe get the easels set up.

Then the very next Saturday morning, when Wills started into the building, the first thing he saw was Roscoe's posters on the new glass doors. Wills took the posters down and put them on easels near the doors. He knew Roscoe would see them the next day, so he called Roscoe and told him what he had done. Roscoe was not pleased with what the pastor had done but he did not make much of a fuss about it.

A few weeks later, one of the women's leaders asked Wills about putting up some posters about their work on these same glass windows, and Dr. Wills went through all the reasons not to put the posters on the beautiful glass doors. The woman looked at him and said, "Well Richard, would you pray about this?" Well, what's a pastor to do? Would the pastor pray about it? Sure. Of course!

Dr. Wills said, as promised, he prayed. He said he told the Lord about their new windows and the fact there were other places to put posters etc. To make a long story short, the Lord said to this pastor, "Richard, are there no lost souls in your community to be concerned about? Are there no hungry people? No lonely people? Are there no children to be taught love and cooperation? Are there no more important things for you to be concerned about than where to put posters?" So Richard went back to the woman and told her what the Lord had told him and told her to go ahead and put the posters on the windows.

Then he remembered Roscoe, and it was Saturday again! So he called Roscoe and told him the story. He told Roscoe he could use his own judgment about where to put posters. Roscoe paused a second and said, "Is that really you, Richard?"

In our Scripture lesson in John 17, we have the longest recorded prayer of Jesus. Jesus is headed toward the cross and He is praying for the disciples. He prays that his disciples will be "one." He prays also for all who will come after these disciples down to us sitting here on Sunday morning. Jesus prays for us! Jesus prays that we, as the body of Christ, will be united as one, in love for God and love for one another, and love for our broken world.

William Temple, Archbishop of Canterbury, once said, "We meet in committees and "construct schemes of union," but he added, "How paltry are our efforts compared to the call of God."

God wants us to know that the way to the union of Christians does not lie in committee rooms, although there are tasks to be done in committee rooms. The way we can be united with others is in our mutual personal relationship with the Lord.

When we are one in Christ - in spite of our varying understandings - in spite of our liberal or conservative political backgrounds - in spite of our diverse colors, ethnic origins, ages, denominations or stages of growth - we are, in fact "one in the Spirit and one in love." We are "the family of God."

What William Temple said is that our union as Christians is more than just togetherness. It is more than just appealing to our common humanity! The unity for which Jesus is praying here is deeper, richer and more consuming than sharing the same skin as Donne alludes in his famous poem.[79]

No Man Is an Island

No man is an island,
Entire of itself,
Every man is a piece of the continent,
A part of the main.
If a clod be washed away by the sea,
Europe is the less.
As well as if a promontory were.
As well as any manner of thy friend's
Or of thine own were;
Any man's death diminishes me,
Because I am involved in mankind,
And therefore never send to know for whom the bell tolls;
It tolls for thee.
~John Donne~

What Jesus is talking about when he prays for Christians to be "one" is more than sharing a common humanity. He is telling us God in Christ has brought us together in the unity of the family of God!

We had a family reunion at my house last Labor Day. I am the youngest and the last of my parents' eleven children, nine of whom

---

[79] "No Man Is an Island" by John Donne

lived into adulthood and marriage. So we had a bunch of my nieces and nephews and their families present.

Among my parents' grandchildren and their spouses, there is every level of education, from at least one who did not finish high school to several with Ph.Ds. There are some in pulpits every Sunday and some who rarely attend church. Probably you see some of the same things in your family. Nevertheless, we had a great time because we were joined by blood ties and our love and respect for each other, our parents and grandparents. Even in our diversity, we are family.

> *Our unity in the church is more than our common humanity; it is also a blood tie.*

Our unity in the church is more than our common humanity; it is also a blood tie. How like God to use the analogy of the blood of Christ as a means of our eternal life! If we lose enough blood we die. The Red Cross reminds us of the importance of blood when they say, "Give Blood. Give Life." As Christians, we are "blood kin" though the blood of Jesus.

Jesus reminds us of this in the institution of the Lord's Supper. As in the chorus we sometimes sing; "I'm so glad I'm a part of the family of God, washed in the fountain, cleansed by His blood. Joint heirs with Jesus as we travel this sod, I'm so glad I'm a part of the family of God."

One of my cousins came to the reunion Monday. I asked her about her brother. She told me her brother's wife is angry with her about how her mother's estate was handled and is not speaking to her. I am not usually so quick to give direct counsel but I said, "Mary, find a way to make amends. Life is too short to not talk to your brother."

Most families do not have constant agreement and cooperation. Sometimes we disagree and it brings on anger and hard feelings. So it is sometimes difficult but important that we find common ground, if possible.

> *Life is too short and eternity too long to live in dis-harmony.*

The church, as the family of God, also has "blood tie" characteristics similar to other family units but with even more possibilities for disagreements and dissention. What I told Mary about her small family is even more important in the church family. Life is too short and eternity too long to live in dis-harmony.

We sometimes have to forgive others not only for what they do but for who they are. Paul recognized this and called for reconciliation. Paul tells us God has reconciled us to Himself by Jesus Christ and in verse 19 tells us "God has given us the ministry of reconciliation"[80]

As Christians, we are given the awesome and glorious ministry of reconciliation. To reconcile is to bring into harmony. Not to make everyone sing in unison but in harmony. Musicians have a good choir, not by having the entire choir sing soprano or having everyone sing alto or baritone. It is not unison but harmony that is needed. Reconciliation does not erase differences; it seeks to bring them into workable accord - into harmony.

Those of us born into a segregated society have been enriched by ties with the black church which were not possible when the races were segregated. In 1963, at Trinity, we had an African American caretaker, Silas Johnson. When Mr. Johnson's wife died, he asked Rev. Charles Shaw, Trinity's pastor, to assist in the funeral at Metropolitan Methodist Church.

On the day of the funeral service, Charles went early to meet with the pastor. Miss Lottie Duncan (the church secretary at the time) and I went to the funeral. When Miss Lottie and I walked into Metropolitan church, we were a little uncomfortable. It was the first time I had ever been in an African-American Church. The people went to great lengths to make us feel welcome. We sat down, and I noticed right away the Methodist hymnals in the hymnal racks.

---

[80] John M. Braaten, page 118-120, Sermon "Beyond Togetherness."

(This was before we became United Methodist by uniting with the Evangelical United brethren).

We were worshipping the same God, reading the same Bible and singing from the same hymnal. After the service I met the minister. He was in his late thirties - about my age at the time. He had also been raised in Newton County, the county in which I grew up. We were both Christians reared in Methodist churches, but tradition and custom had kept us from unity in Christ.

In our Scripture lesson in John 17, Jesus prays his last public prayer before going to the cross to die for our sins so that we may be reconciled to God and thus reconciled to one another. We may not always sing the same musical line, but we are one family in God, regardless of color or denomination or worship preferences when we each claim Jesus as our savior and Lord.

And thus we are to seek harmony until we become a uni-verse, one verse, one song in praise of God's awesome grace in Jesus Christ. Amen.

Do You Know about Easter?

Luke 24:1-12 and Mark 16:1-7

But on the first day of the week, at early dawn, they, and certain other women with them, came to the tomb taking the spices they had prepared. They found the stone rolled away from the tomb.
~Luke 24:1-2 (NRSV)~

One of the stories making the email rounds is about an elderly woman named Edith. Edith asks individuals at every opportunity, "Do you know about Easter?" The opening scene in the story has Edith in her doctor's waiting room, asking a young woman, "Do you know about Easter?" and then telling the woman about Jesus and leading her to Christian faith.

Meanwhile, Edith's doctor is preparing to tell her that tests show a malignancy in her body. Her time is short. Edith's final scenes are in the hospital. She is dying but still looking for every opportunity to happily ask everyone who comes in her room, "Do you know about Easter?"

Edith is kind and cheerful, but the cynical head nurse, Eleanor, is impatient and verbal with what she calls "Edith's fanaticism." Edith's major prayer is that she will not die until the Lord gives her the opportunity to talk to Eleanor about Easter and to lead her to faith in Christ. This complete turn-around for Eleanor does finally happen. Eleanor observes Edith's joy in Christ and her consistent life and testimony.

The last scene in this drama has Nurse Eleanor walking out of the hospital room after Edith's death asking the first person she meets in the hallway, "Do you know about Easter?"

Mark tells us[81] that very early in the morning on the first day of the week, some of the women came to the tomb to anoint the body of

---

[81] Mark 16:1-7

Jesus against the decay. To their fear and dismay, they found an empty tomb. This was the last straw in a series of tragedies. Jesus had been beaten and crucified, was dead and buried. Now the body had been stolen away! What else could go wrong?

Jesus had told his disciples that he was to die and, in three days, rise again. But they had their own agenda for throwing off the yoke of Rome and winning freedom for their generation. They could not believe Jesus came to bring salvation to the whole world, Gentiles as well as the Jews. They could not believe Jesus came to bring salvation, not only for their generation but also for every generation.

The disciples, like us, were too busy arguing over non-essentials like who would sit on the right hand and on the left when Jesus finally got the Romans off their backs and established His own kingdom.

When my husband, Charles, and his Marine buddies came home from the South Pacific at the end of World War II, he said he would never forget the sight of the Golden Gate Bridge in San Francisco. Everyone who knew Charles is not surprised that he came up on deck very early to get a glimpse of the famous bridge as soon as it came in view.

War veterans, who spent time in the South Pacific, still see the Golden Gate Bridge as one of the most beautiful sights in the world. They see it as the gateway to home.

I read a story recently about a veteran who had stopped overnight in San Francisco just to see the historic bridge. He went out early in the morning, but to his dismay the bridge was enveloped in fog. Then just before he had to leave, the fog began to lift, and he could see the upright towers and all that lay between but nothing of the anchorage at either end. He could see the suspension span but not the massive supports that held it up.

Life is like that. It comes out of an eternity we cannot see and leads into an eternity we do not know. We just see from birth to death, and it is so very short. Like the early disciples, we worry.

When I was a student at Georgia State University, a student in one of my classes told us about her mother who had Alzheimer's disease. She said, "I looked at her and I thought, 'That's not my mother.'"

I began to think about the question of when a person is not the person they have been. This mother was in the same physical body that had given birth to her daughter, had the same hands that had fed her and looked after her needs. She had the same feet that had run to protect her child from danger. Why was she not now her mother? What this girl was really saying is there is more to life than the physical.

Actor Christopher Reeve was asked what he had learned from being paralyzed. He said he had learned "We are not our bodies." Christopher may or may not have known it, but this is what Easter is all about. There is more to life than the physical.

We must be prepared to see this other dimension. In other words Jesus promised his followers that what we call death will not have the final word over what God calls life. The Easter message is that there is more to life than "eat, sleep and work so you can retire early with a good pension." Job's ancient question, "If a man die, shall he live again?" was answered from an open grave by Jesus Christ when he walked out of that grave saying, "Because I live, you shall live also."[82]

As a mother, I like the analogy of birth that I first heard Dr. Paul Echols use when he was pastor of First Presbyterian in Atlanta in

---

[82] Did Jesus Rise from the Dead? Former "hatchet man" of the Nixon administration, Chuck Colson - implicated in the Watergate scandal - pointed out the difficulty of several people maintaining a lie for an extended period of time. "I know the resurrection is a fact, and Watergate proved it to me. How? Because 12 men testified they had seen Jesus raised from the dead, and then they proclaimed that truth for 40 years, never once denying it. Everyone was beaten, tortured, stoned and put in prison. They would not have endured that if it weren't true. Watergate embroiled 12 of the most powerful men in the world— and they couldn't keep a lie for three weeks. You're telling me 12 apostles could keep a lie for 40 years? Absolutely impossible. "

the 1970s.[83] It put into words some of the thoughts I'd had as a mother. It speaks to my logical mind because I believe we accept the Gospel of Jesus Christ by faith, but it is not a blind faith. There are reasons to believe.

Albert Einstein said "the fairest thing we can experience is the mysterious - the fundamental emotion which stands at the cradle of true science." Einstein and other prominent scientists have concluded there is room in a rational universe for incomprehensible wonders.

I believe with Elton Trueblood that there are three areas that need to be cultivated if faith is to be a living faith: the inner life of devotion, the intellectual life of rational thought, and the outer life of human service.[84] I believe that God is calling some of us to address this area of rational thought as well as the other two.

As Echols reminds us, our life began in the watery warm world of our mother's womb. In biology, we learned that in the beginning we looked like a speck of transparent jelly. But the body, the mind, the spirit, the emotions - all the vast potentialities of life were hidden away in that tiny dot of transparent computer-like genetic information (DNA) - tiny as a grain of sand.

As an unborn baby, we adapted to the environment of the womb. Had we been aware of it, we would have been frightened at the possibility of leaving the secure environment of the womb for an outside world.

In the womb we lived without breathing. How could we possibly live by breathing? In the womb we lived without light. How could we possibly live with all that light shining around us? In the womb we lived in water. How could we possibly survive with air all around us instead of water? Frightening possibility! We'd be like a fish out

---

[83] The analogy of the baby in the womb is from a sermon by Dr. Paul Echols televised while Dr. Echols was pastor of First Presbyterian Church in Atlanta 1977-1988. I do not know if he cited another source. I found Dr. Echols's sermon interesting. I have used some of these thoughts in funeral sermons.
[84] Elton Trueblood. *A Place to Stand.* p.18

of water. Dead. It makes sense. Being born out of the womb would certainly seem like death. We come into the world crying while everyone else is smiling when they hear that first cry.

Why not cry? How in the world could an unborn child know that it is necessary to leave the womb to be born into a larger world? How could we have known that the womb is just a preparation place for a larger world? In the darkness of our mother's womb, eyes were being formed for light we had never seen. In the stillness, ears were being formed - fashioned for sounds we had never heard. In that airless environment, lungs were being formed for oxygen we had never breathed. In our mother's womb our brain cells were being prepared for thoughts we had never had. And finally we were born.

And here we are. What if this big world on the other side of birth is a big round womb? This world of spring flowers and sunshine, of tornados and floods, this world of loving care, and wars, and crime, and pain, and death, and people who say, "How can a God of love allow pain and untimely deaths?" What if we are being fashioned and prepared for another world? A world as different from this one as this one is different from our mothers' wombs?

There is something about the very structure of this world that whispers to me and to you, "There's something more." There is more to life than just what we are able to see and touch and handle. As children we first sensed this when we learned to count. We quickly learned there is no stopping place. There is always one more number. Infinity! The same is true of every human discipline – history - electronics - microbiology - botany.

There is something uncanny about infinity. Science keeps documenting our intuitions about infinity. For example, look at the human ear that was formed in the womb for things it could not hear there. The ear is an amazing receiver set, picking up sounds between sixteen cycles and eighteen thousand cycles a second - a range of 11 octaves. Radios and dogs and bats keep reminding us that what we hear is only a little of all the sounds around us.

Our eyes were formed in our mother's womb for things we could not see in the womb. With normal eyesight, we see all the glorious rainbow colors of nature but no more. But we know that there is more than our eyes can see. There is infra-red at one end of the scale and ultra-violet at the other end. Beyond that there are X-rays - gamma rays - cosmic rays - and the Lord only knows what else.

And that is the point! The Lord alone knows what else. We are learning a little about DNA, but the Lord only knows all. But we do have the equipment built into us right now to know that we hear and see only a small amount of the world's sights and sounds. Equipment like our untiring curiosity, our sensitive spirits, our believing hearts that bring us together Sunday after Sunday to celebrate and hold firmly to things we do not fully understand.

So when Paul tells us, "Eye has not seen, ear has not heard, neither has it entered into the heart of man the things that God has prepared for those who love him," we just know that we know it is true!

> *I feel a great sadness for fragile, dying human beings who ball up their puny little fists and say "no" to God's truth.*

This is the first step - the decision to believe. I feel a great sadness for fragile, dying human beings who ball up their puny little fists and say "no" to God's truth. I feel sad for people who say, "This world is all I know. I'm not going to believe in a world I cannot see with my own eyes."

On that first Easter, the disciples had grieved for three days. God had stood aside and let them kill the physical body of the only sinless person who ever lived. But just as he said, on the third day Jesus was raised. Jesus was alive! They saw him. They ate with him. They knew him. He was alive in a body they recognized; but it was a body without limitations, a body that could walk through doors and be ascended into heaven.

Do you know about Easter? What God did once in a graveyard in Jerusalem, he can and will do on a grand scale for all of us who know Jesus as Savior and Lord.

Death has never been the same since it took on Jesus. Paul reminds us, "Jesus is the first fruits of the resurrection." The first fruits! Against all odds, the terminal shall be made alive. God came down and wept with us on Good Friday so that some glad morning we will laugh with Him. Do you know about Easter? Alleluia! Christ is alive. He is risen indeed! Amen.

How Does God Sign His Name?

Matthew 25:31-46

The King will reply, 'Truly I tell you, whatever you did for one of the least of these brothers of mine, you did for me.'
~Matthew 25:40 (NIV)~

Back in the seventies, I read a story I have never forgotten. It was about two ten year old girls who lived in the early days of our country. One day they went with their entire church to attend an all day Sunday School Convention meeting in a historic old church. They rode in horse drawn buggies to one of the oldest churches in the country, a church building dating back to the American Revolution.

As the afternoon wore on and all the speaking continued, the children began to amuse themselves by looking around and reading the initials carved on the backs of the rough, hand-hewn wooden pews.

One of the girls pointed to the initials "J. A." and whispered to the other, "Maybe those are the initials for John Adams." The little girls thought, from some of the history of the church that there was a possibility that, as a child, John Adams could have sat in that very pew and carved his initials.

This was a fascinating thought. They might actually be sitting in a pew where one of our earliest presidents had sat. Then they began to excitedly look for other initials of famous people. There might be a "J.M." or a "T.J." or a "G.W." Could it be that James Madison or Thomas Jefferson or even George Washington had once sat on these same church benches?

They whispered to one another about all the important and historic people who might have sat in those pews as children and carved their initials on the rough pews in this early American church building.

Then one child whispered to the other, "Maybe God carved his initials here? How about God's initials?"

"That's silly," the other child said, "God cannot write."

"That's silly again. God can write if He wants to," responded the other child.

Then the thought struck them: If God wrote something, it would not necessarily be in English or any other language. God's writing would not have to be like our writing. As they began to look around the building, thinking of the concept of God carving his initials, one of the girls noticed a tiny blue violet growing in a crack in the floor. She quietly whispered to the other, "Look, God signed his name there."

Their excitement grew as they began to look around and point out place after place where God had put his signature. One pointed out a dimple in a baby's neck in the lap of a young mother in the pew in front of them. Then they noticed smile wrinkles on a grandfather's face. Then they saw a small intricate spider web.

The writer, one of the girls in the story, ended the article by saying, "I knew that Molly and I would spend the rest of our lives looking for places where God has left his imprint, where God has placed his signature, a place where God has signed His name."

Epiphany comes at the beginning of the New Year and is the season in the church year to reveal to us more about God and how God has manifested Himself in our world.

Just a year or so before my husband, Charles, had his first heart attack, we were on the exit ramp of the expressway on our way home when we noticed a man on crutches beside the road, falling down. Since we had already passed him, we drove back. Charles asked me to stay in the car as he got out to talk with the man. The man was "falling down drunk," on crutches, and had a broken leg.

After finding out he was homeless, Charles put him in the car, took him home with us and helped him get a bath. We found some clean clothes for him to wear while I put his clothes in the washing machine and prepared him something to eat. Some days later, Charles was able to get him into a Christian home for alcoholics nearby.

> *God signs His name with open arms to all of us, more especially to the persons with the most immediate need!*

So be it! God's signature is seen, sometimes in dramatic ways and many times in the pastor's ordinary work day. God signs His name with open arms to all of us, more especially to the persons with the most immediate need! God signs his name to the "least of these."

I accepted the invitation to pastor at East Point Avenue United Methodist Church after reaching mandatory retirement age (age 70) and served there for four years (June 1993 through June 1997). The dear people at East Point Avenue United Methodist Church were always available to help with secretarial duties as they did not want me to risk being in the church alone because of its downtown location.

One afternoon I happened to be alone when I heard a knock at the door and thought "Oh no" when I saw that it was someone who would be asking for financial help. I thought of how much easier it would be for Christian pastors if we had never read Matthew 25:31-46 where Jesus reminds us that God signs His name as "one of the least of human beings." Jesus tells us that "whatever you did for one of the least of these brothers of mine, you did for me." (Matthew 25:40 NIV)

Mother Teresa was asked why she picked up filthy dying strangers off the street to bathe and feed them and minister to their every need. It was because she saw Jesus in every destitute helpless person and thus ministered to them just as if he/she were Jesus Christ Himself.

"Then the King will say, 'Come you blessed of My Father, inherit the kingdom prepared for you from the foundation of the world. For I was hungry and you gave me food. I was thirsty and you gave me drink. I was a stranger and you took me in. I was naked and you clothed me. I was sick and you visited me. I was in prison and you came to me. Inasmuch as you did it to one of the least of these, you did it to me.'" (Matthew 25: 34-40).

> *God looks beyond our sins and sees what we can become with His amazing grace!*

We come to Jesus just as we are - clothed in the garments of sin, spiritually starving and sick unto death. We are welcomed by Christ (and hopefully by Christians). We are accepted as a son or daughter, bathed in God's love and forgiveness, transformed and clothed in his grace. We are given a place at his table of grace. God looks beyond our sins and sees what we can become with His amazing grace!

I heard Dottie Rambo tell of praying for her brother who had become an alcoholic. Dottie's brother finally came to God, was saved to God and from his sins. Dottie wrote one of my favorite of all her songs in honor of this brother.

He Looked Beyond my Fault and Saw my Need
Amazing grace shall always be my song of praise
For it was grace that bought my liberty.
I do not know just why he came to love me so,
He looked beyond my fault and saw my need.
I shall forever lift mine eyes to Calvary
To view the cross where Jesus died for me.
How marvelous the Grace that caught my falling soul!
He looked beyond my fault and saw my need.

Matthew tells us God looks beyond our fault and sees Jesus who identifies with the lost and least of us.

God writes His Name as One who loves each one of us as if we were Jesus the Christ Himself and is holding out His arms of welcome to each one of us. Amen.

God Put A Rainbow in the Clouds. Hallelujah!

Genesis 9:7-17

And God said to Noah, This is the sign of the covenant which I have established between Me and all flesh that is on the earth.
~Genesis 9:17 (NKJV)~

God is good, all the time! All the time, God is good! And nowhere is this great truth that "God is good" illustrated more than in our Scripture lesson today.

We read in the first chapter of the Bible, Genesis 1, God's saying, "It is good" about the earth and all that he created the first five days of creation!

Then on the sixth day, God created man and woman and He said about us, "It is very good." So in the first two chapters of Holy Scripture, we see life understood as a divine gift when God united physical matter (the dust of the ground) with spiritual matter (the breath of life). Thus man became a living soul. And it was Good! Very good!

But In Chapter 3, the story changes dramatically when the serpent comes on the scene. He tells Eve that God is not good, and he tempts Eve to defy God in prideful disobedience. Things were no longer good.

Paul expresses the implications and enormity of how Eve's actions, and later Adam's actions, had universal effects when he tells us, "By one man's offense, many died," or "In Adam, all die."

We can illustrate and clarify this by using the analogy of Einstein's splitting of the atom. When Einstein published his Theory of Relativity, we are told there were only twelve men knowledgeable enough to understand anything about it.

But 40 years later when the first atom bomb was dropped on Hiroshima, all of us were ushered into the Atomic Age, whether we understood the theory or not. There was no going back, and there were no exceptions because Einstein's atomic reality had come to all people on earth.

With Eve and Adam's sin, we were all ushered into a fallen - that is a "full of sin"- world. Adam and Eve tried to hide from God, but they learned, and we are learning, there is no place to hide. Our world has become a neighborhood and we have yet to learn how to be neighbors.

So our problems are spiritual. I do not have to tell you this - we all know this. This is why we are in church today, and this is the reason people have met and are meeting all over the world in small and large churches. The answers to life's questions are spiritual.

Sin entered the world through the first family, and in the second generation, the downward spiral of violence and rebellion continued. The psalmist put it in a nutshell when he wrote, "We are all born in sin."

We certainly saw the fallout effects of drugs when cocaine and then crack entered our society. We are all affected by it. The increase in crime and disease has affected us all.

I was at a doctor's office some time ago, and they had a new rule that everyone had to present a photo identification because (they told me) someone had lent another person an insurance card. The owner of card had died and thus the card was canceled. The person using the card had to finally come forward with the truth. One patient's crime affected all of the patients.

When we get to Genesis 6:6, we read that God was grieved and His heart was filled with pain that He had created humanity. God decided He would have to bring a flood to destroy all flesh and start over. But He found one man who did not follow the crowd.

We take sin lightly. We indulge in sin. We laugh at sin. We watch it acted out on television each day. But this narrative about Noah brings us face to face with the fact that God takes sin very seriously, not as an angry tyrant but as a troubled parent - as a loving father grieving over the alienation of his children.

As Sam Jones, a lawyer turned well-known Georgia Methodist evangelist and pastor at Trinity United Methodist Church in Rome, Georgia in his early days, loved to say, "Don't follow the crowd. The crowd is going to Hell." But, like the people to whom Sam Jones preached and the people in Noah's day, we today also like to follow the crowd. We do not want to stand out from the majority of our friends and neighbors.

So Noah entered the Bible with what Walter Brueggemann[85] calls, "a minority view." The Bible tells us Noah was a just man. Noah regarded God's commandments as promises that God had already written into our bodies and our psyches before he put them in the Bible. They are the instructions for a good life. So God tells Noah how to build the ark. He orders Noah to take his family and also to take and preserve representations from every species of the things that God had created.

Thomas A. Kempis, in his classic, *The Imitation of Christ*, said "If your heart is right, then every created thing would be a mirror of life and a book of sacred doctrine. There is no creature so small or worthless that it does not show forth the goodness of God." So God was interested in Ecology before we were.

We are told Noah had a minority view. He did not follow the crowd. The devil has given us a majority view. We hear people parroting back the words and ideas spread abroad by the agnostics and unbelievers in our world. We hear, and our children are told, every day, "We do not need to talk about God outside the church. We can be Christian without going to church."

---

[85] Walter Brueggemann is an Old Testament scholar and theologian. He is considered one of the most influential Old Testament scholars of the last several decades.

Several years ago I went to visit and pray with a man who was having heart surgery. Redmond Hospital values pastoral visitation, and so it has set aside three parking places for pastors to park for hospital visitation. I pulled my car into one, as I had done numerous times before, and was walking toward the hospital when a guard came over and told me the place was for pastors only.

He was not sure he could take my word and asked me to show him some evidence that I am a pastor. So I began trying to think of what evidence I had. I usually leave my purse in the car and put only my small Bible and car keys in my pocket, and so I had no church bulletin. Then I remembered I still had a Redmond hospital pass that goes over the auto mirror in front. The Pastor at Trinity had given it to me back when I was doing much of Trinity's visitation. The guard and I walked back to the front of my car so he could see the "evidence."

The guard said, "Well you know we do not see many women pastors." I asked him if he was a Christian and he said "yes." I asked him what church he attended and was not surprised when he said, "I do not go to church, but me and the Lord communicate."

This is the "majority view" Hollywood and academia are promoting: It is OK to believe in God, but we do not have to go to church. In the friendly conversation that I had with this man, I did tell him that we, as Christians, are told in scripture "to forsake not the assembling of ourselves together."

Noah built the Ark. He took his family and all that God had instructed him to take with him into the ark, and they all rode in that huge ungainly Ark for over a year before they could step out on dry land. Meanwhile every living person and thing outside the ark was destroyed.

In Genesis 9:8-17, after the flood, God makes his first covenant with Noah and his descendants and with all of us - including you and me in church here today. God said in Genesis 9:11, "I establish my covenant with you that never again shall all flesh be cut off by the waters of a flood, and never again shall there be a flood to destroy the earth." When God put a rainbow in the clouds after the flood, he indicated to Noah the covenant was between God and all future generations and not just with Israel.

The covenant was not only with human beings but also with all creatures on the earth. God was interested in ecology long before we were. We read in Genesis, "seed time and harvest… fowl and cattle…all things God made at creation." Most dramatically of all, in this rainbow covenant, only one party to the agreement speaks. God is speaking and no response from Noah or his sons is called for or given. Not even their acknowledgment or acceptance.

> *There comes a time, in the clouds of life, when there is need for a rainbow.*

When God put that first rainbow in the clouds, he was remembering us, in an act of gracious engagement with us, as his covenant people. There comes a time, in the clouds of life, when there is need for a rainbow.

Today we sometimes feel that we are in chaos and crisis almost as dreadful as the flood. We are shadowed by clouds of terror, drugs, alcoholism, pornography, crime, hate, unrest. But our lesson in Genesis 9 reminds us that God put a rainbow in the clouds. Hallelujah! A rainbow in the sky almost always brings an excited response from all of us. Can you imagine walking outside and seeing a rainbow and not pointing it out to someone?

When we were at Lake Junaluska for a family reunion a few years ago, the large house in which we stayed overlooked the Lake. We had rain nearly every afternoon. One afternoon my son Terrell walked out on the porch and looked across the lake and called for all of us to come out a see the rainbow. The whole family stood there on the porch for a long time drinking in the view and enjoying the amazing beauty of a very large rainbow in the sky and its reflection on the beautiful Junaluska Lake.

There is something about a rainbow that brings a smile. Robert Cunningham said, "It is good to know there are some areas of life beyond our power to mess up. We humans have harnessed the babbling brook and stripped trees from our forest and split the atom, but we have not yet found a way to mar the rainbow.

> *When we see a rainbow, we remember that God remembers us. We are not alone.*

Our lesson today tells us to see the rainbow as a sign of God's goodness and grace! A rainbow is not just a sign to us. It is also a sign to God. The Bible tells us we are to remember that God remembers us. When we see a rainbow, we remember that God remembers us. We are not alone.

It is grace coming after the rain and after the pain - not as a fleeting hope but as a sign of God's love,` amazing goodness and grace.

It is a sign that God is good, all the time! All the time, God is good. God still remembers us and is available, even today, to save each of us and to walk with us - all the way home! Amen.

The Golden Calf

Exodus 32:1-14

Now when the people saw that Moses delayed coming down from the mountain, the people gathered together to Aaron, and said to him, "Come, make us gods that shall go before us; for as for this Moses, the man who brought us up out of the land of Egypt, we do not know what has become of him."
~Exodus 32: 1 (NKJV)~

When my husband Charles was a student pastor, we had to be out of town one weekend, and Charles asked another pastor to preach at the church on Sunday. When we returned on Monday, Charles called one of the church lay leaders and asked how the service went. The lady told him, "Well, Brother Shaw, attendance was down - not many people were present. You know the old saying, 'When the cat's away, the mice will play.'"

In today's scripture lesson, Moses had been away for 40 days. He had been up on Mt. Sinai in the Holy presence of God, receiving the revelation of the law, including receiving the Ten Commandments. It was an experience unmatched before or since.

Meanwhile, the Israelites down below became impatient with their leader's absence. The people began murmuring and complaining about needs both real and imagined. And, like the little mice, while Moses was away, they played! Verse 6 tells us, "The people sat down to eat and drink and rose up to play." They went to Aaron and told him, "Make us gods we can see who will go before us."

Just a few weeks earlier they had agreed to bind themselves to the covenant that had begun with Abraham, Isaac, and Jacob-Israel, and then Jacob's twelve sons who became the twelve tribes of Israel. They had told Moses, "All that the Lord hath spoken, we will do and be obedient." The frame of reference here is the Covenant. The Covenant is the thing that binds us to God and to one another - the thing that brings us back to church and joins us together as the people of God.

In today's Scripture lesson, we see them going a step farther than their complaining and murmuring. We see a rebellion that is threatening the life of the community. It is a rebellion that is rupturing the covenant relationship with the God of their fathers.

They wanted a God they could see and manage, a God of their own making, and a God that provided them what they wanted! The people said, "Our needs are simple. We just want food of our own choosing. We have manna and quail but we would like a richer variety in our diet. We have leadership, but we need direction at every turn. We have a God, but we cannot see our God like our neighbors see their many gods.

I will never forget an incident in our children's Sunday School Class when I was pastor at Rico United Methodist Church, the first church I served as pastor. Pat Foster was the teacher and, for several Sundays, had been teaching the children a unit from the Old Testament about Moses. One Sunday morning, Pat introduced another lesson about Moses. Six-year-old Laura spoke up and said, "Miss Pat, do you think we could talk about somebody else today? I'm getting kind of tired of this guy Moses."

Apparently these Israelites were getting tired of waiting for Moses to come back to them. Moses had been on his mission on Mt. Sinai for 40 days. So, like children, they complained to Aaron, the second in command, "Where is this guy Moses when we need him?"

We first met Moses as a baby. He was born in Egypt after Pharaoh had decreed that all Israelite boy babies be killed at birth. Moses was rescued from his little basket-boat in the Nile River where his mother had hidden him. He was rescued by the Pharaoh's daughter. And through the care and cleverness of his mother and his sister Miriam, his mother was hired to nurse him until he was weaned at about age three.

But Moses knew who he was, even though he was raised in the Egyptian palace as the Pharaoh's grandson and as the Prince of Egypt! One day, when he saw his people being mistreated at the hands of the Egyptians, he killed the Egyptian who was brutalizing an Israelite.

The very next day Moses saw two Israelites fighting. Moses was appalled and asked them why – why in the midst of all the violence AGAINST them – why? Why would the people of God fight among themselves?

This was a marvelous question for then and for us today. But these Israelite ruffians told Moses to tend to his own business, and furthermore, they told Moses they had seen his violence against the Egyptian the day before.

So Moses fled from Egypt to become a shepherd in the land of Midian. There he married Zipporah and became a father of two sons. Moses was tending sheep in the land of Midian, trying to live his own life and trying to forget his people who were slaves back in Egypt.

Meanwhile, back in Egypt, God heard the groaning of the Israelite slaves and God saw and knew their condition. The Bible tells us that God "remembered His covenant with Abraham, Isaac and Jacob."

God came down in the burning bush experience to Moses. On that day, Moses was out in the fields and saw a bush that was burning but was not being consumed. Moses stood with God on Holy Ground. The God of his ancestors was no longer just the God of Abraham, Isaac and Jacob. He became the God of Moses, and Moses forever after became probably the most faithful of any of the patriarchs of the Old Covenant.

The amazing story of the golden calf began in Moses' absence while he was on the mountain in the presence of God and receiving the Ten Commandments. The Israelites below became impatient and resentful of their leader's absence and requested a substitute to take Moses' place in leading them.

They went to the second in command, Aaron, and demanded, "Make us gods who can go before us!" as Moses went before them in the wilderness experience. They wanted gods that could be fabricated and managed.

If Aaron offered any resistance to their demands, the record does not tell us. Aaron called for all the gold jewelry, and the Bible tells us he used the jewelry to form a golden calf. The people called it their god and built an altar and worshiped the image. So the people's sin of idolatry was in breaking the first two commandments. This is the first theme in this passage.

The second theme is about the role of Moses as mediator. Moses stood between the people and God and communicated in both directions. There was no threat to Moses, but he responded to God's threat to the people and identified with his people.

In other words, Moses, as all great leaders, was in solidarity with the people. When speaking of the people, Moses said "we" instead of "I" and "they." Moses believed in the people more than the people believed in themselves. Moses believed in the people more than the people believed in Moses. After all, they had been ready to write Moses off after a forty-day absence.

> *The willingness of God to forgive and restore runs like a golden thread through the entire story.*

Moses said to God, "If you are going to blot their names out of your book, blot mine out also." Moses kept interceding for the people. He saw more in them than they saw in themselves.

The willingness of God to forgive and restore runs like a golden thread through the entire story. God's love and forgiveness makes renewal of the covenant possible. In the tenth verse, the Lord announces His decision to destroy these people for their idol worship and for breaking the covenant. At the same time, God left room for grace.

God said to Moses, "Let me alone that my wrath may burn hot against them." God, here, is indirectly inviting Moses to intercede for his people. In other words, we could understand it to mean, "If you do not let me alone, if you intercede, I will not destroy the people."

Because of Moses' intercession, God changed His mind. Moses did not offer any excuse to God for the people. Moses did not plead that they deserved forgiveness. He simply reminded God, "God, these sinful people are not just my people; they are also Your people." Moses appealed to the faithfulness and mercy and grace of God.

This is the foundation for the prayer of intercession. It is the foundation for our prayers for our hurting and lost loved ones as well as our prayers for ourselves.

God's faithfulness and mercy and amazing grace make renewal of the covenant possible.

> *Twas grace that caused my heart to fear*
> *and grace my fears relieved.*
> *How precious did that grace appear*
> *the hour I first believed.* [86]

Praise God! Praise God! Amen.

---

[86] This is one verse of the hymn "Amazing Grace" written by John Newton (1725-1807)

Asking the Right Questions

Zechariah 7:1-10 and Luke 20: 27-28

Then the word of the Lord came to Zechariah, saying, "Thus says the Lord of hosts: 'Execute true justice. Show mercy and compassion everyone to his brother. Do not oppress the widow or the fatherless, the alien or the poor. Let none of you plan evil in his heart against his brother.'"
~Zechariah 7: 8-10 (NKJV)~

We cannot ask the right questions and learn the right answers to the questions of life and death if we refuse to see truths that are beyond the physical. A columnist for the *Kansas City Star*, Bill Tammeus, speculated about why some journalists and some scientists refuse to see truths that are not physical.

When Pope John II visited Mexico, huge crowds were present wherever he spoke. In San Juan, Los Lagos, it was estimated that the crowd that gathered in a meadow to listen to the Pope numbered over a million people. Why did these people in enormous numbers seek out this man? Would you believe that most of the news stories which covered the visit of Pope John Paul II never asked such a question? Bill Tammaeus did ask the question, "Why are they so interested in a man who can give them only sermons - not jobs, not food, not shelter?"

The prophet Zechariah received a delegation from the sanctuary town of Bethel in 528 B.C. The delegation represented some of the returning Jews from the Babylonian exile, and they asked the prophet Zechariah a question. They asked if they should continue to maintain the quarterly fast that was instituted to remind them of the destruction of the temple in Jerusalem years earlier in 587 B.C. A new temple was being constructed. Should they continue to fast in remembrance of the destruction of the old temple?

The word of the Lord came to Zechariah with a question for his people. Did you fast unto the Lord?[87] In other words, what was

---

[87] Zechariah 7:5

your motivation in fasting? Were you fasting to learn the will of the Lord or was it sentimental observance or self-pity? Did you fast to understand why the temple was destroyed? Did you understand why God had been offended by your backsliding, by your lack of love for one another, by your blindness to the poor, and by your neglect of the commandments of God? Zechariah, like Amos and Micah before him, called for moral and ethical righteousness.

The ritual fast was important; but more important than any ritual, especially one that has lost its original intent, was the charge to refrain from oppressing weaker persons. In other word, we are supposed to live by what we profess to believe. What we ARE speaks so loudly that people cannot hear what we are saying. Verses 7-10 tell us, in answer to the question of whether or not to continue the fast, "Execute true judgment. Show mercy and compassion. Do not oppress the widow, the fatherless, the stranger, or the poor." There is more than one way to oppress. We oppress when we ignore or put temptation in their way.

An old Levite law provided that a brother marry his brother's childless widow to provide an heir (Deuteronomy 25:5-6). In Luke[88] we read that the Sadducees did not believe in the resurrection, and when they could not find a way to trap Jesus as a blasphemer, they came in with another attack. They came to Jesus, moving from the sublime to the ridiculous, by posing an answered question to try to disprove the resurrection.

Jesus knew that the Sadducees refused to see truths that were not physical. Jesus knew that they wanted to make the possibility of resurrection appear to be ridiculous rather than a reality. But Jesus answered their question about the woman who had been widowed seven times: "Whose wife will the woman be?"

I thought, as I read this, that after burying seven husbands, the woman probably would not want to be anybody's wife! First, Jesus answered their question by telling them that resurrection is not the same as a continuation of this life. You have to die to be resurrected. It is an entirely new life that is given by God to those

---

[88] Luke 20:27-38

who are believers. Death has to precede resurrection. Then God lifts us up to a level of existence that is completely different because it is one that will last forever.

> *The resurrection of Jesus took place with such power that the disciples gave their lives to preach it.*

Second, Jesus told them that the resurrection hope is a reality, not a fantasy. Jesus taught the resurrection as he headed toward His own death on the cross, and He demonstrated what He taught. The resurrection of Jesus took place with such power that the disciples gave their lives to preach it.

Every Sunday we celebrate the resurrection. That is why we meet on Sunday instead of on the Jewish Sabbath. And every Sunday I look for better ways to tell the story of the glorious, historic resurrection of Jesus Christ. It has been twenty centuries since that first Easter morning. It has been preached from every pulpit in the world, and the story has been read millions of times. People have witnessed to it in churches, homes, offices, factories, campuses and military bases. IT IS NOT NEW NEWS!

But are we any different than those frightened women who first went to the tomb to anoint the body of Jesus expecting to encounter the smell of physical decay but instead found the body gone? They did not say, "Glory Halleluiah, He is risen!" They asked the wrong question, "Who stole the body?" A world of resurrection was not a world that they were familiar with. It is not a world that we are familiar with. Our world is a world of 8 to12-hour work days, a world of death, taxes and elections - a world of automobiles, business deals, income taxes, electronic media, and grocery shopping. It is not a world of resurrection, empty graves and visiting angels. Or is it?

The Sadducees refused to believe in truths they could not understand. They didn't know there was a world of transcendent reality just beyond this world. This is what Dr. Luke's gospel lesson in chapter 20 is all about.

We must start asking the right questions and seeing another reality. The Bible teaches that our life here is just a beginning. For the Christian who dies, heaven will be a much better place. Death is simply a passageway into that eternal life. This is the answer to the question about resurrection.

We live in a world that pounds its message of "Eat, drink and be merry; for tomorrow we die." Many very fine people today live by the creed of eat, drink, and work, so that you can retire early with a good pension. The resurrection message is that there is more to life than eat, drink and be merry and prepare for retirement! The story of Jesus does not end with His death; it begins a new chapter with His resurrection. Job's ancient question, "If a man die, shall he live again?" was answered from an open grave by Jesus Christ.

"Because I live, you shall live also!"

I remember the first time I knew this. I was eleven and sitting in church with my widowed mother. We were singing:

> *Was it for crimes that I have done*
> *Christ died upon the tree?*
> *Amazing pity, grace unknown,*
> *and love beyond degree.* [89]

I thought, "How could my sins today have anything to do with causing Christ to die on the cross nearly two thousand years before I was born?" That was the first of many times that I have pondered theological questions. Something in me – only 11 years out of my mother's womb – somehow made the connection; and I knew in my heart that Jesus not only died for the whole world, but he also died for me! That is the most important decision I ever made in my life – the decision to believe God as revealed in Jesus Christ - the decision to believe in the resurrection.

Every other important decision has been built on that one, and I

---

[89] Hymn, "At the Cross" by Isaac Watts

feel a great sadness for the fragile, dying human beings who ball up their puny little fists and say "No" to God. I feel sad for people who ask the wrong questions and come out with the wrong conclusions. They say, "This world is all I know. I don't understand it. It does not make sense. I'm not going to believe it. I'm going to eat, drink, and be merry, for this world is all there is."

To my mind, the world does not make sense, except for the truth of Jesus Christ that has changed and is changing multitudes of lives. I read recently that science is almost beginning to hint that matter itself is spiritual; the stuff of the world that once was considered solid and motionless is in reality a whirling mass of electrons.

Scientists now say, for example, that this solid pulpit is actually a whirling mass of electrons and if I knew how to do so, I could put my hand through it. In other words the line is becoming increasingly blurred between matter and energy, between visible and invisible. They tell us it is no longer simple to distinguish between the physical and the spiritual.

Sometimes, looking back, I feel that I awoke as a child with God on my mind. The older we grow, the more we become aware of how little we know with our flawed human understanding

Flannery O'Connor wrote: "Dear God, I cannot love Thee the way I want to. You are the slim crescent of a moon that I see and my self is the earth's shadow that keeps me from seeing all the moon. The crescent is very beautiful and perhaps that is all one like I am should or could see; but what I am afraid of, dear God, is that my self shadow will grow so large that it blocks the whole moon, and that I will judge myself by the shadow that is nothing."[90]

Consider memory - that amazing capacity to record and preserve and later reflect upon impressions received by one body even though our bodies have changed. Our bodies change every seven years. The tired blood and worn-out cells go, but the memory

---

[90] For 18 months in the 1940s, Flannery O'Connor kept a notebook in which she wrote a series of entries addressed to God. This is one of them.

stays." I have memory of that experience in church when I accepted the truth of Christ into my life. If it is true that we get a completely new body every seven years, these memories go back beyond many bodies. That physical body that sat in church when I was eleven years of age and accepted the truth of God is gone. But the memory remains. The spiritual new-birth remains.

Paul explains that the things that are seen (bodies) are transient; but the things that are unseen (God, persons) will live forever. This body will die; the body will be resurrected into a body that will never die; and we will go on forever.

Strong men placed the lifeless broken body of Jesus in that tomb and rolled the heavy stone in front of the tomb. The women who went to the tomb on Sunday morning discovered that God doesn't pay any attention to the stones we roll in front of anything. God doesn't give up or fall apart or roll over and stay dead simply because we hang Him on a cross and crucify Him and place Him in a tomb and seal it with a heavy stone. Death has never been the same since the day it took on Jesus Christ!

With Jesus Christ as our Savior, we will step out of this life into a world as different from this one as our mother's womb is different from the world into which we were born. That bit of transparent computer information that is the REAL US will be transformed into a different kind of body.

> *The world is not merely a random conglomerate of atoms. There is eternal purpose and meaning in human life.*

This is the answer to the question of the resurrection. The world is not merely a random conglomerate of atoms. There is eternal purpose and meaning in human life. There is a just intelligence behind everything which will only tip the scales. One day God will even up the score. Those who are self-sufficient and those who pile up riches at the expense of others will find themselves helpless and without resources. Those who refuse to see truths that are not physical will find that the truth of God is the only truth that will abide forever! The truth of the resurrection is that the lion will indeed lie down with the lamb and that a cup of cold water given in the name of the Master will have its reward. The truth is that we need never be disheartened or discouraged in well-doing because the risen Lord is preparing the way before us.

Are you not quite sure which questions you should ask and which reality is the true one? Weigh the reality of everyday living of working, eating, sleeping, watching TV and planning for retirement against the other reality of the risen Christ which gives meaning, purpose and joy. If you are only living in the reality of this present world, you are as unaware of life as a baby in the womb of its mother is unaware of a world of air and oxygen and sight and hearing.

The difference is as great as the difference between the gloominess of Good Friday and the glory of the Resurrection! In His resurrection, Jesus has not only broken the bonds of sin and death, but he also has broken the limitations of space and time and the weakness of earthly existence. Jesus said in our passage today, "Neither shall they die anymore, for they are equal unto the angels and are the children of God, being the children of the resurrection." (20:36) Like Mary on that first Easter, we are to come and see and go and tell. Amen.

What a Friend We Have in Jesus[91]

John 2:1-11

Now both Jesus and His disciples were invited to the wedding. And when they ran out of wine, the mother of Jesus said to Him, "They have no wine."
~John 2:2-3 (NKJV)~

The first recorded miracle of Jesus took place at the wedding of a friend in Cana of Galilee! All of us who have attended a wedding or who were married by a Christian pastor probably heard the pastor say, "We are gathered together in the sight of God and in the presence of this company to join together this man and this woman in Holy Matrimony, which Holy estate Jesus adorned and beautified by His presence in Cana of Galilee."

So it was at a wedding in Cana of Galilee that Jesus "adorned and beautified with his presence," not as an officiating minister, but as a friend. He went to the wedding to share daily life and celebration with friends. It was here that Jesus did his first miracle, or as John tells us, "His first sign." John saw this and other miracles of Jesus as "signs" of His Lordship and Divinity.

Weddings in Galilee, at the time when Jesus walked on earth, were great and grand occasions. Marriage has rich meaning in Jewish and Christian thought, and having family and friends to be a part of the marriage celebration has always been important. It still is! We do not have many weeks to go by at the church I attend[92] when we do not read in the church newspaper an announcement about a wedding or a wedding shower.

At the wedding at Cana of Galilee, Mary, the mother of Jesus, seems to have had some responsibility as hostess in the wedding. The Bible tells us Mary comes to Jesus to tell Him there is a problem. There is a shortage of wine for all the guests. The wine

---

[91] The hymn, "What a Friend We Have in Jesus" was written by Joseph Scriven (1819-1886).
[92] Trinity United Methodist Church, Rome Georgia.

has all been used.

It is interesting! Mary does not ask Jesus to do anything. John Brockhoff, in commenting on this, says it is kind of like a wife saying to her husband, "I can't get the lid off these pickles." Mary, his mother, just shows Jesus the problem - trusting he will fix it!

What Mary is saying to the son she knows to be, as John tells us in John 3:16, "the only begotten Son of God" is "I need your help." Jesus responds, as many of us have testified, with the answer to our needs!

I like the story of two small children looking at a picture of Queen Victoria and one said to the other, "What is she doing?" The other child replied "She doesn't have to do anything, she's reigning."

Jesus is speaking to us in the only way we can truly understand - by becoming one of us.

John would have us know throughout the gospel of John that Jesus is the King down from heaven to earth - not just with words from God or about God, as prophets of the Old Testament had done, but as the WORD - a summary of all that God wants to say to us as human beings. Jesus is speaking to us in the only way we can truly understand - by becoming one of us.

In fact John, the beloved disciple, places Jesus right in the midst of life's indispensables! John tells us Jesus is the water of life. We can't live without water! Jesus is the bread of life. We can't live without food! John tells us Jesus is the way, the truth and the life. In fact John uses the same term "I AM" that we see used for the name of God when God speaks to Moses at the burning bush!

When our oldest daughter, Janice, was about to graduate from college and planning her wedding later in the summer, she had asked a couple of friends to be in the wedding, but her sister Joan was to be maid of honor and the junior bridesmaids were to be her other three sisters. I was trying to find time for making the 4 bridesmaid dresses and because of a real shortage of money, I was also planning to make the wedding gown.

When Janice got home from school, she and I went from our small town with no fabric store to Rich's in Atlanta to buy fabric. While we were looking at fabric and patterns, I had a sudden inspiration that turned out to be an answer to prayer.

I said to Janice, "Lets' go up to Rich's Bridal shop and see what we would buy if money were no object and also to get some idea about the pattern and material we need to buy." When we got up to the bridal shop, we found exactly what we would have bought if we had had a fat bank account. It was a stunningly beautiful ivory-colored silk gown with alencon needlepoint lace, seeded pearls and a traditional train!

Great News! The sales lady told us the gown had been part of a bridal fashion show a day earlier, and so they were just then marking it down to about a fourth of the original price. The gown fit Janice as if it had been made for her. We were able to buy the gown at the new price and went home with a light heart that one of the items in our wedding plans could be checked off the list!

It seems almost irreverent to say, but could it be that the king of the universe, Jesus - this friend of sinners - was also a friend in need to this sinner in our little wedding plans as Jesus was a friend in need that day when the wine ran out at the wedding in Cana of Galilee?

John wants us to know Jesus is the king of the universe, stepping down to become a friend of sinners. Jesus performed this miracle out of compassion and friendship for his host. What a friend we have in Jesus!

One of the things I learned as a pastor's wife involved in the weddings of our people - and even more as the mother of the bride or groom - is that we want our friends to share in these celebrations and festivities. We do not want them to just send a gift but to come to the wedding! We appreciate friends taking time to come to help celebrate. Jesus was this kind of a friend in this Scripture lesson! He dropped everything else he had to do and came to the wedding.

In Galilee, a newly married couple would hold open house not just a few hours as we do now, but for a whole week. And the week of festivities was a high moment in the lives of the people when there was much poverty and hard work! Running out of refreshments would be an embarrassment - much more serious to the host than dropping a ring or missing a line in the wedding liturgy.

So at this wedding that Jesus adorned with his presence, the unthinkable happened: the wine ran out - a terrible embarrassment to the host in the midst of the wedding festivities.

We need to know that the wine they had in that agricultural society was prepared at home and was not more than 4% alcohol. One would have to "tarry with the wine" for a long time to get intoxicated. This was brought out on the day of Pentecost when the Holy Spirit came and they were so excited, people accused them of being drunk. And they said it was impossible for them to be drunk seeing as it was only the third hour of the day.

In our society, the wine sold in our liquor stores and in most grocery stores is some 16% proof. So today it is possible to get drunk before the third hour of the day and millions do, including many children. It was upsetting to read in our local News Tribune recently of the increase of alcoholism among younger and younger children.

But in this first century agricultural society, the host at the wedding, to his great embarrassment, had not prepared enough wine and there was no corner store where they could buy more. Only a miracle could save the day. So Jesus was a friend when he took an impossible situation and changed it into a miracle.

The wine made out of water was so good that the master host of the feast complimented the bridegroom! The master host thought the bridegroom was responsible and missed the opportunity to speak to Jesus!

This sort of thing happens all the time, doesn't it? We often give ourselves and others credit for various blessings in life - blessings that come from the hand of God.

However, the disciples of Jesus were thoughtfully watching and saw the miracle with the water. The disciples saw this first "sign," and they knew Jesus was not simply a magician or a miracle worker but the Messiah of God. The significant point about this is that the message is revealed and also concealed. That is why John calls it a sign. Some get the point while others scratch their heads and wonder what it is all about, and others see nothing at all.

At that point they had no way of knowing just how far they would go when they later saw Jesus alive after he had been beaten almost to death and then crucified to death on a cross and buried in a tomb.

As a little girl of 11, when I sat in church with my widowed mother, and I chose to believe in Jesus and to accept Him as Lord and Savior and decided to give my will over to Him to lead me, I had no way of knowing just how far that decision would lead.

At Candler School of Theology, one of the requirements for the Master of Divinity degree was a professional assessment paper on a major doctrine of the church. I wrote a twenty page paper on the doctrine of the Holy Spirit and entitled it "Friendship with God." The idea was a part of what has shaped me and molded and enriched my life as a Christian - the good news that we are not drafted (we have been given free will) so we are not conscripted into service. We have been given the wonderful invitation to become a friend to Royalty!

We choose whether or not to accept His gracious invitation. The God who created the universe has invited us into His very presence, and this friendship with God (as I tried to tell a disturbed woman recently) makes our lives sacred!

Jesus was accused of being a friend of sinners! Imagine that! He still is a friend of sinners. What a friend we have in Jesus!

Mary told the servants to do whatever Jesus told them to do. Jesus told the servant to fill the water pots with water when what they needed was wine! How ridiculous! But, strange as it sounded to them, they did as Jesus told them and out of their obedience came success.

> *The Lord gives us a choice. We get to choose whether or not to accept the Lord's gracious invitation.*

Have you ever had a divine call that did not make sense? It makes about as much sense as calling a timid girl or boy to preach the Gospel! The Lord gives us a choice. We get to choose whether or not to accept the Lord's gracious invitation. God has invited us into His very presence and offered us His friendship.

A small boy was asked what his Sunday School lesson was about, and he said it was about Jesus going to a wedding and turning water into wine. When he was asked what he had learned from the lesson, he said, "If you are having a wedding, make sure Jesus is there!" What a Friend we have in Jesus!

The Mother of Jesus said to Him, "The wine has run out." Jesus responded with the answer to her needs. Sooner or later, the wine runs out for all of us. Sooner or later we all face shortages in life - a shortage of wisdom or courage - a shortage of faith - of strength - of health - and finally of life itself. Sooner or later life runs out for all of us. We need a friend.

I have visited in many hospitals, nursing care places, funeral homes and even prisons in my short years since 1986 when the Lord opened a door and pushed me into the preaching ministry. As a minister I have learned that we can do much, but we can go just so far with those in need. We can go just so far with even our dearest loved ones. The best of medical people can do just so much. The most loving of doctors sometimes have to say, "I have done all I can do."

The good news that brings us together to a celebration of worship is that we have a friend. We have an Awesome Friend that can carry us all the way home. What a Friend we have in Jesus! Amen.

Draw Near With Faith

March 2:1-6

And when they could not bring him to Jesus because of the crowd, they removed the roof above him; and after having dug through it, they let down the mat on which the paralytic lay.
~Mark 2:4 (NRSV)~

Life in Palestine was very public. In the morning, the door of the house was opened and anyone who wished might come in. The door was never shut unless a person deliberately wished for privacy. An open door meant an open invitation for all to come in.

As I thought about this message, I realized that this was not a great deal different from the small town in Newton County Georgia where I grew up in the late 1920s and 1930s. Neighbors never rang a bell or knocked. They would pause briefly at the door and say, "Hello! Mrs. Baird, I coming in."

Someone has remarked that television and air conditioning have changed neighborhoods more than any other modern invention. They are two inventions that keep people inside their homes. In the thirties in my small town there was no TV and no air conditioning.

Many of our neighbors gathered in our kitchen or on our front porch in the late evening to rest and talk after a hard day's work. While the adults talked, the children played in the yard, in the front of the house, or in the road that rarely saw a car or sometimes a horse and buggy. During my childhood, we had one man who came to our street each week in a horse-drawn buggy to sell, milk, eggs, and vegetables.

In our Bible lesson today, Jesus had completed his tour of the synagogue and returned to Capernaum. Jesus was visiting in a home where the crowds began to gather. Such large crowds gathered that there was no room for anyone else to get in, not even around the door. Into this crowd came four men carrying on a stretcher a friend who was paralyzed. They could not get through the crowd. But these four were men had recourse.

The roof on a Palestinian house was flat. It was regularly used as a place of rest and quiet, and it had an outside stair leading up to it. The roof consisted of flat beams that had been laid across from wall to wall. The space between the beams was filled with brushwood packed with tight clay. Sometimes grass grew on the roof. So the men could probably dig out the filling between the beams and not do too much damage to the house. We are told it was all easy to repair.

So the four men dug out the filling between the beams at the top of the house and let their friend down directly at the feet of Jesus.

When Jesus saw the faith of these four friends that would overcome any barrier - men who "drew near with faith," he looked at the man and said, "Child, your sins are forgiven."

This may seem to be an odd way to begin a cure. William Barclay said that to the Jews, a sick man was a sinner, and a sinner was a person with whom God was angry. The rabbis had a saying that no sick person could be healed of his sickness until all his sins were forgiven. We are told today in some remote parts of the world that disease is considered such a defilement that even converts to Christianity do not dare come to communion when they are ill because they consider themselves spurned by God.

We gather at the Communion table at out Lord's invitation. Communion should be a conscious experience of the presence of the Lord. We come not because we are worthy but because we know we are unworthy. We remember that while we were yet sinners, Christ died for us. We hear the words of the Communion service: "We are not worthy so much as to gather up the crumbs under Thy table." As someone once remarked, "It takes a lot for most of us to feel anywhere near that humble in a society today where we have been taught to have a good self-image."

As I was meditating on the passage of Scripture, I kept thinking of the phrase in the Communion service, "Draw near with faith." When they got to the place where Jesus was and could not get in because of the crowd, it would have been easy for these four men to have said, "Well we tried. We can't get in. It was not meant to be this time." Not these men! They found a way to get their friend to Jesus.

We are to draw near with faith. We are not to draw near with pride. We are not to make a mental calculation of all the good things we have done and decide we have a credit balance and have earned brownie points.

In Matthew 8:5-13, we have the story of the centurion who came to Jesus on behalf of his servant who was at home paralyzed and in terrible suffering. When Jesus told him that he would go and heal the servant, the Centurion replied, "Lord I do not deserve to have you come under my roof, but just say the word, and my servant will be healed." Jesus was astonished and said to his disciples that they had not found anyone in Israel with such great faith. So here we have a man who admits he is unworthy and yet dares to believe that Jesus will help him.

In dealing with sin, the Bible focuses on human pride. Christ tells of two men who went up to the temple to pray. (Luke 18:9) One reviewed his good works. The other asked for mercy. Jesus said only the second left justified. When we think of "drawing near with faith," not pride, we have to remember that sin is subtle. C.S. Lewis said that each of us is inclined to look at other people's valleys from our own mountain tops. This insulates us from our own particular sins, or we explain them away in psychological terms.

All of this adds up to one thing. If we have no problem, we need no solution. If we are not under condemnation, we need no salvation. If we are successful in living, we do not need grace.

Our first step in application is to draw the proper conclusion: that pride, self confidence and trust in our own personal goodness can bar us from salvation. It can bar us from drawing near to God in faith. In other words, Communion is for sinners, not for the self-righteous.

We are also to "draw near with confidence." We are not to draw near with dread and self-abasement. We have the hallmark upon us "made by God." We are told to come boldly into God's presence with confidence, thanksgiving and praise!

It means we are reminded of our great heritage, as having been created in the image of God and made for him. It means that we come at his invitation and therefore we come with confidence, not because of anything we have done but because we have been able to hear and respond to his gracious call.

God loves us and has a wonderful plan for our life. G.K. Chesterton once took a train trip and on the way got so engrossed in his reading that he forgot where he was going. At the station stop, he called his wife and asked her. She told him to look at his ticket. The irony of today's living is that some of us seem to have forgotten that we once had a ticket. God knows the destination for each of us. We can draw near to God in faith because God is our Father. We are a member of the family.

I like the chorus of praise:

> I'm so glad I'm a part of the Family of God,
> I've been washed in the fountain, cleansed by His blood!
> Joint heirs with Jesus as we travel this sod,
> For I'm part of the family,
> The Family of God.[93]

One day Robert Lewis Stevenson went into his bedroom with a wracking cough and terrible pain. His wife came in and said, "I suppose you will tell me that it is a glorious day." He replied, "Strange, that is what I was going to say." Then, looking at the sunlight streaming through the windows, he said, "I refuse to let a row of medicine bottles be the circumference of my horizon."

---

[93] "Family of God," written by Bill and Gloria Gaither

The four friends of the paralytic refused to let a crowd keep them away from Jesus. They found a way to get to Jesus.

J. Wallace Hamilton[94] told the story of Marian Anderson[95] who sang in the home of the great composer Sibelius.[96] The composer listened to her lovely God-given voice and said, "My roof is too low for you."

This is the truth that I believe - like I believe in God: When we draw near with faith to God, the world will have too low a ceiling.

The eternal God, the creator of the universe, the one who in the beginning said, "Let there be light!" is here to shine in our hearts , through the grace of our Lord Jesus Christ. The invitation is out, not only for communion , but for eternal life. It is too wonderful to miss. Come! Amen.

---

[94] James Wallace Hamilton (1900-1968) was a well-known Christian author.
[95] Marian Anderson (1897–1993) was an African-American contralto and one of the most celebrated singers of the twentieth century.
[96] Jean Sibelius (1865-1957), born Johan Julius Christian Sibelius, was a Finnish composer of the late Romantic period.

In Gold We Trust?[97]

Luke 12:13-21

Then one from the crowd said to Him, "Teacher, tell my brother to divide the inheritance with me."
~Luke 12:13 (NKJV)~

One week-end many years ago I visited my daughter Janice and her husband Gilbert when they were working at Taylor University. We went to church Sunday morning at the United Methodist Church in Matthews, Indiana, where Gilbert was to be the guest Lay Speaker. We had Sunday dinner with friends who were members of that congregation. We had known them for many years, since our daughters, Janice and Joan, were college classmates and friends of their daughters.

Matthews, Indiana was a small farm town, with picturesque, tall silos around. As we sat around our friends' Sunday dinner table, the husband told us an interesting story. He said that in 1902, Matthews, Indiana, was a booming oil town! Imagine that!

In 1902, oil was discovered in Matthews and people drove in, setting up camp and expecting to get rich in oil. It was like a gold rush, he said! Liquor store people moved in and set up 20 saloons in the small town which had only one grocery store and two

---

[97] Luke 12:13-21: Someone in the crowd said to him, "Teacher, tell my brother to divide the inheritance with me." Jesus replied, "Man, who appointed me a judge or an arbiter between you?" Then he said to them, "Watch out! Be on your guard against all kinds of greed; a man's life does not consist in the abundance of his possessions." And he told them this parable: "The ground of a certain rich man produced a good crop. He thought to himself, 'What shall I do? I have no place to store my crops.' Then he said, 'This is what I'll do. I will tear down my barns and build bigger ones, and there I will store all my grain and my goods. And I'll say to myself, 'You have plenty of good things laid up for many years. Take life easy; eat, drink and be merry.' But God said to him, 'You fool! This very night your life will be demanded from you. Then who will get what you have prepared for yourself?' This is how it will be with anyone who stores up things for himself but is not rich toward God."

churches. The old timers said that many people had oil lights burning on their property day and night. They reported that night was so lit up (maybe "lit up" in more ways than one) that it was hard to tell day from night. But, alas, in a few years the oil was gone! He said they had thought they had an endless supply and wasted it.

How timely that 1902 story is to today. In our community, Kroger moved out a few years ago in order to build one huge luxury grocery store in another part of town. As someone who grew up in the South during the great depression, I am just amazed at our wealth and conspicuous consumption. I see many of us shopping in luxury places like there is no tomorrow, and our waste is like the gold rush in California and the 1902 oil rush in Indiana.

It seems Wall Street and Main Street in America thought we had an endless supply of money and resources, and we wasted it. We are in a world where many of us have so much stuff that we have to rent storage places, and our houses have larger and larger storage closets and attics.

> *It seems we all have been guilty of worshiping the almighty dollar more than believing in the Almighty God!*

Perhaps some of us have learned a little from the past what others of us have to painfully learn now. But none of us, certainly not I, can point a finger at someone else. Selfishness and wastefulness is an all too common trait. We are all sinners and self-centered in one way or another.

It seems we all have been guilty of worshiping the almighty dollar more than believing in the Almighty God!

We have "In God We Trust" on our coins, although there are people in our nation seeking and lobbying to get that important phrase removed from our currency. In fact some are seeking to remove all vestiges of Christianity from our culture and even distort or delete it from our history books.

In our scripture lesson (Luke 12:13-21), Jesus was asked to settle an inheritance dispute, and it gave Him the opportunity to deal with the insidious blight of money and "things" on our souls. (Verses 13-15)

Jesus was not showing indifference to the claims of legal justice but was insisting that there are greater gains in life than getting an inheritance and greater losses in life than losing an inheritance.[98]

The rich man that Dr. Luke tells us about in this lesson looked upon his possessions as his and only his. He saw them not as gifts. We read, "My barns, my grain, my goods, my soul." He seemed to think possessions made life, and here came Jesus reminding us that possessions not only do not give life; possessions do not even give "existence." As Jesus told the rich farmer, death separates us from any possession - anything and everything we think we own.

Our God of love has given us guidelines for what it means to be a civil and liberated human being as well as what it means to be a covenant person and a follower of Jesus Christ.

So Jesus goes on to teach us that our life is in God's hands. He reminds us of God's bounteous provision for the birds of the air and the flowers of the field. His care of things which are transient indicates his major concern for us who have an eternal destiny. It is all too easy sometimes to forget that God is more aware of our needs than we are. It is all too easy to forget that it is "In God We Trust" and slip into the concept and behavior of "In Gold We Trust!"

In our scripture lesson Jesus called the man a fool for basing his life on money. The passage starts out with a man coming to Jesus out of the crowd and asking Jesus to settle an inheritance dispute between him and his brother. Barclay and other commentaries tell us this was not uncommon for people then to take their unsettled disputes to respected rabbis. But Jesus refused to get mixed up in this kind of family dispute about money.

---

[98] *The Layman's Bible Commentary*, pages 110-111

Then Jesus turned to the people, "Take care. Protect yourself against the least bit of greed." Life is not defined by what you have, even when you have a lot. Jesus loves us and wants to protect us against the destruction that greed brings into our life. (*The Message*)

Jesus also had some things to say about the place of money for those of us who have little money as well as for those of us who have an abundant supply of money. Jesus came to reconcile us to God and to each other and not to re-apportion wealth. But Jesus reminds us here and in other scripture passages that possessions do not give life its meaning, and he illustrates it with the "Parable of the Rich Fool."

This man was rich and getting richer. He thought his only problem was to find a place to store and to invest! He needed to expand. He had to make a decision. He said to himself, "I will pull down my barns and build greater!" He faced a problem to which many of us aspire. Yet, Jesus said he was a fool! He certainly would have been successful in our society. We would consider him anything but a fool.

Success is something tangible. It can be measured economically by our bank accounts, our stocks and bonds and our property. Success can be measure socially by our popularity, our education, our accomplishments and name recognition.

It seems to never have occurred to this man to give any of it away. Jesus tells us that a person's life does not consist in the abundance of the things he possesses. (Luke 12:15)

> *. . . he saw many houses of mercy by churches of many denominations, but not even one by an atheist or humanist.*

Malcolm Muggeridge was a successful TV personality in England who became a Christian. He went to India to interview Mother Teresa who was working among the dying in India. He reported that he saw many houses of mercy by churches of many denominations, but not even one by an atheist or humanist.

We all talk about teaching our children the value of money. But Jesus is also teaching us here of the value-less-ness of money.

There is a difference in possessions and ownership. It is said that shortly before the crash of 1929, a man gave Emory at Oxford enough money to build a large building. After he and other wealthy people lost most of his money, he said, "What I gave away is all I have left."

All of us are amazed to see people work to get to what the world calls success. Then when they have achieved that success, they realize that happiness is not found there. Often these people self-destruct with alcohol, other drugs and even suicide.

Jesus warns us that possessions - our storage buildings, our gold or bank accounts - may have become a weight that prevents us from rising to the heights that God has prepared for us.

It is good to have "In God We Trust" written on our money, but it also must be written in our hearts. Amen.

Life Plus

Romans 8:31-39

No, in all these things we are more than conquerors through Him who loved us.
~Romans 8:37 (NRSV)~

On September 11, 2001, we were jolted out of much of our security and complacency. I think our scripture lesson today speaks to us in our kind of world. Indeed, the book of Romans has been used by God to bring change and growth to some of our great Christian reformers.[99] When Martin Luther read in Romans, "the just shall live by faith," it set in him a personal faith that resulted in the Reformation and consequently a reform in the Roman Catholic Church.

It was when John Wesley went "quite unwillingly" to a meeting at Aldersgate and heard someone reading Martin Luther's preface to the Book of Romans that Wesley felt his heart strangely warmed and he knew that Jesus not only died for the sins of the whole world but also for him, AND GOD HAD TAKEN AWAY HIS SINS and saved him from the penalty of sin and death.

Both these great reformers, who were already great churchmen, were enlightened and dramatically changed by the grace of God while listening to the great truth of the book of Romans.

I remember in my own life, at a difficult time, reading the 12th chapter of Romans, and verse 2 leapt off the page. Paul wrote: "Be not conformed to this world, but be ye transformed by the renewing of your mind." We are told that we can be transformed, and I found it to be true. We are told here that we can even have a new mind. It is true.

The epistle to Romans was written about 58 A.D. while Paul was in Corinth. Paul wrote this while he was, like some of us here today,

---

[99] Romans 8:31-39

classified as "old." And Paul had also suffered the loss of many things, and yet he had the spirit of youth.

The book is one we need to read over and over again. Romans 8 begins: "There is therefore now no condemnation for those who are in Christ Jesus who walk not after the flesh but after the spirit." This chapter ministers to me each time I read it.

We read in the book of Corinthians about some of the intense pain that Paul endured: Five times Paul received 39 stripes. He was beaten with rods 3 times, once he was stoned, 3 times he was shipwrecked, for 24 hours he was adrift on the open seas. Paul was constantly on the road, meeting danger from rivers, terror from robbers, and danger from false friends. He went without sleep, was hungry, thirsty, and suffered from the cold and exposure.

Yet Paul tells us here in Romans 8 that "In everything, God works for good." This verse is often quoted and often misquoted: "We know that in everything, God works for good with those who love God and who are called according to His purpose."

This does not mean that every single thing that happens to us is "for good" as people often say. We are living in a fallen world. God's will is not being done on earth as it is in heaven. But God does gather up the good and the bad and uses them all to bring about good in our lives when we love him and seek His purpose and will for our lives.

When Paul was writing this, Nero was in Rome ruling with a high hand in the palace. Nero saw himself as a conqueror. He was boastful and arrogant. It is said that Nero had a colossal hundred-foot statue of himself with the inscription "Conqueror of the World." But Paul was not too impressed with 100 foot statues of conquerors. Paul knew that, in Jesus, a person can be not just a conqueror but "more than a conqueror."

The Bible tells us in Genesis 1:25 that we were created in the image of God. But in the third chapter of Genesis we read that the human race fell into sin in prideful disobedience. We became something less than we were created to be. In Genesis 5:7, we read that Adam begat a son in his own likeness - after Adam and Eve's own image. The fallen image, at best, is a poverty stricken likeness of God's intentions for us.

In Hebrews 1:3, we are told that God the Father sent Christ Jesus that we may be conformed - remade - to the image of Jesus. Wonderful news!

Today's lesson in Romans 8:31-39 presents the climax of Paul's great exposition of God's plan for our being re-made. This is what the first 8 chapters of Romans are about - God's wonderful plan for our re-birth.

This scripture presents some of the most wonderful words from the pen of Paul. Paul wants us to know the truth that the battle of life, the aim of life is for us to live victoriously. We can live life abundantly - life plus!

The immediate battle for Paul and for those to whom he wrote was persecution. It was 58 A.D. Paul was an old man but with the enthusiasm of a young man in Christ Jesus. Meanwhile Nero was the ruler. Only a few months later, Nero would saturate the bodies of Christians with oil and would drive his chariots by the light of their burning bodies.

It was a time when it was dangerous to be a Christian. To say Lord Jesus and not to also say "Lord Caesar" often meant to sign your own death warrant. Christians were being fed to the beasts in Rome's arenas. When Paul said, "If God be for us, who can be against us," it was good news. It was relevant good news. Paul was not speaking figuratively, but literally. Daily men and women faced these terrors of tribulations, persecution, sword and death because of their faith.

While we may not face the immediate problems Paul faced, our soldiers and our Christian missionaries are facing some of the same kinds of terror in radical Islamic countries, and we as a nation are in war. Since 9-11-01, we have become aware that there are those who are ready to kill us.

And we daily fight enemies peculiar to our age that threaten to separate us from God - an increasingly pagan society, materialism, consumerism, humanism, political confusion, 24/7 news filled with lies and hate, the multi-billion dollar alcohol industry and now the multi-billion dollar pornography industry as well as the gambling industry that has declared open season on our children and on us. Increasingly, large numbers of people face company downsizing, which is a new term for job loss and financial problems. Then we all face the common human enemies of aging, illness, cancer, heart problems and death.

Yet Paul tells us that even in the worst of circumstances, we can be conquerors, and indeed "more than conquerors." We can have life plus.

> *God is committed to the task of developing us, firming us up and deepening us - doing whatever it takes so that the image of His son . . . will begin to take shape in us.*

Probably most of us remember hearing about Oprah's weight loss plan and the fact that she was able to achieve this by having a personal trainer - a personal trainer who ran with her and worked out her diet and exercise program. It occurred to me as I was reading the Bible recently that God is committed to being our personal trainer. God is committed to the task of developing us, firming us up and deepening us - doing whatever it takes so that the image of His son, the character traits of Jesus, will begin to take shape in us.

I had been having problems with my furnace. The heating and air people I contracted with sent a man out to get it started again. However, it went out a second time. When I called them a day or so later, another man came out and found a crack in it. He told me that it would either require another unit or a replacement of an important part that would be almost like buying another unit. As it turned out, it was still under warranty, so I would have to pay only for the labor which would be about 400 dollars.

This was on a Thursday and I told him to repair it since a blackberry winter was predicted. The part came in Friday but it was raining Friday, so they could not come out until Monday. My reply was a curt, "I can see I am not very high up on your list of priorities." As soon as I hung up the phone I felt I had been rude to the lady who had little, if anything, to do with their decision.

She called back Saturday and said the manager would come out and put space heaters anywhere I needed them. I apologized for my impatience the day before and told her I was comfortable since my son-in-law had brought over an electric heater in case I needed it.

In the scripture, we see that we are God's top priority. Jesus will be our personal Savior.

A good analogy to my mind here is the difference in just painting over the mess in a shabby old house, and that of restoring the house - taking out the rotten planks and the tacky stuff. We are not just doing a cover-up but restoring from the foundation up.

Most of us come to Christ wanting to be re-painted, to cover up the old mess we have made. But when the Lord comes in and starts hammering and pulling up planks, we yell and scream and sometimes call off the project. We just want to be respectable, Lord. We want to be saved from Hell. We want to be healed from our diseases and have a decent life. We want to be happy, but we do not want to be too good. People won't like us if we are too good.

The youth at our church did a play a few years ago. One of the fine young men played the part of a Jesus who was like the Jesus we like to invent - a Jesus that keeps nodding and smiling at us even when we act like spoiled, self-centered brats and do self-destructive things. We want a Jesus that pats us on the head and places his stamp of approval on whatever we do and however we live. This is not the Jesus of the Bible. Yes, Jesus loves us, but He died on the cross to save us from our sins - not in our sins. Jesus has a high view of our possibilities.

Chuck Swindoll[100] gives an analogy about the cod fish that are such a delectable dish and a big commercial business in the Northeast. There is a big market for Eastern cod fish, but the problem is in the shipping. At first they froze the cod, but the freezing took away the flavor. They tried shipping them alive in the sea water, but the cod still lost much of the flavor and became soft and mushy. Finally a creative person solved the problem. The codfish were placed in a tank of water along with their natural enemy, the catfish, and the ornery catfish chased the codfish all over the tank, and the codfish arrived on the west coast as fresh as when they left the East.

Many of us have a few catfish in our tanks along life's way. The greatest lesson we can learn is to thank God for the irritants that come our way and pray that God can use them to "work for good" to help make that image of Christ emerge in us.

Paul tells us that even these catfish that aggravate us cannot separate us from the love of God. They can actually help us to be more than conquerors. They can be used of God to give us life abundant - life plus.

The exciting culmination of this eighth chapter of Romans:

> *Nay in all these things,* (all these irritants that are a part of life in a fallen world), *Nay in ALL these things we are more than conquerors through Christ who loves us. For I am persuaded* (I am sure. I am positive) *that neither death, nor life, nor angels , nor principalities, nor powers, nor things present, nor things to come, nor height, nor depth, nor any other creature shall be able to separate us from the love of God which is in Christ Jesus!*

This has been called the grandest expression of faith in all literature.

---

[100] Chuck Swindoll is an evangelic pastor, speaker, author, and educator. He founded *Insight for Living* which is headquartered in Plano, Texas.

In all these things. What are the things Paul is talking about? Paul has just listed them in the previous verse; tribulation, anguish, persecution, famine, nakedness, peril, sword. These were everyday happenings in the life of the first century Christians. The church was born in occupied territory and under ruthless dictators. Paul tells us, "Even in occupied territory under ruthless dictations, we can be more than conquerors."

How in the world can we be more than conquerors? Wouldn't it be enough to just be a conqueror? Alexander the Great was a conqueror. Napoleon was a conqueror. Hitler was a conqueror. However, they were not more than conquerors. Being more than a conqueror is the plus of life - good measure on the side of character, integrity, justice, consideration, good will, joy, peace of mind, love, and eternal life.

Being a conqueror would mean material gains, prosperity, fame and fortune. By that definition we are living in a world of conquerors, people who have achieved much that the world has to offer and yet are saying with amazement, "Is this all there is?" These things are not enough. They must be matched by moral and spiritual gains. Paul knew what Jesus taught: that the problems of our world are spiritual problems.

One of the things evident that I observe in our world is the paradox of the greatness and the littleness of our society. The greatness of our technology - and the selfishness. The littleness of much of society as emphasized by crime rate, the drug rate, child abuse, child pornography, sin and deceit in high places.

Our machines are bright, but the faces of our people are not as bright as the machines we prize and struggle to purchase. The continued production of good machinery is dependent, not just on advanced technology, but on the integrity and trustworthiness of those who design and make and repair our machines. If we cannot trust the integrity of the service manager or the mechanics who look after the airplane we board or the car we drive, then all the technology in our nation is useless - worse than useless.

If we cannot trust the people who inspect our food, water and medicine, then all the medical advances are of little value

Our machines are bright and impressive, but some of our shiny lawyers and bright politicians and hypocritical priests and doctors and golden media personnel will look the other way or do anything if the price is right.

What Paul wants us to see in this lesson from Romans is that our problems are not technological but spiritual. We need to be re-made, re-birthed by the power of God in Christ Jesus.

In the midst of this kind of world - a world in which we see unfaithfulness, mixed up values, misery, jadedness and absurdities - the Bible reminds us that we can be more than conquerors through Christ who loves us and gave Himself for us.

The last word in this long text is "our Lord." It is the personal application of the reigning and ruling Lordship of Jesus Christ that is necessary. It is making Jesus "my Lord" that brings salvation from the realm of possibility into our hearts and lives - in transforming power. Amen.

What Made Jesus Angry?

John 2: 12-22

When He had made a whip of cords, He drove them all out of the temple, with the sheep and the oxen, and poured out the changers' money and overturned the tables. And He said to those who sold doves, "Take these things away! Do not make My Father's house a house of merchandise!"
~John 2:15-16 (NKJV)~

Have you ever met a person and have one initial impression of the kind of person he or she is, but when you get to know the person by talking to him/her or being around him/her, the person ends up being quite different from your first impression?

We do not know a person unless that person communicates somehow. We can communicate with others in speech, gestures or facial expressions. Unless we communicate, we remain a mystery. God was a mystery until he broke His silence. In Genesis we read that God spoke once, and all creation sprang to life. He spoke again, said the Disciple John in the New Testament, and that Word became flesh and dwelt among us in the Person of Jesus Christ.

We have four gospels. The Synoptic Gospels, Matthew, Mark and Luke tell the story of Jesus from birth - his life, his crucifixion, his resurrection and his ascension. John assumes we know about the birth and the basic facts that took place in Bethlehem and Nazareth and the villages around Galilee. John interprets the life of Jesus theologically.

John selects vignettes from the life of Jesus that represent not more than twenty days out of his three year ministry and arranges them to have us know a Messiah who knows where he came from and where he is going. John would have us know Jesus as the Son of God who came to earth to do the work of the Father.

The first three Gospels reveal Jesus as the Messiah more gradually. John presents Christ as a participant in the original creation who came to earth as the Word made flesh, a summary of all God wants to say to us, God speaking to us in the only way we can truly understand - by becoming one of us.[101]

In other words, all down through the Old Testament, God sent his prophets with words about God and about God's love for us. But somehow we did not understand. Then the word was made flesh and we beheld his glory.

All four gospels tell us about Jesus cleansing the temple. Matthew, Mark and Luke place the account near the cross as if running the money changers out of the temple was kind of the last straw in the decision to kill Jesus.

John puts the story near the beginning of the events he tells about so that it may be understood as the theological event that it was. There is not any contradiction here. John and the other disciples are telling the story of Jesus from different points of view. They do not contradict but complement each other. Matthew, Mark and Luke concentrate on the ministry of Jesus in Galilee; John focuses on the ministry in Jerusalem.

John is not interested in the cause of Jesus's death. John sees the life of Jesus as not shaped by causes or circumstances and historical contingencies. Those who blame the Jews (or the Romans or whomever) miss the point. John tells us Jesus laid down his life and he took it up again.[102] Jesus rose from the dead; He took his life up again. This is the reason we in the church still sing what some have negatively called "bloody hymns" with lyrics such as: "There is a fountain filled with blood drawn from Emmanuel's veins, and sinners plunged beneath that flood lose all their guilty stains."[103] Any other blood will stain, but the blood of Jesus washes our stain away. The Red Cross tells us to give blood - the gift of life. The Bible tells us that Jesus's blood is the "gift of life - eternal life."

John wants us to know this is a conflict between what Jesus stood for and the values of the "money changers." The temple, built as a

---

[101] Philip Yancey in Insight.
[102] John 10:17, 18
[103] United Methodist Hymnal, p. 622

witness to God and as a means of drawing people to God, is being used as an end in itself.

What made Jesus angry? To see Jesus with a whip in his hand is an awesome sight. His anger was not the kind of thing we tend to get angry about.

I am a pretty even-tempered person, but I remember getting very angry one night when I was a student at Emory. As students, we were required to buy a parking permit each semester. The parking permit was actually for the privilege of looking for a place to park which was usually in Pevine Parking decks about five or six stories high. I have parked on the top floor and walked down the flights of stairs carrying heavy book bags. There are no elevators! Then I would walk some distance uphill to Bishops Hall. Then I would walk up still more flights of stairs to my classrooms.

So to avoid that, I got up before daylight every morning to get to Emory an hour before my 8 o'clock class to parallel park in one of the few parking places on the street behind the buildings. (Incidentally, I think I may be prouder of how well I finally learned to parallel park than I am to have earned a Masters of Divinity degree!)

One cold day, I had to go back out to Emory in the late afternoon for choir practice for those of us singing in the Candler Chorale. There were no parking places available behind the buildings. I drove up and around Pevine and found no parking place. In the parking provided at the foot of Pevine, cars were parked on the grass and on the yellow stripes at the end of the rows. What was going on? So, running short of time, I pulled in a space with yellow stripes at the end of a row, making sure there was still room to go around me.

The Candler Chorale was practicing for a Christmas program. It was dark when I, dog-tired and hungry, came back for my car. My car was gone! Every friend I knew at Emory was gone! I would have to drive for over an hour in heavy Atlanta traffic to get to my home in South Fulton County after I found my car.

To make a long story shorter, this was the day the powers that be decided to haul away all the cars parked incorrectly.

My family will tell you I rarely, if ever, get angry. But I was angry! I fussed and fumed for a while trying to find out why my car was gone. Apparently all the people who knew had gone home or gone to dinner. I finally had to call a taxicab to go several miles in DeKalb County and pay a fine to retrieve my car.

What made me angry? Some of the students did not bother with buying a parking permit. They would pay the small fee if they were caught in a parking place without a sticker permit. The cars with no stickers were not the ones hauled away that day. I bought a parking permit every semester. My car had a parking permit on it, but there was no parking place available because some who bought no parking sticker were in the parking places.

What made me angry that cold day at Emory is not the kind of thing that made Jesus angry enough to chase the money changers out of the Temple of God. Jesus was not angry at a personal inconvenience. He was not angry, as I was, at a bunch of unknown students who took all the parking places and took a few hours of my time.

> *Jesus was not angry because of an inconvenience or even personal loss or injustice. He was angry because of injustice to the vulnerable and the poor . . .*

In our lesson in John 2:13-20, Jesus was not angry because of an inconvenience or even personal loss or injustice. He was angry because of injustice to the vulnerable and poor who were paying more than double to be able to worship in the Temple.

The Passover was the greatest of all Jewish feasts. It was the feast commemorating when the death angel passed over the Hebrew children when they were slaves in Egypt. According to the law, every Jewish male who lived within 15 miles of Jerusalem was required to attend the Passover. So a large number of Jews assembled in Jerusalem to attend the Passover. And every Jew over 19 years of age was to pay a Temple tax. The tax was a half shekel. This was equivalent to about two day's wages.

So Pilgrims arrived from all over the world with all kinds of coins. In the Temple courts sat the money changers. If their trade had been straightforward, they would have been fulfilling an honest and necessary purpose. In addition they also sold oxen and sheep and doves for those who visited to make a sacrifice. In other words it was extortion at the expense of poor and humble pilgrims, and that was bad enough. But what moved Jesus to anger was the fact that it was perpetrated in the name of religion. They were using religion to swindle the pilgrims and enrich themselves.

We sometimes drive by liquor stores and pawn shops with signs offering loans without reference, and we immediately see them as people out to fleece desperate and vulnerable people - someone willing to take advantage of a person afflicted with an alcohol problem or desperate for money. We do not really expect better from loan sharks or liquor store people, but we expect better from the church, the temple and from Christians and Jewish believers.

Jesus, on the cross where he was crucified with trumped up charges, prayed, "Father, forgive them for they know not what they do." But Jesus was moved to anger in the temple, when he saw the money changers' exploitation of the pilgrims who had come to worship. Amen.

Palm Sunday Parade

Mark 11:1-9

Then they brought the colt to Jesus and threw their cloaks on it, and Jesus sat on it.
~Mark 11:7 (NRSV)~

I love a parade! In that first Palm Sunday parade, Jesus, a lone rider, entered a great city on the back of a donkey. A crowd began to gather to watch - some probably out of curiosity, not knowing what it was about. Someone rushed forward and spread his cloak in front of the donkey.

There were many people who knew Jesus. They had wanted to make Jesus their king after seeing his miracles. They wanted someone to save them from the heavy yoke that Rome had placed on them.

As Jesus rode into Jerusalem on a donkey these people began to wave branches of willow and myrtle and palm. And they sang "Hosanna," which means "save us." Soon this first Palm Sunday parade was over.

In a few days, Jesus, this Man who chose to ride a lowly beast of burden instead of a white charger, was killed by his enemies and buried in a borrowed grave. Three days later, He walked out of that grave. And thousands of people today - over two thousand years later - are gathered in churches large and small to celebrate this amazing good news. Why? Why do we celebrate that Palm Sunday parade?

The first time my husband and I visited the Holy Land in 1978, I determined to play the tourist role to the hilt. I tend to be timid around animals, and so I had to be intentional. I determined to ride all the animals other people in our group would be riding. I found myself high up on a camel in front of the King David Hotel in Jerusalem. Then near Cairo in Egypt, I took another longer ride on a tall camel all the way from the pyramids down to the Sphinx. I rode a horse down a long narrow path into Petra. I was told ahead of time the only way to get down into Petra in Jordan was to ride a horse. I did not look forward to the ride, but I rode the horse into that strange little city.

I used to tell my children it was "good for their character" to do important things they did not want to do. All this riding of animals, hopefully, was good for my character. I breathed a sigh of relief, congratulating myself on being a good sport! Wow! I had ridden all the animals I would have to ride. Then out in some remote village everyone in the group was riding a donkey. I rode a donkey! What's with these tourists? Are there no animals to ride at home?

When you are on a donkey you are still at eye level with the people, not lifted high above them . . . . The lowly donkey is the animal Jesus rode in order to set forth his availability to people.

As you know, a donkey is not an impressive looking animal. But at least, on a donkey, you are not very far off the ground so I was more comfortable on the donkey than on a horse or high up on a camel. The most common, the cheapest, the most usual and most useful beast of burden in the Holy Land for human use is the lowly donkey. When you are on a donkey you are still at eye level with the people, not lifted high above them as on a camel or in a chariot or mounted on a horse. The lowly donkey is the animal Jesus rode in order to set forth his availability to people.

This lowly donkey is what Jesus chose for what we now call, "His triumphant entry into Jerusalem." Triumphant kingly entry?

The two books of Kings in the Bible begin with King David's death. David was Israel's king during its golden age. David's son Solomon had great qualities but became unfaithful. The story of the kings of Israel continues through the destruction of the Northern kingdom in 722 and ends with the destruction of Judah and Jerusalem in 587. The word "king" is synonymous with the word "power." And the book of Kings presents an inscrutable picture of the resilient power of God hidden in the shadow of the posturing of earthly kings with their vested interests.

The Old Testament focuses on this when we see God's prophet Nathan stand before Israel's beloved King David after King David had committed his sinful deed against God as well as against Bathsheba and Uriah. This prophet of God tells Israel's powerful King to his face, "Thou art the man!"

Hold that thought because we must remember that God's power, as leaven in bread, is sometimes hidden. We see this in "the rest of the story" of David. And we see it today amid the strutting of the rich and famous and powerful - the terrorist, as well as the powerful in Hollywood, Washington and in Georgia and even in your small town and mine. It is for all those of us who live as if we do not know we are terminal - all of us who live as through we do not know we are dying as we are reminded on Ash Wednesday as we kneel at the altar of the church and hear the pastor's words from the Bible, "Remember you are dust and to dust you will return." We live as if we do not know that even in the midst of our prosperity we have an alarming rate of suicide.

A few years ago I taught a workshop titled "Grief Tentacles" at Taylor University in Indiana. It was about how grief over a loss tends to reach out in many directions. My workshop was one of four. We had a workshop on Prayer, one on Self- Esteem, and one by a medical doctor on AIDS. I did not get to attend the other workshops because they were going on simultaneously. I taught three classes of about fifty women each.

In one of my classes were two women - attractive, intelligent and devout women. Each of them had a son in his twenties who had killed himself. These mothers were, of course, devastated and seeking answers as to how to handle their grief.

As parents, any of us can imagine the horror and grief of having your child die, and especially by suicide. The death of their sons had forced these young mothers to look for ultimate answers to life's problems. Otherwise they might not have attended a meeting of Christian women on a Saturday morning.

Why do we commemorate a man riding a donkey into Jerusalem to celebrate the Jewish Passover? Why do we call it the beginning of Holy Week and look to Easter the next Sunday? Why do we come today to tell about that first Palm Sunday parade, with our children waving palm branches to welcome that solitary Palm Sunday rider into our hearts and into our lives?

The most talented artists the world has ever known have tried to tell the story of Jesus on canvas, in crafts, in all the fine arts - music, poetry and literature. Handel captured the beauty of the story in his poetry and music that lifts us to our feet singing; "King of Kings and Lord of Lords, forever and ever. Hallelujah!" The purple paraments on the altar and on our rugged cross near the road are purple for royalty as we come today to recognize Jesus Christ as King of Kings and Lord of Lords.

As Jesus rode into Jerusalem, knowing he was headed to the cross, the crowd shouted, "Hosanna, Blessed is the King of Israel!" All Jerusalem - all the crowd - was stirred on that first Palm Sunday. Jesus's enemies said, "Behold the world has gone out after him." It was a demonstration of the power of Christ to do whatever he willed. He was their king and ours. But he refused their crown and he did not sit upon a king's contemporary (and temporary) throne in Jerusalem.

That first Palm Sunday ended in disappointment for the crowd who wanted an earthly king for that generation of Jewish people. Their vision could not encompass a Savior of love and grace for the whole world and for every generation. So Palm Sunday was followed by Good Friday. Every generation of us are helplessly caught in our own trap of sin.

Jesus came to snatch us from that deadly trap. Augustine said, "Proud man would have died had not the humble Christ saved him." Jesus comes to the very door of our hearts with lifting love and amazing grace. The question on Palm Sunday is, "Will we open the door and invite him to come in?" Amen.

The Power of the Dream

Genesis 37:1-29

"Here comes the dreamer," they said to each other. "Come now, let's kill him and throw him into one of these cisterns and say that a ferocious animal devoured him. Then we will see what comes of his dreams."
~Genesis 37:19-20 (NIV)~

We hear a great deal about the American Dream and about the right to life, liberty and the pursuit of happiness. We talk about the power of hard work, honesty and thriftiness to work out into success and to work out into the fulfillment of our dreams.

When the Olympics came to Georgia in July of 1996, I enjoyed so very much watching the Opening Ceremony on television until well after midnight. I was then, and still am a morning person and usually drop into bed exhausted about 10 o'clock each night. Even so, I did not want to miss any of the dramatic and fascinating Olympic opening events carried on television. Gladys Knight's beautiful singing of "Georgia on My Mind" was an early highlight, especially to us native Georgians.

As some of you remember, there was a bombing incident on that Saturday. At the ceremony to re-open the Centennial Olympic Park on the Tuesday after the bombing, a young woman with a beautiful voice sang, "The Power of The Dream." The song was not a Christian song; not even a religious song, except in the sense that "humanism" is a religion. But it did glorify, and did an admirable job of glorifying, the best in the human spirit to achieve greatness by dreaming great dreams.

Our scripture text today is about a dreamer named Joseph. The story of Joseph is a story about the power of the dream. Joseph was a dreamer. Joseph was the eleventh of Jacob's twelve sons and was the first by Jacob's beloved Rachael. The scripture tells us Joseph was Jacob's favorite son! The fact that his father favored him over his brothers was the first of Joseph's troubles! Jacob played favorites with his children. Choosing a favorite of one's children is always a mistake - a mistake for the favored one as a well as for the rest.

Our lesson today in Genesis 37 tells us that Jacob loved Joseph more than all his children because he was the son of his old age. Jacob went so far as to make Joseph a very special coat - a coat of many colors! When his brothers saw that their father loved Joseph more than them, they hated Joseph and would not speak peacefully to him. The scripture tells us his brothers shunned Joseph.

In childhood Joseph had this dream of success. He dreamed that his brothers were bowing down before him. Joseph made the mistake of telling the family about his dream. Joseph was a great deal younger than his brothers. Perhaps he told the dream, not to brag, but to let his big brothers know that he was somebody, too. After all, a dream is not an accomplishment. However, telling about the dream to his brothers only added to Joseph's estrangement from his jealous brothers.

One day the brothers entered into a conspiracy to kill Joseph, but when they saw a band of Egyptians traveling down the road, they decided they should get rid of him in a less drastic way. So they sold him to the Egyptian traders, and they thought that was the end of the dreamer. Then they killed a goat and dipped Joseph's special "coat of many colors" into the goat's red blood to make sure their father believed their story that Joseph had been killed by a wild animal.

When the brothers brought the coat to their father, Jacob said, "It is my son's coat. An evil beast has devoured him." Jacob rent his clothes, put on sackcloth and refused to be comforted, saying, "I will go down to my grave mourning for my son."

The story of Joseph is also about the hidden God! Joseph had this dream of power - a dream of God's plan for his life and the life of his family and his nation. The power of Joseph's dream kept living, even in the midst of his long story of suffering, trials and temptations!

Joseph's story is the story of a dreamer, but more. Joseph's story, like that of his great-grandfather Abraham, is the story of a man committed to trust in the faithfulness of God in spite of any and all evidence to the contrary - and in spite of pagan disbelief all around him.

After his brothers sold him into slavery in Egypt, Joseph continued to believe in the God of his fathers as his God. The Bible tells us that the Lord was with Joseph.[104]

In Egypt Joseph finally rose to a place of honor and responsibility in Potiphar's household. But Potiphar's wife, apparently with too much time on her hands, noticed that Joseph was a good looking man. Most of us would say, "Where was God when Potiphar's wife lied and got Joseph thrown into prison?" In the contingencies of history, the purposes of God are at work in hidden and unnoticed ways! But the purposes of God and the power of the dream, although sometimes hidden in the shadows from our understanding, are reliable and will come to pass.

In the life of Joseph, the dream was alive! Not as in the life of Abraham when we are told plainly that God tested Abraham.[105] We are not told that God tested Abraham's great-grandson Joseph. We are not told that God demanded radical faith and trust of Joseph as God certainly did in the life of Abraham and Sarah when they were told they would have a son and their descendants would be as numerous as the stars on a clear night. Abraham believed in the midst of circumstances to the contrary. We are told that Abraham's faith was credited to him as righteousness.[106]

The eagle soars when it is caught up in the jet stream of the wind. It does not soar in its own strength. The bird's innate capacity is multiplied by the power of the wind which lifts and impels it. So it is with us when we wait for God. God's spirit has the power to infuse the tissues of our impotent mind, our depleted emotions, our wayward wills and our weary bodies. God's omnipotent power is

---

[104] Genesis 39
[105] Genesis 22
[106] Genesis 15:6

gloriously revealed in the energizing, vitalizing and uplifting of our human nature. We were created to be inadequate until filled with God's magnificence. Joseph's hidden God is at work.

Regardless of human actions and human efforts or human knowledge, we are finally shown that the hidden God was at work in the life and dreams of Joseph, in spite of human efforts to destroy the dream and to kill the dreamer.

Neither Joseph nor his brothers could possibly have known until much later that God was really in charge to bring good out of evil and to bring about God's purpose. One of the successful business men of a former generation said, "I go to church on Sundays to be reminded of who is really in charge here."

In our kind of world with our piddling little news from the Associated Press, our boring, managed and subjective news that sometimes seems to mold news rather than report it, we sometimes forget it is neither Hollywood, nor the International Olympic Committee, nor the President, nor the FBI, but God, who is in charge.

So the promises of Abraham and the future of Israel were in the hands of young Joseph. But Joseph's jealous older brothers wanted to kill the dream and the dreamer. Joseph had this dream that he believed was a message from God, a statement of who he was and the plans God had for him. But the dream interfered with business as usual for the brothers. They were living in the present. They thought they were in charge! So they set out to destroy the dream by killing Joseph. When we get to the end of the chapter, even Jacob, the father believed that Joseph, the dreamer, was dead.

> *The purposes of God are at work in our lives –*
> *sometimes in unnoticed ways.*

The main character in this powerful drama is God - the hidden but powerful God. The purposes of God are at work in our lives - sometimes in unnoticed ways. But the purposes of God, the power of the dream, even sometimes hidden in the shadows from our understanding, are reliable.

Joseph's brothers thought they had seen the last of Joseph, the dreamer, when they sold him into slavery. How could they know they would meet Joseph, the dreamer, again as the powerful Prime Minister of Egypt, when a famine in their land brought them to Egypt to buy food? Amen.

Actions Speak Louder than Words

James 1:22-25

But be doers of the word, and not hearers only, deceiving yourselves.
~James 1:22 (NKJV)~

In Hebrews 11, the Faith Chapter of the Bible, faith is described using the nouns, "substance" and "evidence." Faith is defined as "the substance of things hoped for and the evidence of things not seen."

However, in the book of James (James 1:22), faith is also a verb. Faith is something we do. Christianity is more than a religion or a philosophy. It is a lifestyle - a way of doing as well as a way of being, and it is based on the heart-changing and life-changing amazing grace that we receive when we accept Jesus Christ as Savior and Lord of our lives.

James (James 1: 22-25) tells us that willingness to do what one hears from God is what characterizes genuine faith. "If we just listen and do not obey, it is like looking at our faces in the mirror. As soon as we walk away, we forget what we look like." Some of us, as we get older, may want to forget what we look like.

When I speak to senior citizen groups I remind them (and me) about one of the laws of compensation. As we age, our eyes get dimmer, so when we look in the mirror we don't always see all our wrinkles and age lines.

Ode to Myopia

My face in the mirror
Isn't wrinkled or drawn.
My house isn't dirty;
The cobwebs are gone
My garden looks lovely
And so does my lawn

I think I will not
Put my glasses back on.

~Cary Fellman~

James advises us to "keep looking steadily and clearly into God's law - not just to mirror our own finite thoughts, but to get a word from the infinite God."

I am not a sports fan, but someone called my attention to an article in the *Atlanta Journal* about a fullback with the Atlanta Falcons. His name was Bob and his faith in Christ was worked out in what he did and how he lived. He was an eighth grader when his parents invited Christ into their lives. Bob witnessed the dramatic change in his parents' lives. So Bob became a Christian a few months later.

When Bob, who is a graduate of Northwestern University with a degree in Electrical Engineering, was playing in Chicago someone asked about his lifestyle. He knew they might make fun of him when they learned he took seriously the teachings of the Bible. However, he decided that if speaking out helped just one youth, it was worth any harassment.

> *We need to give our young people reasons for*
> *not drinking.*

Bob said something I believe. We, as Christian adults, are letting our youth down when we know what is right but are not getting the information out to our young people because it is politically incorrect by the standards of Hollywood and academia. We expect our youth to take on our values. At the same time we are not giving them practical reasons for practicing sexual abstinence before marriage in a world of AIDS and other sexually transmitted diseases. We need to give our young people reasons for not drinking. In a world of high powered automobiles and DUIs, when one out of ten people who drink becomes alcoholic almost from the beginning, and, according to stats, many more become problem drinkers, we need to set the example.

If the church does not tell the truth, we can be sure people who have a vested interest in a multibillion dollar alcohol industry will not. So it is good to have successful sports figures not just talking the talk but walking the walk.

I read a story recently about a poor farmer. He had one horse he depended on for his living.[107] His horse pulled the plow and was his only means of transportation. One day a bee stung the horse and it ran away into the mountains. His neighbors in the village heard and came by to tell him how sorry they were to hear about his "bad luck" in losing his horse. The old farmer said to his neighbors, "Good luck, bad luck - who is to say?"

A week later the horse came home, and with him were twelve fine wild horses. The old man and his son corralled these fine horses. Again the news of the farmers windfall spread throughout the village and his neighbors came back to congratulate him on his good luck. Again, the old farmer just shrugged and said, "Good luck, bad luck - who is to say?"

The only son of the farmer was one day trying to tame one of the fine wild horses and the horse threw him off and his leg was broken in three places. When word of the accident spread the villagers came back saying, "We are sorry to hear of the accident and the bad luck of your son getting hurt. The old farmer just shrugged and said: "Good luck, bad luck - who is to say?"

Two weeks later war broke out between the provinces, and the army came through conscripting every able bodied man under sixty. The son did not have to go because of his injury which turned out to save his life because every soldier in the village who went was killed in battle.

The old farmer was wise in accepting the fact that we human beings, regardless of advantages or education or money, are not wise enough to make final judgments on what is good luck or bad

---

[107] John Claypool, *The Library of Distinctive Sermons*, General Editor, Gary W. Kingston. P. 31.

luck. He was profoundly wise in accepting his inability to make a final verdict until all the evidence was in.[108] As Paul tells us, "Now we see through a glass darkly."[109]

Verse 17 in James 1 tells us that God is the father of lights with whom there is no variation or shadow of turning. We are wise to remember that we are not in a position to make a final judgment on some things that happen to us. Some events that have every appearance of bad luck, in the mysterious unfolding of life, may turn out to bring unexpected good. We may flex our muscles and spout off our learning in the arts and sciences, but (I visit in hospitals and nursing homes enough to know) we are not always in charge of our own bodies.

The arts and the sciences are constantly being revised and "new" scientific truth is brought forth, and yesterday's "old" scientific truth is discarded.

In one sense, I had the privilege of going through seminary twice. My first degree from Candler was a PHT (Putting Hubby Through). When my husband was a seminary student at Emory in the 1950s, because of my interest and calling, I read most of the books he brought into the house. Rudolph Bultmann was one of the major theologians in the fifties with his works on form criticism and "demythologizing" the New Testament. Martin Buber, the Jewish thinker, was cited often with his "I and Thou" relationship theology. When I attended the same seminary in the 1980s, neither Bultmann nor Buber was on our reading lists.

The point is: Human wisdom and the combined wisdom of noted thinkers often change with the times. We see this illustrated in the medical field as well as in theology. How wonderful to be privileged to gather around the timeless wisdom of the Bible - the word of God that "stands written" and is the eternal truth for every generation.

---

[108] Ibid
[109] 1 Corinthians 13:12

This is basically the message of this text in the book of James. James wants us to know that "faith is something we do." Our actions (our behavior) do indeed speak louder and clearer than our words. The Lord wants to rescue us from our damaging lifestyles and sins because God loves us and wants the best for us.

Therefore, when the Bible gives clear, direct and strong moral proclamations about certain behaviors, you do not have to be a religious fanatic or a bigot to take it seriously. The people who are handing out condoms in public schools in the name of "raging hormones" are giving kids the mistaken idea that hormones do not rage beyond youth; so they had better take advantage while they can.

Too often, our youth are advised to sell their future blessings for a mess of porridge like Esau who so devalued his birthright that for immediate gratification he lost his blessing for a lifetime and lost the blessing that would have gone to his children.

God wants to lead us into whatever changes are needed in our lifestyles, even if those changes are painful in the short run. God's changes for us will bring blessedness now and, in the long run, joy for a lifetime and beyond into eternal life.

In 1997 (8-17-97), I turned on the TV to "The Christophers," an interview program hosted by a priest. I tuned in just in time to hear a distinguished guest talking to the host. He was telling how he had been invited to speak a few years earlier at John Brown University. He wondered about the origin of the name - "John Brown University." He decided it would probably not be named for the John Brown of "John Brown's body lies a molding in the grave" fame, and so he wrote for a brochure. He learned that the John Brown who founded the university had been a traveling evangelist.

As he was preparing to go to the school and give his speech, he admitted he felt "a little condescending." He said he was identifying the term "evangelist" with some radical TV evangelist. On the morning of the speech, his father called from Tennessee and asked about his day and what he was about. This distinguished speaker mentioned to his dad that he was about to catch a plane to go out west to speak at John Brown University.

His dad replied, "Oh yes, I know about that university. It was under John Brown's preaching that my dad was saved."

Later, in relating this story on "The Christophers", he turned to his host and explained that "saved" is the term commonly used in some church groups for becoming a Christian.

The rest of the story is that this distinguished speaker's grandfather had been from a non-Christian, poor, very disadvantaged family in the hills of Tennessee. At the age of 16, he had struck out on his own. He happened to encounter John Brown's preaching and became a Christian. When he was ready to get married, he married a Christian girl, and they established a Christian home. Thus, his life and the life of his family and descendants were guided by, and thus blessed by, God.

I thought as I heard this story, "What better word could be found in the entire dictionary than the word 'saved' to describe what happens to individuals and even families when Christ comes into a person's life?" Not just saved from the "wrath to come" that John Wesley and the early circuit riders preached about, but also saved from illiteracy, ignorance, poverty - spiritual poverty and often economic poverty also - as we join our disability with God's ability.

Christians established the first hospitals, schools and the Ivy League Universities in our nation. James speaks of looking into the prefect law of God, not to mirror our own flawed wisdom, but to point us beyond human understanding to the liberating message of God's mercy and grace. Amen.

The Ten Maidens

Matthew 25:1-13

Then the kingdom of heaven shall be likened to ten virgins who took their lamps and went out to meet the bridegroom.
~Matthew 25:1 (NKJV)~

Have you ever been working on a project and needed more paint or a certain type of tool, and you looked at the clock and thought, "If I hurry, I can get to the store before it closes so I can finish this tonight." So you dash out, but the traffic or something delays you and you get there just as the manager locks the door and turns his back. And if you've got the nerve to knock, he ignores it. You just got there too late.

You knew the business hours, you could have taken stock of your needs earlier, or maybe you couldn't. No matter what the excuse, it's too late now. This is the first thing I thought about when I read this parable of the Ten Maidens.[110]

Of course, the second thing we think about is that this parable is more serious than a delayed household remodeling chore because in this parable, the management will not open up again at seven in the morning. The door is closed, period. It will not be re-opened in the morning or ever again. And the need in this parable is not about a temporary item but something that will make an eternal difference. This parable of the ten maidens is found in Matthew and similar, shorter fragments on the same theme in Luke 12 and 13.

In the parables that Jesus taught, there are two basic types of endings. The happy ending surprise type and those that end as we generally expect - those that follow the direct course from cause to effect.

Some of our favorite and most familiar are the happy ending

---

110 Matthew 25: 1-13

parables. We love those that offer a happy surprise of grace at the end of the parable, such as the parable of the prodigal son, which ends with a party for the prodigal illustrating the fact of forgiveness of a Heavenly Father who runs with arms outstretched to his wayward son.[111]

Another parable of happy surprise and grace is the one of the Pharisee and the tax collector. The tax collector was justified and given grace simply because he knew he needed God and prayed "God be merciful to me, the sinner!" The law-keeping Pharisee went out unjustified and still a sinner because he was "self-righteous" and did not know he needed to be "God-righteous."

The most amazing parable of happy surprise and grace is the parable of the workers. The man who only worked one hour but received a full day's pay. Grace, graciousness.

Then there are the parables that end as we sinners would expect - parables that follow the direct course of cause and effect. People get what they deserve. These are parables of justice, not grace. In this type of parable, there are no parties or gifts at the end, but the harvest comes from what is sown, reaping what was sown. Together these two types of parables present justice and grace, either of which becomes distorted without the other. God is the Lord of justice and grace.

Today's parable of the ten maidens is not one of the happy surprise-ending parables. The five maidens who did not follow the Lord's instructions, who did not put oil in their lamps, simply waited too late. The parable goes from cause to painful effect - the door is shut and will not be opened. There is no Father running out with arms outstretched with grace, graciously saying, "You've come home. We're throwing a welcome party." No full day's pay for one hour's work. This is a parable of warning and confrontation, not comfort. It tells us that there is a time when it will be too late - that the day of grace is not forever.

---

[111] Luke 15

This Bible and this parable do not teach universal salvation. It was not the coming of the bridegroom that made five of the maidens wise and five foolish, but it reveals who is wise and who is foolish. It reveals who is prepared. It reveals who believed the truth and based their actions on this truth.

The content of Matthew, Chapters 23-25 concludes Jesus's public ministry and also his interchange with the scribes and Pharisees. Chapter 23 begins with a message to the crowd about the scribes and Pharisees, exposing them as false shepherds.

Jesus then spoke to them of the seven woes in contrast to the statements of blessings in the first seven Beatitudes in Matthew's gospel. These final statements are the teaching of Jesus and his interaction with his enemies as he heads towards the cross.

> *These final chapters help us to see Jesus as an authentic person, able to have anger without violence. He shows us that love is not spineless.*

We see several things here. We see his expressions of judgment upon unbelievers. These final chapters help us to see Jesus as an authentic person, able to have anger without violence. He shows us that love is not spineless.

He commended these leaders for their teaching of Moses's Law, but he points out two glaring weaknesses. For one thing, they did not practice what they preached! Jesus pointed out the disparity between what they taught and what they practiced. And second, Jesus condemned them for their love of having the best places. He warned us, his followers today, that we also do not practice what we preach when we insist on the best seats and the best titles.

The first beatitude, in which Jesus said blessed are the poor in spirit, is in contrast with the Pharisees' attitude of "self-confidence." None of us really wants to be "poor in spirit" or poor anything. We would much rather be self-confident, but the truth is we have to get down on our knees in humility - not a good self-image - to get understanding of the deceitfulness of our hearts.

The pronouncements of judgment are for the very opposite behavior from that which Jesus declared to be blessed. This is illustrative of God's judgment, which is unequivocal. We cannot succeed on borrowed religion, whether borrowed from our parents or anyone else.

The unprepared could not borrow oil from the prepared; the prepared had already gone in. Three of the saddest sayings in the parables of Jesus are found here. (1) Our lamps have gone out. (2) The door is shut. (3) I do not know you.

We see Jesus here rebuking the leaders for their sins and talking about the serious consequences of sin. Jesus is warning us about the foolishness of sin and the foolishness of being unprepared - the foolishness of never coming face to face with who we can be in Christ Jesus.

Along the roadside, traveling north on I-75, there used to be signs every now and then - I don't know if they are still there or not - that read "Prepare to meet thy God" or "Jesus is coming soon." That is what these texts in Matthew and Thessalonians[112] today are about: the second coming of Christ and about being prepared.

The most commonly used term to describe Jesus' return to earth is "parousia," meaning presence or appearing. The parousia was identified with the Old Testament Day of the Lord. To the Israelites, all of history consisted of two ages, the present age and the age to come.

The end of the present age and the beginning of the age to come would be inaugurated with the Day of the Lord. The Day of the Lord will end this sinful fallen age and usher in the gold age and the abolition of sin, suffering, war and death. It will also mark the final judgment of God.

---

[112] Thessalonians 4: 13-18

In the passage in Thessalonians, Paul is answering the believers' questions about the return of Christ, bringing them assurance, declaration and comfort. Jesus, in the parable of the ten maidens, would have all of us to know that there will be a time when it is too late, when the door is shut and will not be opened.

Paul focuses on the same theme over and over. He also is answering the questions of believers about the end times as regards their loved ones who have already died as believers. Verse 14 tells us "God will bring with Him on His return those who have died."

The destiny of the dead in Christ lies with the God who raised Jesus from the dead. As Paul said, "Jesus is the first fruits of the resurrection." There is more to come. What God did in a graveyard in Jerusalem, he can and will do on a grand scale for us. Against all odds, the terminal shall be made alive.

> *Our hope is a blessed hope because it is unlike any other hope, for it is grounded in the fact of the resurrection of Jesus Christ.*

In verse 13, he enters into their grief because of the death of their loved ones, and he gives them assurance, blessed assurance. He assures them that they need not sorrow as those who have no hope. In his letter to the Corinthians[113] he writes, "If in this life only we have hope in Christ, we are, of all men, most miserable or most pitiable." Our hope is a blessed hope because it is unlike any other hope, for it is grounded in the fact of the resurrection of Jesus Christ.

For burial services, I like to use a committal at the graveside that I first heard my husband use in services he conducted. The poetic words:

> *"Cherishing memories that are forever sacred, sustained by a faith that is stronger than death, comforted by the hope of a life that shall endless be, all that is mortal of this person, we commit to its resting place, in*

---

[113] I Corinthians 15:19

the assurance that if the earthly house of our tabernacle be dissolved, we have a building from God, a house not made with hands, eternal in the heavens."

I heard Dr. Howard Eddington from First Presbyterian in Orlando on the AIB Network tell about two men sitting side by side while traveling on a train. The older man took out a Bible and began to read, and the young man asked him what he was reading. He told him he was reading the Bible and the account of Jesus feeding 5000 people with a few barley loaves of bread and three fish and that everyone ate and even had some left over.

And the young man said to the older man, "You don't really believe that, do you?" And the older man told him he certainly did believe it. The younger man said that he was a scientist and he did not believe anything that could not be proven in a laboratory.

When the younger man reached his destination and the train stopped, he said goodbye to the older man and said, "By the way, I did not get your name." The older man reached into his pocket and handed him his card. The young man looked at it in amazement. He had been talking to Louis Pasteur, the most imminent scientist of his day! Pasteur was also a very devout Christian. Pasteur - a man intelligent enough to know there is more than one way to define "truth."

As Albert Einstein said, "The fairest thing we can experience is the mysterious. It is the fundamental emotion which stands at the cradle of true science. He who knows it not and can no longer wonder, no longer feel amazement, is as good as dead."

Paul believed, Pasteur believed, Einstein believed, and I believe that we are being fashioned by all the things that happen to us. We are being fashioned if we allow ourselves to be fashioned and prepared for another world as different from this one as this one is different from the world we lived in during the months we lived in our mother's wombs.

We are all here in church today because there is something about the very structure of the world that whispers to me and to you, "There is something more." There is a truth, more real, more truthful than anything that can be proven in a scientific laboratory. Thank God. Amen.

Blood Kin

Hebrews 9: 1-17

For if the blood of bulls and goats and the ashes of a heifer, sprinkling the unclean, sanctifies for the purifying of the flesh, how much more shall the blood of Christ, who through the eternal Spirit offered Himself without spot to God, cleanse your conscience from dead works to serve the living God?
~Hebrews 9:13-14 (NKJV)~

One of my favorite stories is of the little boy who was giving directions to a church and he said, "It's that building down the street with a big plus sign on top." Good Friday is about how a "Bad Friday" - a very bad Friday - became "Good Friday" and a big plus sign.

The great "good news" the writer of Hebrews explains in lawyer's language, is that we are the heirs of Jesus.[114] We all are the beneficiaries of the "Notarized Will of Jesus." All the debts have been paid. We just need to step up and accept our inheritance as the blood kin of Jesus and thus realize we are the beneficiaries of His last will and testament.

I finally went to see the Mel Gibson movie, "The Passion of the Christ." As I sat watching, I found myself turning my head away from the relentless scenes of blood and violence. When I went home, I read again the passages about the crucifixion in all four gospels - passages I had read many times - but now realized that just as I had covered my eyes from seeing the blood in the movie, I had read hurriedly past the blood and gore of the scourging and the cross in the Bible record. I suppose we all would like to imagine - and re-imagine - a Gospel without dripping blood. It is an unpopular theme.

I sing a lot around the house, and this week I was looking at the large number of hymns about the cross and the blood of Jesus. It seems so central in the Old Testament as well as the New

---

[114] Hebrews 9:1-17

Testament. Blood is not only in hymns like "The Old Rugged Cross" and "There is a Fountain Filled with Blood," but hymns like "Blessed Assurance" with the line "Born of his spirit, washed in his blood."

Just the phrase "washed in the blood" had also raised questions in my mind as a child: "How could anyone be washed in blood and come out clean? Who in their right mind would be interested in being washed in blood?" And, how we all like to think we are in our "right mind." We are not like those "fundamental" Christians. That is why we memorize John 3:16 and read quickly and dismiss Hebrews 9.

> So "washed in the blood of Jesus" means being washed in life, real life - the essence of life - the plus of life.

When we read the American Red Cross slogan, "Give blood. Give the gift of life," we are reminded of the value of life-giving blood. We know loss of blood means loss of life. So "washed in the blood of Jesus" means being washed in life, real life - the essence of life - the plus of life.

Blood is the vehicle of transferred life in medicine as well as in the Bible. In Exodus 24:5, we see Moses in the old blood covenant taking the blood of a lamb and sprinkling it on the people. To our ears this sounds strange, and the people may not have been happy to have blood sprinkled on them. But this blood of the lamb used in the Old Covenant is also in our Scripture in Hebrews today. It points to the cross and eternal LIFE through the shed blood of Jesus, God's spotless "Lamb of God."

As we know, Communion symbolizes the blood covenant we have entered into in remembrance of Jesus' last supper and the sacrifice of Jesus for our salvation.

One of our family stories is about the first time my granddaughter Lillian took Communion at age four or five. When she was at the altar with her parents and sister and heard the pastor say, "This is the blood of the New Covenant," she apparently was listening to the words because she clamped her mouth tight and shook her head and refused to drink it.

Later, her mother, Sheila, talked to her about the meaning of Communion and told her she could not go up and take Communion if she refused to drink the grape juice. Grape juice? Now she knew for sure what was really in the Communion cup, and at the next Communion, she not only drank it but smacked her lips, and rubbed her little stomach and smiled up at her mother to show she was not only obeying by taking Communion but was doing so joyfully.

I think this kind of aliveness and joy is an appropriate response to Communion for a 4-year old or any of us as we realize that this life-giving blood of the new covenant is to bring us, as beneficiaries of Jesus, back from the deadness that sin has placed upon us.

On C-Span recently I heard a sad looking girl, who identified herself as an atheist, talking about how she does not need a God - that she is in control of her own life. Poor child! There comes a time when even the strongest among us are helpless and not in control of anything.

It takes a long time for some to realize our best minds are too weak to comprehend all of the mystery of God and our arms are too short to box with God. We accept Christ by faith but, thank God, it is not a blind faith!

Albert Einstein said, as I have quoted before, "The fairest thing we can experience is the mysterious - the fundamental emotion which stands at the cradle of true science." Einstein and other prominent scientists have concluded there is room in a rational universe for incomprehensible wonders.

On the cross Jesus identifies with us in our helplessness and brokenness. It is his blood transfusion that brings about vitality and transformation in our life.

A few years ago I went with some of my family and other Trinity friends to Daisy United Methodist Church in the Chattanooga area to hear my grandson Benjamin sing with his College Glee Club and Bell Choir. One of the young students gave her testimony. She was the daughter of a Methodist Minister. A few weeks earlier, her grandmother had died, a friend died and her father was transferred after a nine-year pastorate. Moving after nine years in her young life was a traumatic event. Then in the midst of the move, her mother had a heart attack. It put a great deal of the packing on her young shoulders. She said she kept looking up and asking "Lord, I know you are there, but why? Why is all this happening in my life?"

Most of us do not live long until we realize we need more than just a few religious band aids to patch up our brokenness. No ritual "first aid treatment" can heal the grief-bruised and sin-sick soul. Spiritually, we are told throughout the New Testament, we need a heart transplant - a blood transfusion. We need God.

I heard Vic Pense, from Peachtree Presbyterian Church tell the story of a man driving his car in Eastern Washington State one day and having to stop and wait because a large flock of sheep was crossing the road. As the man watched the sheep, the phrase "Lamb of God "kept drifting through his mind. As he waited, he got out of his car and walked over to the shepherd and asked him, "What does the phrase 'Lamb of God' mean to you?"

The sheep herder told him, "Each year at lambing time, there are some baby lambs as well as some mother sheep that die. Inevitably there will be a ewe that is full of milk, but her lamb has died and she refuses to feed a lamb she does not recognize as her own. There will also be a baby lamb whose mother has died so it is starving because no other mother ewe will accept and feed it."

The shepherd said he'd learned that he could take the mother sheep's dead lamb and cut it throat and pour the blood over the little orphaned lamb. Then the mother sheep would recognize the blood and accept and welcome the lamb that had the blood of her own lamb on it. Through the gift of being washed in the blood of the lamb that had died, the living lamb is recognized and accepted and nourished and saved.

Dr. Pense went on to say, "When we are covered with the blood of Jesus - the Lamb of God, God sees us through rose colored glasses. God sees us as His own through blood-tinted glasses!"

So we do not come to the Communion table today to have a priest of the old covenant sprinkle blood over us or dip his finger in the blood of a spotless lamb and place it on us. We come forward to take the blood and body of Jesus inside us as in the Jeremiah prophesy that one day - one great "plus sign" day, God would put his new covenant inside us - in our hearts. Thus, by accepting his sacrifice for us, we share in his body and blood and become blood kin to Jesus and blood kin to one another.

Thank God! Amen.

Ash Wednesday Meditation

Luke 15:1-10.

Just so, I tell you, there is joy in the presence of the angels of God over one sinner who repents.
~Luke 15:10 (NRSV)~

When our daughter, Deborah, was critically ill at age 2 months, her Daddy and I sat in the waiting room of the hospital where other people with sick children were waiting. If you have spent many days in a hospital waiting room, you realize how you begin to interact with people. You listen to their stories and tell them yours. You become concerned about their loved ones and appreciate their concern for yours. Each individual patient is precious to someone. Charles and I were so distraught that someone asked, "Is she your only child?" I replied, "She is our fifth child, but she is our only Debi."

Jesus came to earth to tell us the amazing news that each individual one of us is precious to God. We each have our own fingerprint, our own voice accent, our own DNA. God so loved each one of us that he sent Jesus that whosoever believes in Him will not perish but have everlasting life.

The Pharisees thought God rejoiced in the death of sinners. In Luke 15, Jesus tells us there is joy in heaven when each one of us repents of our wandering and believes this greatest Good News the world has ever heard!

The story of Adam and Eve in Genesis 3 is our story. When we, as human beings, left the garden, we left the presence of God, and we have been homesick ever since. As Augustine reminds us, "We were made for God, and we are restless until we find our rest in God."

Jesus tells us the exciting greatest good news the world ever heard - that God loves us! God so loved the world that he gave his only begotten son, Jesus, that whosoever believes in Him will not perish but will have everlasting life. (John 3:16)

When Jesus was on earth he sought out the lost in unlikely places. He ate with the lost people, thus offending the religious leaders.

Bruce Larson, in his comment on Luke 15, reminds us there were four lost items- a sheep, a coin, a prodigal son and the elder brother. It is obvious that the first three are lost. However, the elder brother is the tragic one because he is lost and he does not know it.[115]

Shakespeare said that the wise man knows himself to be a fool. The fool thinks himself to be wise. In other words, the wise person knows when he is lost and understands the source of his homesickness and returns to the father who loves him.[116]

The great English preacher, P.T. Forsyth, said, "The only way to get to the Father is through the far country." The "far country" may not always be moral dissolution. He says we are in the far country when we get to a point in our life when we are disappointed to the point of thinking, "Is this all there is?" And Forsyth ends by saying, "The Father answers, 'Of course that is not all there is. Come home.'"[117]

> *The ashes of Ash Wednesday are to remind us that our physical bodies are dying. The sign of the cross is to remind us that we are more than our physical bodies.*

The ashes of Ash Wednesday are to remind us that our physical bodies are dying. The sign of the cross is to remind us that we are more than our physical bodies.

It is Ash Wednesday, but Easter is coming! Ash Wednesday begins Lent and the believer's journey to Holy Week and Easter. It is a journey of individual repentance and prayer. In the Service of Ashes, we kneel at the altar and the pastor marks the sign of the

---

[115] *Communicator's Commentary*, Luke, page 226
[116] Ibid
[117] Ibid

cross in ashes on our foreheads.

When I checked into the doctor's office recently, they asked to see my health insurance cards. I told the doctor's receptionist she already had all that information, but I was told they have to have it fresh at every visit now. She handed me a leaflet in large print: "We now require a copy of your insurance card and a picture ID at every visit. This is to protect you, the patient, from insurance fraud. Thank you for your cooperation in this matter." It seems someone lent his/her insurance card to another person. So we are all paying in time and money for the cost of insurance fraud.

We are told in the Bible, our Book of Faith (Romans 6:23), that the wages of the sin of fraud are also coming from the pockets of all. Peter talks about those who have forsaken the right way and who love the wages of unrighteousness (2 Peter 2:15).

None of us have clean hands. It is all too easy to confess other people's sins instead of our own. Ash Wednesday is to remind us of our own sin and our own mortality.

Ash Wednesday reminds us to get life in focus and to get our priorities straight. We need to be reminded we will not live on this earth forever. This life is a short "dry run" even if we should live 100 years. We are all dying people. We are going to spend eternity somewhere. So we are reminded again on Ash Wednesday: "Remember. Dust you are and to dust you will return." Thus we need to repent of our own sins. Repentance is the doorway into eternal life.

Ash Wednesday is also the signal that winter is on the way out and Easter is on the horizon! Amen.

The Four "R's" of Deuteronomy

Deuteronomy 26:1-11

And it shall be, when you come into the land which the LORD your God is giving you as an inheritance, and you possess it and dwell in it, that you shall take some of the first of all the produce of the ground, which you shall bring from your land that the LORD your God is giving you, and put it in a basket and go to the place where the LORD your God chooses to make His name abide.
~Deuteronomy 26:1-2 (NKJV)~

I went back to school after my children were grown, and so I aged into the study of aging. While working on my degree at Georgia State University, I also earned a certificate in Gerontology and did an internship at a large complex for elderly and disabled people.[118]

During the course of the time I was at the convalescent center, I taught a poetry class to a group of elderly residents on Saturday mornings. Some of them had arthritic fingers and thus had difficulty holding a pencil. So I would have them tell me their poems - something about their lives, an event, or a memory - and I would write it down in poetic form and read it back to them and to the group.

I learned much from these elderly citizens. I especially remember an elderly nurse, Rose, telling her story of when her mother called all the children in at night for supper, and she was always the child "sitting on the highest limb of the tallest tree".

When I read Rose's poem out loud to her and her cohorts in nurse care, her wrinkled face lit up with joy as she relived this remembering.

Mr. Roberts, an elderly man in a wheelchair told me his poem. He recounted:

---

[118] This large complex included individual homes for elderly or disabled couples or individuals, a Convalescent Center, a Nursing Care building and an Alzheimer's Unit.

Everything was not good
In the good old days.
Everything was not safe
In the good old days.
One day when I
Was about knee high,
Not more than four years old,
I took a stick of dynamite
Out to the railroad track.
My father used dynamite
To clear his land for plowing.
Dynamite made a loud noise!
I wanted to make it
Make a loud noise!
My mother looked out and saw me.
My mother trembled
As she came to get me.
My mother was afraid to call me.
My mother's hands trembled
As she reached out to me
And took the dynamite!

As I read Mr. Roberts' poem back to him and to the group, I no longer saw only an elderly man in a wheelchair. I also envisioned a small, precocious boy, a child who had loving parents - a father he wanted to emulate and a mother who would risk her very life to protect him.

By the gift of memory, by remembering, this disabled and elderly man was a young child again, remembering who he was. He was somebody. He was loved. Probably in Mr. Roberts' early memories he thought primarily of the danger he had encountered in this childhood escapade. Now, elderly and disabled, the smiling Mr. Roberts was remembering a strong daddy who worked hard to support him and a young mother's love for him and her bravery on his account.

This gave him added status in his own eyes and in the eyes of his cohorts in the nursing home who were now his neighbors and were hearing his story. Although he was an old man in a wheelchair, he was thus able to share more of himself with others around him. He remembered who he was and was able to share his story.

When Jesus was baptized by John in the Jordon River, a voice from Heaven said, "You are My beloved Son." In the gospel lesson about the temptations of Jesus, Satan tells him, "If you are the Son of God, command this stone to be bread. If you are the Son of God, cast yourself down from this mountain." "If you are." The Devil suggests to Jesus that there is some doubt about his identify as the Messiah of God.

The temptations of Jesus at His baptism were not designed so much to get Jesus to do something wrong as they were attempts to get Jesus to forget who He was and to lose sight of His mission.

I remember when I was a little girl, I listened to my mother tell family stories. She told about one Sunday when their preacher described how one busy Saturday afternoon he mashed his finger painfully and lost his temper. The preacher told how he yelled and slammed things around until finally, he said, the devil looked at him gleefully and said, "What are you going to preach about tomorrow?" In other words, he had forgotten who he was.

In Deuteronomy[119] we read one of the great creeds of the Bible. The descendants of Jacob (Israel) had been led out of slavery in Egypt. After 40 years as wilderness wanderers, they were standing on the verge of Jordon looking over into the Promised Land. The Lord was giving them some last minute instructions about remembering who they were and what kind of people they should be when they got to the Promised Land. Much of it had to do with remembering who they were as people of God!

One sociologist has suggested that we hyphenate the term re-member to distinguish it from ordinary recollection or reminiscing. Re-membering is the reconstructing of one's members, the reconstructing of the figures that properly belong to one's prior selves. Through re-membering, a life is given shape and form and

---

[119] Luke 4

extends back into the past and forward into the future as an edited story. Through re-membering, one's entire life is put in perspective. Without re-membering, we lose our history and ourselves.

People who have never been humbled haven't learned much.

Good news! The Lord God of Israel knew about the importance of re-membering long before the sociologists found out about it! All the way back to Deuteronomy, the God of Israel, the God that Jesus called "Father," kept telling the children of Israel to remember. "And you shall remember all the ways which the Lord your God has led you these forty years in the wilderness, that God might humble you, testing you to know what was in your heart, whether you would keep God's commandments or not."[120] That God might humble you. People who have never been humbled haven't learned much.

My daughter, Joan, tells about how schools often, in attempting to teach children "self-esteem," praise them for inconsequential and insignificant acts rather than for real accomplishments. Her experience with children in school has convinced her that, while children certainly need positive reinforcement and personal attention, they learn self-esteem primarily from remembering their work done well.[121]

"**R**emember" is the first of the four R's of this lesson. The others are **R**ecite, **R**espond and **R**ejoice. The people of God here displayed their gratitude to God in tangible ways. They responded. They brought "first fruits" of their harvest to the temple. This is not the same as reminiscing. I learned in working with the elderly that there is a difference in the people who just recollect things about their past and those who re-member.

---

[120] Deuteronomy 26
[121] *Daddy's Roses*: Weblog by Joan Shaw Turrentine

In other words, the people of God were to begin their worship liturgy with a recitation of remembrance. Re-membering - giving shape and form to their entire story which included those who had gone before them as well as the God who had led them. And a central part of their worship liturgy was the reciting of the ancient confession of remembering. They were to remember and tell the source of their strength. They were to recite their story as a witness and to respond with "first fruits" and rejoicing. They were to remember who they were. Since the days of Abraham they were no longer just a "no people," they were "God's people." We rejoice!

They were like the man in the nursing home, who, even in the life-threatening dynamite story, re-remembered his mother risking her life to save him. He was "somebody." He had a history. He was loved!

The people of God were to begin their worship liturgy by remembering. To me this is one of the tragedies of the alcohol and drug problems today. We see people trying to escape, trying to forget, rather than to live, to really live, this incredible privilege of life.

We get this picture in Old Testament passages like Deuteronomy 26, where the people of God, as they close the door on their wilderness experience, are to take God's hand saying, "Thanks for the memory. Thank you, God, for being there even in the oppression."

In this Old Testament lesson, the Hebrew people were to understand who they were. It began with Abraham, a wandering Armenian, who had believed in the promises of God.[122] We read of God telling Abram that his descendants would be as numerous as the stars, even though he and Sarah were already elderly and childless. The Bible tells us that Abram believed God and it was put into his account as righteousness![123] So here we see his descendants standing in the door of the Promised Land with their first-fruits in their hands. And they are recounting their story and it

---

[122] Deuteronomy 8:2
[123] Genesis 15:1-12, 17. 18a

is also God's story! It's a beautiful liturgy. "A wandering Armenian was my father and we had bad times. In fact, we were afflicted. We were oppressed. But we have a God. And God acted on our behalf!"

The last "R" in this text is rejoice! In verse 11 they were commanded, "And you shall rejoice." Wouldn't it be wonderful if Christians started joyfully affirming one another at every opportunity?

In Luke 2 we read about a prophet named Anna. It is easy to skip over Anna. But here she is, a lady prophet right in Luke's account of the birth of Jesus.

Luke tells us when Mary and Joseph brought the baby Jesus into the temple, "coming up at that very moment was Anna, and she remembered and re-membered and rejoiced!" Anna told the story of Jesus to all "who were looking for the redemption of Jerusalem."

When something bumps into our lives, what spills out tells a great deal about us. It tells whether we go down complaining or come up being thankful. It tells what has shaped and formed us.

So right here in the book of Deuteronomy, we get a glimpse of God who was not just a God "within the shadows, keeping watch," but a God of action.

Jesus on the very night when he was betrayed, took bread and when he had given thanks, he broke the bread and gave it to his disciples saying, "Do this in remembrance of me" - a ritual of remembrance, reciting, responding, and rejoicing. Amen.

Love in Every Language

Acts 2:1-13

And they were all filled with the Holy Spirit and began to speak with other tongues, as the Spirit gave them utterance.
~Acts 2:4 (NKJV)~

Pentecost Sunday in the book of Acts gives us a cameo picture of the life-changing experience and vitality of the 120 men and women disciples as they gathered to observe the feast of Pentecost and to prayerfully wait in Jerusalem for the coming of the Holy Spirit - as Jesus had instructed them to do. (Acts 2:6)

When we read Acts 2, we know it sounds a little different from some of our ways of having church. In fact, there was so much excitement that people looking on accused them of being drunk. Imagine that!

I was baptized as an infant and grew up in church. But I do not remember being taught much about the Holy Spirit.

When Dr. Thomas Long was teaching a Confirmation class and came to the topic of Pentecost, he proceeded to tell the children that "Pentecost was when the church was in a group and the Holy Spirit landed on them like tongues of fire on their heads." The children took all this in stride, all but one little girl who looked wide-eyed and said: "Gosh, Rev. Long, I must have been absent that Sunday."

In the church I grew up in we had Sunday night services but we were back home after about an hour. The Pentecostal Church on the edge of town was still going strong at 8:30, 9:30, 10:30, and all over town we could hear their singing and shouting and everyone praying at the same time. Some people laughed at these people. My mother did not allow me to laugh, but she said it was "extremism" and "fanaticism."

One thing I respected about these people, though, was that they were willing to be different. We, in the mainline churches, try to fit in with anything Hollywood and the popular media send our way, and sometimes we just reflect the views of the society around us, rather than setting Christ-like standards. We adult Christians are letting our children down when we do not give them information and instructions to offset the life-damaging sexual messages and self-serving alcohol propaganda they are getting daily in the media and even in some of our schools.

But my mother was right - at least somewhat right - in her assessment of that particular branch of Pentecostalism in our town. In our text today, it was not an unknown tongue, as they taught, but a miracle of language.

The work of the Holy Spirit in our Bible lesson today, as well as in the Gospels, is to bring about right relationships! The Holy Spirit does not create chaos or confusion, but love and community in order to bring the goods news of God's love and salvation to people everywhere. The fire of the Holy Spirit empowers us for ministry and for making disciples, as it did for those 120 disciples.

Visiting in Jerusalem for this feast of Pentecost were Jewish people from all over the world. When these visitors heard the commotion coming from where the Christians had gathered, they were curious and went over to see what was going on. They heard the Christians speaking in foreign languages about the great things God had done in Jesus Christ, and miracle of miracles, they understood in their own language. Miracles of miracles, thousands were added to the church that day.

What the Holy Spirit began that day was an extension of His work among God's people in fulfilling the promise of Jesus in John 14, 15, and 16.

John tells us in chapter 14 that Jesus and the twelve are gathered in the upper room. The earthly Jesus was beginning his "goodbye" to his twelve disciples. Jesus began with the verse we often hear at funerals, "Let not your hearts be troubled."

In our language, the Holy Spirit - the Paraclete - translates to us, not as just one word, but many: comforter, counselor, helper, encourager, the spirit of truth, someone to stand alongside.

Since 9/11 we are living in a world of fear. Oh, how we need a comforter. How we need a counselor. How we need this spirit of truth.

I heard the story of a little girl in the days when people rode trains with sleepers. The child was put to bed in a top bunk and was very fearful in her strange surroundings. So her daddy told her God would watch over her. As everyone got quiet trying to sleep, the fearful child called out, "Mommy, are you there?" The mother assured her she was there. A little later, she called out louder, "Daddy, are you there?" The father tried to reassure her that he was nearby also.

After this went on for a while, one of the other passengers in the sleeper car lost his patience and said, "Yes, we are all here. Your mommy's here. Your daddy is here - your brother, all your aunts and cousins. Now please settle down and go to sleep." The little girl was silent for a moment and then quietly asked, "Mommy, was that God?"

> *Part of the work of the Holy Spirit is to grow us up to "Christian maturity" - maturity that manifests itself with love in every language.*

Jesus, in offering us His Holy Spirit, does not treat us like frightened children - not impatiently saying, "Shut up and get quiet. I'm giving you whatever you want." Sometimes God has to say "no" to our requests - like a loving parent who understands our needs and who wants to "grow us up." Part of the work of the Holy Spirit is to grow us up to "Christian maturity" - maturity that manifests itself with love in every language.

I am a long time student, and I taught Christian history in many of the churches where my husband was pastor. The early Methodist circuit riders rode west with the first settlers in this country and their spirit-filled sermons were used to change the face of America.

I am told most early Methodist sermons had 4 points.

> *First: All of us are sinners*
> *Second: All of us can be saved (none are predestined to be lost)*
> *Third: All of us can know we are saved ("the doctrine of assurance")*
> *The fourth point had to do with the work of the Holy Spirit in daily life. That is, we can live like "Christian" people. This is not "sinless perfection" but "perfect love" or "Christian maturity."*

John Wesley talked about having his heart "strangely warmed" and referred to the Holy Spirit later as "perfect love" - not always perfect judgment or perfect ability - but perfect intentions and perfect love for God and others.

I like the story of the little boy who was tagging along in a field as his dad was plowing on a hot humid day. Soon the little boy ran to the house to get his Dad a glass of ice water. He returned to the field smiling as he gave the glass to his dad. The dad noticed the little boy's muddy fingers had been holding on the inside of the glass and mud was seeping down inside the large glass of water. The child's intentions were perfect. His love for his Dad was perfect. But his performance, his ability (sometimes like ours) was not perfect. The boy's father took the glass, and thankfully drank every drop of the water.

In the United Nations, modern technology has now been perfected to the degree that each representative has ear phones rigged in such a way that a person can be speaking in French but the English and American representatives hear it in English. The Spanish people hear it in their native language – The Germans hear German. All the delegates hear in their native language. When I read about this technology I thought, "Praise God, the Lord knew how to speak His love in every language 2000 years before the computer people in the United Nations perfected that kind of technology."

When we understand the complicated mechanism of articulation through the system of the brain and how difficult it is for us to understand one another - even when we speak the same language, we begin to understand what a marvelous thing happened on the day of Pentecost.

These fearful Christians were so filled and under the influence of God's Holy Spirit that God was able to utilize their mechanism of speech to enable the believer to articulate God's love in languages they had not learned previously.

There was a best seller some years ago titled, *Men Are from Mars, Women Are from Venus.*[124] None of us who are married or have ever been married would disagree. Men and women are fascinated with one another, but we certainly do not always understand one another. However, on the day of Pentecost and since, the Holy Spirit enabled men and women to better understand one another and to love one another in spite of differences.

The Holy Spirit enables people who look different from one another and who speak different languages to love one another. Most preachers will agree that it is not our ability, but our availability to the Holy Spirit of God that the Lord uses to reach people. Amen.

---

[124] John Gray. *Men Are from Mars. Women Are from Venus*

What Do You Say? Say, "Thank You"

Psalm 34: 1-10

*I will bless the Lord at all times; His praise shall continually be in my mouth.
My soul shall make its boast in the Lord; The humble shall hear it and be
glad. Oh magnify the Lord with me, and let us exalt His name together.*
~Psalm 34: 1-3 (NKJV)~

One of the first phrases we teach our children is "thank you."
When someone does something for them or gives them a gift, we
say, "Honey, what do you say? Say 'Thank you.'" "Tell Aunt Mary
'thank you.'" "Tell Grandmother 'thank you.'" And when they
finally say, "Thank You," in their little baby voices, we hug them and
tell them how sweet they are.

The season we are in has been called "Hallow-thank-mas." It starts
each year before Halloween with increasingly elaborate Halloween
decorations and continues through the many festivities of
Christmas. Sometimes it seems that Thanksgiving get squeezed out.

Thanksgiving Day, as a holiday in America, began in the fall of
1621, as the Pilgrim Fathers and Mothers were facing their second
winter. Half of them had died that first winter. The wheat and the
peas they had brought with them failed to germinate. We are told
that at one point the daily rations were 5 grains of corn!

When fall came in 1621, it looked like the few who had survived
that dreadful first winter would not have enough food and shelter to
survive a second. They still had problems. They had not reached
Utopia. But they were filled with gratitude to God. That level of
gratitude would carry them a long way.

I heard a Presbyterian minister tell about a time one summer when
he and a friend took a bicycle tour of Hawaii. They pedaled up a
hill just as a rainbow arched across the horizon. To make it even
more awesome, it happened just as a cooling rain began to fall while
the sun was still shining! In awe, he turned to his friend and said,
"Wouldn't it be wonderful if we could bottle this up and bring it out

some dreary November day?" The friend replied, "You need to do what my father taught me. My father told me to remember my goosebumps."

This is what the Apostle Paul did. When Paul was an old man, writing from a Philippian jail, chained to guards, he kept remembering and rejoicing "in the Lord." This is what we, as we age, should do if we want to have sunshine even during the storms of life.

Moses kept reminding the children of Israel to rejoice. The Israelites had been wandering in the desert for forty years. Finally they were standing on the verge of Jordon and Moses was telling them what kind of people they were to be if they were to keep the freedom God had given them by bringing them out of slavery in Egypt.[125] They must remember. They must memorize their history and teach it to their children.

They were standing in the door of the Promised Land recounting their history in a beautiful liturgy. They were reciting: "A homeless Aramean about to perish was our ancestor and we had bad times. We were enslaved. We were oppressed. We were afflicted. But we have a God! God brought us out of Egypt with an outstretched hand. We are no longer a 'no people.' We are God's people."

Back in the fifties, when my husband was a student pastor, he had driven 90 miles to a church to preach. The children and I usually went with him for a week-end stay in a non-furnished five room "parsonage with a path." But that is another story to tell later.

That Thanksgiving Sunday in 1952, I was home with a sick baby. I had lost a great deal of sleep, and it was a cold and dreary day in a small apartment on a college campus.[126] A little after eleven, baby Deborah was asleep and I decided to turn on the radio (no TV) while washing the dishes and cleaning up the kitchen. A preacher was in the midst of a sermon about things for which to be thankful.

---

[125] Deuteronomy 26
[126] November 1952

He said, "Have you ever thanked God for dirty dishes?" As tired as I was, I thought, "As a matter of fact, I don't believe I ever have."

But another thought followed and I realized: "Dirty dishes mean you have food to eat. People with no food do not have dishes to wash." Have you ever thought that the beggar out on the park bench has no dishes to wash, no floors to mop or furniture to dust?

The preacher read a poem written by a teen-aged girl. I have never seen the poem in print but remember it as something like this:

> *Thank God for the dirty dishes*
> *For they've a story to tell*
> *And from the stack I have to wash*
> *We've eaten very well.*
> *While folks in other lands*
> *Are glad for just a crust*
> *From this stack of evidence*
> *God's mighty good to us.*

Thanking God for the things we usually take for granted is a step in the right direction on Thanksgiving Day and every day. A good place to start is to begin with zero and move up to the level of being grateful for ordinary things of life - food to eat, a clean bed, a warm house, fresh apples, turnips greens and cornbread, the smell of flowers, a Christmas tree, a church. And freedom!

I think I may have gotten a new idea of what zero is when I saw women in Afghanistan a few years ago being thankful for just being able to uncover their faces, and men being free to shave or grow a beard as they wished.

God has made beauty and not just utility.

God has made beauty and not just utility. Food could have all been tasteless and flowers without color or smell. Thank God.

I believe it was C.S. Lewis who said, "There is a profound

democracy in creation. There are some things we all inherit."
All of us - rich and poor, men and women - have inherited the
possibility of knowing God through Jesus Christ who has broken
down the wall of separation and offers us life here and life eternal
in the next life.

Helen Keller, blind and deaf, said, "I thank God for my handicaps.
Through them I have found myself, my work, my God." Whatever
it takes, find God.

One source of ingratitude is lack of thought! "Think" in the Anglo-
Saxon is related to "Thank." A "thank" is a "thought." To "think" is
to "thank."

The Psalmist tells us: "Bless the Lord, O my soul, and forget not all
His benefits." Forget not. Remember. Thoughtful people are
thankful people!

Doctor Luke, in Luke 17, tells a poignant and distressing story
about 10 men with leprosy being healed by Jesus. But only one
came back to express thanks. Where were the nine? Only one
moved up to the level of Thanksgiving. This one gave thanks, and
by giving thanks, he gained more than just physical healing. Amen.

Not Cost Efficient

John 12:1-8

Then Mary took a pound of very costly oil of spikenard, anointed the feet of Jesus, and wiped His feet with her hair. And the house was filled with the fragrance of the oil.
~John 12: 3 (NKJV)~

A few years ago, when a hostage was released from a South American prison, a reporter asked him, "What is the first thing you want to do now that you're free?" He replied that he wanted to eat a good meal, read a good book, and talk with good friends.

Jesus makes a similar choice with his final hours before his crucifixion. In this passage of Scripture today, He is headed toward the cross. Much of His time every day, from other passages we read, were spent, not just with a good book, but with The Book – The Holy Scriptures. And in prayer. In this scripture passage today, he is having a meal with good friends.

At the heart of this story is the approaching death of Jesus. The cross looms large. The scene is Bethany. The time is the Passover. Lazarus, whom Jesus had raised from the dead, is among those sitting at the table with Jesus. The disciples are apparently there (one of the synoptic gospels so states) because Judas, whom John recognizes now as not only a traitor but as a thief, speaks.

And there is the story of Mary. Out of love and devotion, she enlarges an act of hospitality into a drama of devotion and beauty. And Jesus says in another place, "She has done a beautiful thing."

Who is this Mary? John's record identifies her as the sister of Martha and Lazarus. In the privacy of their home Jesus finds respite from public pressure. They probably knew his prophecy of suffering and death. Mary had already shown her sensitivity to spiritual truth because she had become so interested in his message and teachings that she continued to sit at his feet while Martha was cooking the meal one day. And Martha complained that Mary had left her to serve alone. Jesus told Martha that Mary had chosen the good part – to study – to learn. Jesus had later raised Lazarus from the dead, and Mary and Martha were eternally grateful.

Many of our expressions of love are channeled through routines of duty and standard patterns of expression. It is easy to slip into routine and take love for granted. This is a problem in many marriages and in many friendships.

We all laugh with stories of a wife who complained that her husband didn't love her, and he replied, "Well, I married you, didn't I?" Or, the wife who complained that her husband had not said he loved her since the day they were married, and he replied, "Well, I told you then that I love you. If I ever change my mind, I will let you know." Also, there's the case of the man who said, "I go to work every day and bring my paycheck home. That should be enough to tell her I love her." Sometimes, though, loves requires more.

There are times in life when money is no object – when lavish gifts are appropriate. In today's scripture, Mary had to do more. Just preparing a meal or sitting at His feet was not enough. When your brother has been literally raised from the dead and you know that the Messiah of God is sitting at your table, the love and gratitude of your heart cannot be expressed. You forget about the cost. You throw caution to the winds. You throw a party. You celebrate! You don't calmly sit down and figure out how to make the project cost efficient.

Mary could have said, "Let's see. I could water down the perfume and use about a third of it – that expensive spikenard – and still have enough to anoint His feet." No. Mary, if she thought about it at all, said, "I want every nook and cranny of this house filled with the fragrance. We are going to celebrate today! My brother who was dead is alive, and Jesus is Lord. He is here, and we must celebrate!"

Mary, out of love and gratitude, enlarges an act of hospitality into a drama of love and beauty. And for the rest of her life, Mary must have experienced both grief and joy. Grief that she had so recently prepared her brother's corpse for burying – grief that she had unwittingly anointed Jesus for burial – and joy that she had a small part in Christ's redemptive act.

Every small effort is important. Mother Teresa taught that as she ministered to the dying in India, "I can't get to all of them." But she ministered to each one that she could – as if that person were Christ Himself. "Inasmuch as you have done it to one of the least of these, you have done it unto Me." One commentator on this passage said, "All our acts and words have meaning and effects by no means limited to what we intend at the time."

The first time Charles and I went to the Holy Land, he had saved money from performing wedding ceremonies and used those savings to buy me a ring in Haifa, a city in Israel that specializes in diamonds at reduced prices. If my husband had discussed it with me ahead of time, I might have tried to talk him out of it – to spend the money on more practical things. But, I know now that I think about that pilgrimage every time I look at that ring and think of his love and thoughtfulness in getting it for me.

> *There is a fine line between the Christian "vow of poverty" that some Christians are called to and many of us struggle with and the concept that Jesus came to give us life and life abundantly.*

There is a fine line between the Christian "vow of poverty" that some Christians are called to and many of us struggle with and the concept that Jesus came to give us life and life abundantly. But one thing we certainly get from this passage of scripture is that there are times to celebrate – whatever it takes to do so.

In the story of the prodigal son, the father threw a party, a big party, to celebrate the return of the younger son. And the older son refused to celebrate because he had his own agenda, and he could not stretch himself to celebrate with his brother.

People whom Christ redeems from gross sins are often the most extravagant Christians.

In the revival under the Wesleys - a revival that historians said saved England from a revolution – a revival that jumped the ocean and rode with the circuit riders and the pioneers in America that settled this country - many people were converted from damaging sins like drunkenness, adultery, brawling, and profanity. In the joy of their new-found and life-changing faith, they sang and shouted the praises of God. People called them "enthusiasts." People looked at the early Methodists and said, "That is Christianity in earnest."

I heard our great Bishop Moore say, "I hope I live long enough to hear the words, 'That is Christianity in earnest' said about our Methodists again!" We like to hear, "Those folks are excited about Jesus Christ and are practicing what they preach. They are not just carrying on a form, but Christianity in earnest."

In the more than 2000 years since Mary anointed the feet of Jesus, acts similar to Mary's have been duplicated in ways that bless us and also plague us. Especially those who worry about the poor and wonder how much of the Lord's money should be spent on Easter clothes, or paraments, or silver communion sets, or velvet altars, or fancy kitchens, or pew cushions.

The Salvation Army, for example, has focused on plain meeting houses in their efforts at ministering to the poor. Common sense and cost efficient methods tell us to plant beans and potatoes – not roses.

> *God did not create the world in monochrome, but He lavished it with beauty - flowers, multicolored birds and sunsets.*

Oliver Cromwell (Lord Protector in England from 1653-1658) sent some of his people to find gold to melt down for the needs of the country. They came back and said that all they could find was statues of the saints. Cromwell said, "Melt the saints down and put them to use." There are times to be practical and there are times for art and beauty.

About the same time in England, someone said, "If you have only one loaf of bread, sell half of it to buy flowers to feed the soul." God did not create the world in monochrome, but He lavished it with beauty – flowers, multicolored birds and sunsets.

Mary, in her emotional way, allowed her heart to spill over in gratitude and to express her love and caring without counting the cost. To Judas Iscariot and people like him looking on, the whole thing seemed sheer foolishness. Like the elder brother in the Prodigal Son parable, he didn't have anything to celebrate, and his major concern was holding tight the purse strings.

Criticism frequently tells more about the critic than it does about the person who is criticized. Criticism exposes the motive behind what we do. John, in this gospel lesson, hastens to add that Judas was not concerned for the poor but wanted more money to be added to the treasury – because he was a thief. This suggests that his betrayal of Jesus may have grown out of his thievery, his dishonesty, his stinginess, his joylessness in the celebration of God's presence in Jesus Christ.

Jesus rejects the critics and matches the woman's gratitude point for point. First Jesus describes Mary's act as beautiful instead of wasteful. Isn't that wonderful? When we walked into our beautiful place of worship here and saw our beautiful stained glass, it was good to read this passage and think that Jesus could also look at it and say, "It is a beautiful thing they did."

We call our coming together each week "the Celebration of Worship." Our celebration: something wonderful is happening, and we are celebrating God. We come out to celebrate. Every Sunday we celebrate the resurrection together. Every day we try to celebrate with the way we live and relate to one another, the way we love and are loyal to one another.

Now Jesus does not suggest that the poor be neglected, but he credits the woman's perception for a timely and appropriate act. He accepts her gift as something beautiful.

The heart of the story is the approaching death of Jesus. Jesus sat at the table with Lazarus (verse 45) after the raising of Lazarus. The Chief Priest and Pharisees decided that Jesus should die. The closing comment of Jesus that the disciples would not always have Him with them but would always have the poor was not intended as a rebuff of efforts to alleviate poverty by means of charity. It was not meant to play down social concerns.

One of the amazing things to me about the Methodist revivals over 200 years ago was that, along with all the conversions, the church built schools, orphanages and hospitals. The church worked to abolish slavery and child labor. They fed the hungry and took the gospel outside the doors of the church to the poor and disadvantaged.

We are a part of a world-wide church that has always taken social concerns seriously. In fact, the Methodists have been criticized for reaching out to feed and clothe and educate rather than just preaching individual salvation. We have done both. Jesus taught us to do both.

The closing comment of Jesus here is a warning to His followers that they should be struggling with the great sickness in humankind. This sickness was dragging Jesus to His death. The church has to be primarily concerned with the sin problem in our society rather than just glibly spending money to feed a few people. Jesus states clearly in another scripture, "This you ought to have done – and not to have left the other undone."

And the passage from John 12 teaches that love is always in order. Mary, out of love and gratitude, enlarges an act of hospitality into a drama of love and beauty.

The Christian life is essentially a love relationship – being filled with God's spirit and communicating his transforming power – life-changing power – celebrating power.

Mary was celebrating. We are celebrating the One who said to John, "I am the first and the last. I am the alpha and the omega. I am He who was dead and is alive forever. Amen. And I have the keys of hell and of death." (Revelation 1:17-18)

Mary must have got hold of this truth of just who it was that was sitting at her table. Nothing was too extravagant to do. She had been confronted with and taken hold of a love that would not let her go. Amen.

A New Heaven and a New Earth

Revelation 21:1-6   Leviticus 26:11-12

And I saw a new Heaven and a new Earth: for the first Heaven and the first Earth were passed away; and there was no more sea. And I, John, saw the Holy City, new Jerusalem, coming down from God out of heaven, prepared as a bride adorned for her husband.
~Revelation 21:1-2 (KJV)~

Have you ever heard someone say, "He's a saint" or "She's a saint"? What we usually mean when we call a person a saint is NOT that the person has been canonized by the Roman Catholic Church but that the person's life shows a lot of unselfish goodness, or that their life is worthy of imitation by all Christians – a person who is consistently kind, good and holy.

The New Testament definition of the word "saint" is not necessarily a holy person, but simply a Christian - a baptized believer. So the term "Christian" and the word "saint" in the New Testament mean the same thing.

Throughout the church year in sermons and liturgies, we hear about Augustine, Luther, Wesley, Asbury, and Calvin. We may sometimes quote well-known Christians like C.S. Lewis, William Barclay, Arthur J. Moore, or Catherine Marshall.

"All Saints Day" in the Christian calendar is a day to recognize the faith of lesser-known Christians – like your parents and mine. It's a day to recognize people whose lives have witnessed to their faith in Christ – people perhaps not well-known outside their own communities – people who, if their names were called on TV, few would recognize. It includes people who were perhaps known only to God but known and loved by God – people who were known and loved by a small circle of family and friends – people whose lives proclaimed something of the courage and transforming goodness of God - people who, because of their belief and faith in God, were able to overcome their self-centered behavior in their Christian love for others.

So All Saints Sunday is an occasion to stress the grace of God at work in a human life. Even though "saints" is a term used for "believers in Christ," not sinless people, this does not mean that we are to continue in sin. God has called us to go on toward perfection. When we are truly born again, it does make a difference in the way we live. Paul tells us that being saved by grace and not by works does not mean that we continue in sin. When Christ comes into our lives, we want to be good witnesses for Christ, and we want to fellowship with other Christians in the church.

In fact, in this passage, wholesomeness and purity are emphasized, and the "Holy City" is compared to a bride "adorned for her husband."[127]

In Psalm 24 we are asked, "Who shall ascend to the hills of the Lord and who shall stand in His holy place?" The answer comes back, "He who has clean hands and a pure heart; who does not lift up his soul to vanity (or to what is false), nor does he swear deceitfully."

All Saints Sunday is an occasion to stress the grace of God at work in the lives of human beings. Whatever goodness we find in Christian people points away from the person to God, who is the source of all goodness.

---

[127] And I saw a new Heaven and a new Earth, for the first Heaven and the first Earth had passed away, and there was no more sea. And I, John, saw the Holy City, New Jerusalem, coming down from God, out of heaven, prepared as a bride adorned for her husband. And I heard a loud voice out of heaven saying, "Behold the tabernacle of God is with me, and God shall dwell with them, and they shall be His people, and God Himself shall be with them and be their God. And God shall wipe away every tear from their eyes. There shall be no more death, nor sorrow, nor crying and there shall be no more pain, for the former things have passed away." And He who sat on the throne said, "Behold I am making all things new." And He said to me, "Write, for these words are true and faithful." And He said to me, "It is done. I am the alpha and the omega, the beginning and the end." But the cowardly and unbelieving and abominable and murderers and sexually immoral and sorcerers and idolaters and all liars shall have their part in the lake of fire which burns with fire and brimstone, which is the second death.

I remember one year on All Saints Sunday when I talked about "Saints in Unexpected Places" and told how someone had called another member of the congregation a "saint" and wondered if everyone was thinking, "It must be me." Bernice, our music director at Grantville, laughed and said, "Not me - no one would ever accuse me of being a saint." Bernice was so well aware of her failings.

Sadly for the Grantville church and community, Bernice got sick and died after only a few days in the hospital. I was fortunate to spend the day with Bernice on the last day of her life here on Earth. I was privileged to pray with her and comfort her by quoting some scripture to her during her final hour. Praise the Lord, we saw a lot of faith and love as well as courage in her last hours that spoke volumes – not about her faith in Bernice but about her faith in God.

John, in his gospel and letters and in the book of the Revelation, would have us to know that God has prepared a place for those who trust in Jesus Christ as Savior and Lord – and another place for those who refuse his grace. The Bible does not teach Universalism. But John, with great joy, tells us that for the Christian our destination, Heaven, is far better than any place or experience along the journey.

Jesus told us in John 14 that He was going to prepare a place for us. John, in the book of Revelation, gives us another word from the throne. "The place is prepared. It is done," he tells us. Heaven is the destination of God's people.

In today's scripture, we hear the One who sat on the throne – not an Earthly ruler, but the King of the Universe – saying, "I am the Alpha and the Omega, the beginning and the end." Alpha and Omega are the first and the last letters of the Greek alphabet. God is saying in this passage that He is the A and the Z. He was here at the beginning and will be here at the ending.

But this is much more than just that God brackets time and history at both ends. It is saying that God is our source and purpose in history. "And He who sat on the throne said, 'Behold, I make all things new. It is done.'" We are talking about God as the source of our lives on Earth and our destination beyond life here on Earth.

We are saying that "The God who made you didn't make no junk." We are talking about the God who loves you and who has a wonderful plan for your life. We are talking about the God whose commandments and prohibitions are because of his love and for our benefit.

God's commandments are the instructions that come with the body and the soul. The laws of God were written on our bodies and our psyches before they are written in Scripture. The Bible is not only the instructions that come with our bodies and our spirits, but it is also our guide and our road map into His heaven prepared for those who believe.

Free grace is not cheap grace.

We have to say, if we are true to our Scripture, that "believe" means more than many of us seem to see. If I truly believe that this building is on fire, I will get out. I will take action. Free grace is not cheap grace. People who believe in Jesus Christ as their Savior take action to get to know him through His word, prayer, fellowship with other believers and seeking to win others with their words and their actions.

As we read today's lesson, we see the word "new" is used four times to describe Heaven: (1) a new Heaven; (2) a new Earth; (3) a new Jerusalem; and (4) Behold I make all things new. This is emphasized because Heaven will be entirely different from life on Earth. It will be something new!

Our passage of scripture today (Revelation 21:1-6) is not to be viewed in isolation. It is one in a series of visions in which John is shown the victorious Christ. John would have us know that the great God who sits enthroned has a message. The message of the voice is that God's presence is not fully realized. Or, literally, God's tent "is pitched with men" fulfilling the prophecies of the Old Testament in Leviticus 26: 11-12 and other passages where God says, "I will make my abode among you." In Ezekiel 37:27: "My dwelling place shall be with them, and I will be their God, and they will be my people."

This "new heaven" is NEW because of what will not be there. We shed a lot of tears down here on earth. Life is difficult, as Scott Peck begins his best Seller, *The Road Less Traveled*. Long before Peck, Jesus said, "In this world you shall have tribulation; but be of good cheer: I have overcome the world." So there will be no more tears in heaven. God Himself will wipe away all tears from our eyes in heaven. No more death. No more standing helplessly by bedsides. No more pain.

The One on the throne said, "Write this, for these words are trustworthy and true." "You can write it down and take it to the bank," John tells us with great joy.

We sometimes say, "Put it in writing" when we are unclear about something or some promise. God did just that for us. He put it in writing. It is written and none can ever erase it. Nobody can add or take away from it. It comes from the authority of the throne of God; and nothing, NOTHING, can ever overthrow that throne. We are on the winning side, folks.

The most important event today is not taking place in the halls of Washington, D.C. or in any earthly government. The most important events today are in churches, large and small, where God's people gather to read from the Holy Bible and to bring a word from the throne of God. This is where people repent and are changed – their lifestyles changed. We are changed to live our lives in Christ and to proclaim the good news to others with our lives as well as our words.

John saw the "holy city, the new Jerusalem, coming down out of Heaven from God." This suggests that we can have Heaven on

Earth to a certain degree when Christ lives and rules in our hearts. We will not be perfect. We are living in a fallen world where sin abounds all around us. But the joys of Heaven can continue on earth.

The final part of the lesson is negative; and we have to remember that there is a positive and a negative. The Bible talks about a Heaven and a Hell. Verses 5 and 6 remind us that repentance and faith are necessary to enter into this fellowship with the one who is the alpha and the omega. So He gives a list of sinful attributes that are examples of the arrogance and hurtfulness of sin – attributes that hurt and damage.

John tells us that our sins separate us from God because their destiny is destruction, not life. The list is like a postscript, attached to this relationship portrait. Our sins break relationship.

Verse 8 shows by contrast what, in the positive sense, is the will of God. We are not to be fearful or cowardly but to have faith. Not distortion, but truth. Not murder, but life. Not sexual chaos, but wholeness and joy. Not mysticism, but relationship. Not idols, but encounters with the living God. Not lies and deception, but the open face of trust.

> *All the other facts of our history affect us, but they do not define us. We are defined by our relationship to God.*

The book of Revelation is a poetic book – hard to understand fully. But we learn from the book of Revelation to live each day as if it were our last and each day as if there were a great future because of Jesus Christ. Jesus Christ is Lord of history, and we are blessed because of that fact.

History is His story. All the other facts of our lives and our history are important but not final. All the other facts of our history affect us, but they do not define us. We are defined by our relationship to God.

C.S Lewis captured the sense of Biblical meaning in his novel *The Horse and His Boy*. Shasta was the name of the boy, and his journey had been very hard because he had been given the task to warn King Lune of an impending attack by the armies of Tash. In one scary scene, Shasta was the lone rider upon a mountain pass, and he rode an unruly horse who would not obey his commands. But suddenly Shasta was aware of a great presence beside him. That presence was Aslan. Finally Shasta spoke out of his fear, "Who are you?" The great lion Aslan was still only known as a large presence, and he replied to Shasta, "Tell me your sorrows."

Then it was that Shasta complained in a loud voice about his dangerous journey, his frightening experience with the lions, his unhappy childhood, and now the fact that he was cold and hungry. The answer of Aslan is surprising. Aslan told him, "I do not call you unfortunate." Shasta was told that he was blessed because he was on the right road. In other words Shasta was not defined by outward circumstances. Then in successive waves of surprise, Shasta learned many things about his own life and journey. The danger was still real. He was still tired and hungry, but he now knew where he was and WHO he was. And best of all, he had met the great presence himself. He was on the right road.

We don't really know where we are and who we are until we meet God and know Him and are found of Him. Amen.

His Name Is Wonderful

Acts 3:12-26

When Peter saw this, he said to them: "Fellow Israelites, why does this surprise you? Why do you stare at us as if by our own power or godliness we had made this man walk? The God of Abraham, Isaac and Jacob, the God of our fathers, has glorified his servant Jesus. You handed him over to be killed, and you disowned him before Pilate."
~Acts 3:12-13 (NIV)~

The words of today's text come from Peter's sermon, which he delivered in the precincts of the temple in response to the healing of the lame man at the Gate Beautiful.(Acts 3:1-10) This was the first "sign and wonder" done through the apostles. Luke records it here in the book of Acts.[128]

---

[128] Acts 3:12-26: When Peter saw this, he said to them: "Fellow Israelites, why does this surprise you? Why do you stare at us as if by our own power or godliness we had made this man walk? The God of Abraham, Isaac and Jacob, the God of our fathers, has glorified his servant Jesus. You handed him over to be killed, and you disowned him before Pilate, though he had decided to let him go. You disowned the Holy and Righteous One and asked that a murderer be released to you. You killed the author of life, but God raised him from the dead. We are witnesses of this. By faith in the name of Jesus, this man whom you see and know was made strong. It is Jesus's name and the faith that comes through him that has completely healed him, as you can all see.
"Now, fellow Israelites, I know that you acted in ignorance, as did your leaders. But this is how God fulfilled what he had foretold through all the prophets, saying that his Messiah would suffer. Repent, then, and turn to God, so that your sins may be wiped out, that times of refreshing may come from the Lord, and that he may send the Messiah, who has been appointed for you—even Jesus. Heaven must receive him until the time comes for God to restore everything, as he promised long ago through his holy prophets. For Moses said, 'The Lord your God will raise up for you a prophet like me from among your own people; you must listen to everything he tells you. Anyone who does not listen to him will be completely cut off from their people.'
"Indeed, beginning with Samuel, all the prophets who have spoken have foretold these days. And you are heirs of the prophets and of the covenant God made with your fathers. He said to Abraham, 'Through your offspring all peoples on earth will be blessed. When God raised up his servant, he sent him first to you to bless you by turning each of you from your wicked ways." (NIV)

Luke is telling the people here and telling us that Peter and John are prophets of God standing in the tradition of the Jewish faith of Abraham, Isaac, and Jacob. Peter is telling the people and telling us that the healing of the lame man who had sat begging at the Gate Beautiful should be understood as a single episode depicting a prophetic word and deed.

Luke, a Jew and a follower of Abraham, Isaac, and Jacob, speaking to other followers of Abraham, Isaac, and Jacob, tells them that the connection between the sermon and the healing miracle is made in the opening verse when Peter disclaims personal responsibility for the miracle. Peter testifies to the crowd that it was only by the power of Jesus that they were able to heal the crippled man.

> *It is only natural that when a divine miracle occurs, onlookers regard the human agent as the source of divine power rather than its conduit.*

He tells the gathered crowd, "Why do you stare at us as if by our own power or our piety we had made him walk?" Here Peter is telling the people, "We didn't heal him, Jesus did – this same Jesus whom you, in your sins and ignorance, killed but whom God has raised from the dead."

It is only natural that when a divine miracle occurs, onlookers regard the human agent as the source of divine power rather than its conduit. Peter makes it clear to them that it was not the power or the piety of Peter or John that accounted for the miracle. It was the power of God - the power of the God of Abraham, Isaac, and Jacob – the God of our fathers, not just Abraham, Isaac, and Jacob's God, but our God.

This passage of scripture seeks to help the people looking on and those of us today to understand that the Church is the divinely appointed messianic community through which the God of Israel is at work in new and decisive ways.

God has broken into history in the person of Jesus Christ. Jesus is the Messiah of whom the prophets had spoken earlier. In the next chapter of Acts, we read that Peter and John were thrown into jail but not before the people had seen and heard (and 5000 people believed) the truth of the Gospel that day.

The locus of divine activity was now shifted. Formerly, the presence of God, the Shekinah, dwelt in the temple. Now it was focused in the "name of Jesus." Peter tells them in verse 16 that it was in the name of Jesus that this man was healed.

> *His name is wonderful; His name is wonderful.*
> *He is the mighty King, ruler of everything.*
> *His name is wonderful - Jesus our Lord.*

This passage also shows how the temple is being displaced as the place of God's presence and action. As Stephen said in 7:47-51, "The most High God does not dwell in houses made by man."

Peter also tells them in verse 15 that although they asked for the release of Barabbas and crucified Jesus Christ, who was the very author of life, Jesus was vindicated through the resurrection. He reminds them that they had done this in ignorance. The good news that Peter preached here with such power was that the Easter faith would illuminate and overcome human ignorance as well as offer repentance and the forgiveness of sins.

The mark and test of a genuine spiritual awakening is found in this text. Acts 3:19 says, "Repent, therefore, and turn again, that your sins may be blotted out, that times of refreshing may come from the presence of the Lord." So Peter, in this sermon, prompted by the healing of the beggar who sat at the Gate Beautiful, was calling for repentance in the name of Jesus.

Repentance comes first before forgiveness. The moment we begin to repent, the forgiveness comes; as in the story of the prodigal son, the son started home and the father came out to meet him. This repentance cannot be mere remorse for getting caught in something or remorse or sorrow for getting in a tight spot.

Repentance, in the New Testament, is Meta-Noia. Meta means "change" and noia means "mind." So literally it means a change of mind – a change of heart and life wrought by the grace of God. That is why the Lord has called me to preach to the mind as well as the heart or emotion. We act on what we believe.

Thus, repentance is replete with radical implications. A change of mind not only turns us from our sinful past, but it also transforms our lives, our plans, our values, our ethics, and our actions. This change comes when we begin to see the world through God's eyes rather than through our own eyes. When we are truly saved, our minds are changed. We have put Jesus Christ on the throne of our lives. We have taken ourselves off the throne of our lives. That kind of transformation requires the surrender of self.

Repentance is the keynote message of the New Testament. John the Baptist came preaching repentance. Jesus came saying, "Repent and believe the good news." What we believe - what we think about God, ourselves and other people - is what makes all the difference.

Repentance is real when we realize that we need redemption. There is a story of an old lady who always told the preacher after each worship service, "You really told them about it today!" She was really applying the sermon to other people and not herself. One day she was the only person at the church when the preacher got up and preached. After the service she told the preacher, "You really would have told them if they had been here today!" That is not repentance.

Repentance is realizing that I need to make a change. Accepting Jesus Christ as my Savior and Lord is the only thing that will ultimately change me. Not my brother, not my sister, but it's me, O Lord, standing in the need of prayer.

This sounds simple, but there seems to be a tendency in all of us to blame someone else for the things we do wrong. Even in the current, seemingly-epidemic incidence of child abuse, we are told that many people who abuse their children were themselves abused as children. Sometimes this fact comes across as an excuse for the behavior. There is no excuse. But there IS forgiveness. However, forgiveness comes after genuine repentance; and repentance is taking responsibility for our own behavior without putting the blame on someone else. And repentance involves "meta noia" (making a change).

We recognize that there are children who have been made sick by abuse, and they continue this behavior into adulthood; but until they learn to seek whatever help is necessary to make changes - accepting the grace of God in their own lives and then allowing God to change them - they will continue to be sick.

I think that the reason we find a lot of very sick and mixed-up people who claim to be Christians is that they falsely believe that God is going to work everything out without their having to go through a process of cleansing and healing. Many people want to hold on to their sins of bitterness and unforgiving resentments. Many want Christ to come in and set their houses in order because they need redecorating. But when He starts remodeling, tearing out walls and hammering, they say, "That's enough. I already look pretty good in the eyes of my neighbors. They don't have to see everything. I'll clean up the basement later." And they never get right with God.

God loves us and has a wonderful plan for our lives, but we cut short His plans and limp through life. We are troubled and burdened and sometimes actually sick until we seek relief and release in the forgiveness and redemption of God through Jesus Christ. We can find grace and power in His name. His name is Wonderful.

Lloyd Ogilvie tells of a woman at a retreat. When they finished singing "Amazing Grace," she said, "Every time I sing that hymn, I think the words should be, 'I constantly get lost and need to be found.'" She had been a Christian for years, but she said that she sometimes takes Christ for granted and begins to feel miserable.

She begins to pray again, and it seems like she has found Christ again and again.

Jesus dealt with a lot of self-righteous religious leaders who did not acknowledge that they were lost and needed to be found. He told four parables about the lost: a lost sheep, a lost coin, a lost son, and a lost elder brother. And Jesus told them something that was a "hard saying" for them, and sometimes for us. "I say to you that likewise, there is more joy in heaven over one sinner who repents than over ninety-nine just persons who need no repentance." (Luke 15:7)

> *Nothing is more oppressive than unforgiven sin. As long as our sins are not confessed, they remain in our lives as a blinding, disabling force.*

Actually Jesus was making a correction to their fallacious ideas. The Pharisees and scribes projected their religious snobbery on God, saying, "There is joy in heaven when those who provoke him perish from the Earth." They could not believe that God loves the sinner. Repentance is simply confessing our longing to have everything right with God. That longing brings us to our knees in honest, open willingness to have God show us areas in our thinking, attitudes and relationships that need to be turned over to Him and transformed by God's wonderful love.

This is what I seek to do daily before God. After praying for the needs of our brothers and sisters and people in need, I say, "It's me, O Lord, standing in the need of prayer." I pray that the Lord will show me areas in my thinking and my attitudes and my relationships that need to be turned over to God's transforming love and power. It is available. This is what daily repentance is - letting the light of God's presence in. Show me my need.

Nothing is more oppressive than unforgiven sin. As long as our sins are not confessed, they remain in our lives as a blinding, disabling force.

John R. Mott tells the story of "The Barrel of Rotten Apples." He said he always wondered why good apples begin to rot when a rotten apple is placed in a barrel with them while rotten apples will NOT become good when a good one is placed with them in the barrel. He wondered why a sick person with contagious illness could cause the well person to become ill but a well person could not make a diseased person "catch" his wellness. In other words, Mott said he wondered why we live in a world where decay and disease seem contagious and wholeness and health are not.
Mott said that he finally took another look at the so-called "good apple" and found that it was not well at all. It was wounded to the core. The second it was pulled from the tree, it began to decay. The lesson is that whether it be plant or animal or humankind, we are wounded, decaying, dying, when separated from the source of life.

The good news is that Jesus has bridged the gap between us and God. We can be plugged into the source of life. We can be plugged into the source of life – eternal life in the name of Jesus Christ. His name is Wonderful! Amen.

Church Keys

Matthew 16:13-19

And I will give you the keys of the kingdom of heaven, and whatever you bind on earth will be bound in heaven, and whatever you loose on earth will be loosed in heaven.
~Matthew 16:19 (NKJV)~

A few weeks before I was to leave Rico United Methodist Church for an appointment to another church, the new pastor and his wife came to visit with me and have me show them the Rico Church building.

At our Wednesday night meeting at the church a week later, we were all sitting around a table at Bible Study talking about the change of pastors. At that point, the people at Rico had not met the new pastor and they were concerned about a change. They kept asking me questions about him: What does he look like? How old is he? Do you think he can work with us?

Finally, one church member, who had a dry sense of humor, added some smiles to the conversation when he said, "Well, when we meet him, if we don't like him, we will just not give him the church keys."

I moved into the Grantville parsonage after nearly four years as pastor of Rico Church and after finishing Candler Seminary at Emory. I don't know if they had talked about whether or not to give me the keys to the church, but the chairman of the Pastor-Parish Relations Committee gave me a set of their church keys - eight keys on a key chain. Two of the keys were for the front and back door of the parsonage, one for the back door of the Church and another for the church's box at the Grantville Post Office.

I do not remember all the keys, but whatever they locked and unlocked, they belonged to the Church of Jesus Christ and they represented more than authority; they represented responsibility and accountability.

This portion of Scripture in Matthew 16:13-19 is usually titled "Peter's Confession" and is also recorded in Mark 8:27-30 and Luke 9:18-31.

Peter's confession of Jesus as the Christ and as the Son of God was the preface to Jesus giving Peter and his followers the Keys to the Kingdom. Peter's Confession of Jesus here combines the title, "Son of God," a phrase used earlier in Chapter 14:14-33 and "Messiah," which is used for the first time here in this passage. This is the first time in the gospels that Jesus is proclaimed as the Messiah.

We are not given a full understanding of all the meanings of these two titles used here — "Son of God" and "Messiah" — but it is quite clear that Jesus approved of the confession. Peter, in verse 16, proclaimed: "Thou art the Christ (the Messiah), the Son of the Living God."

Jesus said to Peter, "Blessed art thou, Simon, son of John, for flesh and blood hath not revealed it unto thee, but my Father which is in Heaven."

So Jesus knew, first, that God had revealed to Peter the truth of His identity, and second, in Verses 21-28, Jesus also made it clear that a part of what it meant for Jesus to be the "Christ" ("Messiah") and "Son of God" involved Jerusalem, suffering, death and resurrection.

So the fact that Peter was able to identify Jesus as "Messiah" and "Son of God" is not an indication that Peter was more perceptive or intelligent than others. We are told in verse 17, "Flesh and blood has not revealed this truth, but God has revealed it." Peter's insight came by revelation.

This confession – this revelation – is the rock on which Christ built His Church. This passage and the one in Matthew 16:17 are the only places where Jesus refers to the Church. We have the promise of Jesus that the Church shall not be overcome, even by death itself. Jesus said in Matthew 16:18, "Upon this rock, I will build my

Church, and the gates of Hell shall not prevail against it." These words are "an unconditional promise that the Church is God's personal project."

> *This really is God's Church, not our Church. Jesus is the head of the Church. Jesus is also the power of the Church; we have the glorious privilege to be a part of the Church!*

So, God has promised to be here. I want you to know that you are here in the very presence of God Himself. This really is God's Church, not our Church. Jesus is the head of the Church. Jesus is also the power of the Church; we have the glorious privilege to be a part of the Church!

You may have heard about Jumbo the elephant and Flick the flea. They walked across a bridge together. When they got to the other side, Flick said: "Jumbo, Did you notice how we shook that bridge?"

We may be pretty small! In fact, we are very small – sitting here in God's presence, walking with the real power and strength of the Church. And how often, like Flick, we take credit for everything that goes right and yet blame God — or others — when things go wrong.

But Flick, the flea, said to Jumbo the elephant, "We shook that bridge." Flick, this tiny flea, knew he could not shake anything alone. He knew where the power was and how to appropriate it. He stayed right with the elephant.

What a joy, what a privilege to walk with the eternal God and watch His shaking and participate in His shaking. There are many interpretations of this Scripture lesson. But one thing is abundantly clear. The bottom line is the affirmation that the continuity between Jesus and His Church was provided by His apostles, the followers of Jesus. They were chosen and given authority during Jesus's lifetime (Mark 10:1), and the authority was to continue after Jesus's death, resurrection and ascension.

In other words, the Church was established here on this faith in Jesus as Messiah and Son of God. Jesus also declared that the Church will be perpetually invincible. The Church will endure. "The very gates of Hell shall not prevail against the church."

The final death of the Church has been predicted confidently — indeed, in this century — but as Mark Twain quipped about a premature obituary, "The notice of my death has been greatly exaggerated." Voltaire, in his writings, predicted that the world had come of age, and the Church and Scripture would be only a memory in another generation. But shortly after his death, Voltaire's complete works sold for a pittance while one copy of an early Bible sold for a million dollars. The Church is of God, and will be preserved until the end of time. The very gates of Hell will not prevail against the Church of the Messiah, of the Son of God.

So, in Verse 18, Jesus said, "My Church!" And he followed this by giving the keys to Peter as a steward of the Church.

Verse 19: "And I will give unto thee, the keys of the Kingdom of Heaven and whatever you shall bind on earth shall be bound in Heaven. And whatever you shall loose on earth shall be loosed in Heaven."

The keys were normally in the hands of the teachers of the law. The teachers of the law unlocked God's word - interpreted God's word. But these keys were now entrusted to Peter and the other disciples, the body of Christian believers. The laws were now to be interpreted in the light of the Messiah of God who is "The Light!"

Later in Acts 20:1-20, we see Peter unlocking and opening the door of the Church to Gentiles. He opened the doors of the Church. "And, it shall come to pass — I will pour out my Spirit upon all your sons and your daughters, young and old, servants and handmaidens." (Acts 2:17)

Matthew 16:19 tells us that "whatever you bind on earth, shall be bound in Heaven." Holding us accountable and relating us directly to Jesus, the Head of the Church. This is the key for unity and effectiveness.

A missionary, touched by God in the East Africa Revival Movement, said, "If we keep the head in its proper relationship to the body, we won't be biting the little finger."

The matter of binding and loosing is developed in chapter 18 as the disciplinary function of the Church. The new community of believers, the Church, is to be responsible — it must be a responsible fellowship of regenerated people who hold one another accountable for their covenant with Jesus Christ, unlocking the treasures of scripture for the people.

But notice — the scripture says, "whatsoever" you shall bind, not "whomsoever" you shall bind.

The Church of Jesus Christ is to be a fellowship, a "Koinonia," a community of believers, a responsible fellowship, concerned about each other and the world.

The Church is not supposed to be a religious club that meekly endures the scorns, the jibes, the attacks of evil forces. The Church is an army in active service, attacking everything in the world that destroys and despoils humankind. We need to know that the Commandments are more than mere suggestions and are there for our protection, as loving parents make rules to protect and benefit their children.

The Church provides a moral and ethical compass in the midst of relativism. The Church teaches that some things are right and some things are wrong. In recent years, young people have been taught that everything is relative, and so God and the Church should not tell us how to behave. More recently, because of the epidemic of bad behavior and the crises in our culture — teen pregnancy, alcoholism, drugs, crime, HIV/AIDS — these hard facts of life and the chaos in our current society are forcing us back to the true teachings of the Church – that everything is not relative. There are some absolutes.

The Church holds the keys because it still stands as the one clear witness to the highest ideals of human life in the world. The Church holds the keys because it still calls people to the highest character and noblest service. The Church is the only institution dealing with the ultimate issues. When we are pushed into a corner, we have to do "ultimate-type" thinking about death, judgment, relationships, our purpose and meaning in life. We have to think about what life is all about, our identities, heaven and hell. The Church is the only institution that deals with these ultimate issues.

The Church holds the keys because it stretches a helping hand down to men and women who have sunk to the lowest depth. The Church reaches down to the lowest – to lift to the highest – unlocking the possibilities of greatness. The Church holds the keys because it testifies to the reality of spiritual things in a materialistic age.

The Church holds the keys because it insists that men and women are more than animals or machines. The Church provides perspective that gives dignity to humankind. The Church counteracts the prevalent message that people are just a means to an end. The Church teaches that each of us is made in the image of God.

The Church, like no other institution, holds the keys because it has provided motivation for the most lasting, unselfish, essential courageous ministries on earth — unlocking opportunity to all people.

The Church holds the keys because our first schools, our first hospitals, missions, half-way houses, children homes - these institutions were originated by the Church.

Many people today are beneficiaries of the religion of their parents and/or grandparents. They are often the materialistic beneficiaries of Christians who have prospered by their work and savings and ethical lifestyle. Far too often, the descendants of those whose lifestyle and spiritual commitment made these benefits possible are themselves away from God and away from the Church. Too often they take their Christian heritage for granted, often despising the "hand that fed them."

The Church holds the keys because the Church places an inestimable value upon the life of the lowest and the least. The Church declares that God loves us and that Christ died for each one of us.

To become part of the Church of Jesus Christ is to take one's stand by the side of Christ and to take his standard of values for one's life and to be ready to live for Him.

The Church is the place to find true community, healing, compassion and love. It is here that people really care, not because of status or money, but because the Spirit of the God of Love is working.

A good illustration of this is about the Canadian geese and why they fly in a V formation. Specialists in aerodynamics learned that each bird, by flapping its wings, creates an upward lift for the goose following him. When every goose in the V formation does his part, the entire flock has a 71 percent greater flying range. When one goose gets out of formation, the others honk him back in.

The Scripture teaches that we, like those Canadian geese, need to work together. It is too easy in our crowded society to ignore other people. We are to stay involved with each other in the Church. Amen.

The Lion King

Revelation 5:1-9

Then one of the elders said to me, "Do not weep. See, the Lion of the tribe of Judah, the Root of David, has conquered, so that he can open the scroll and its seven seals."
~Revelation 5:5 (NRSV)~

We are being told today that it is important for us to make a will as to how the disposition of our possessions will be handled upon our death.

We use the term "God's will" so casually, but if it is another person's will or a relative's "Last Will and Testament," especially if we might be a beneficiaries, we listen, or as they say, "We listen up."

John tells us in Revelation 5, that we have God's last will and testament, sealed with seven seals! This is priceless information; but there is a problem. A big problem! Who is worthy (and able) to open the seals so that we may know who the beneficiaries are?

And the profound question that echoes throughout the universe is that we have this priceless information, this priceless life and death information, but who can open the seals so we can access this treasure? Who is worthy (and able) to open the seals so that we may be beneficiaries of such priceless information?

In verse 1, we read, "I saw in the right hand of Him (God) who sat upon the throne a scroll written inside and on the back." This scroll written inside and also on the back is a symbolic expression of the whole sweeping history of creation.

In chapter 4, we are told that it is "by God's will that everything existed and was created." In Revelation 4:11, we read "you created all things, and by your will they were created and have their being."

So we are to understand that this amazing scroll, written on front and back and sealed with seven seals, is the narrative of our God and Creator, who has stepped out of eternity into time. He has stepped into the foreground in the life, death, and resurrection of Jesus the Christ!

John, in the book of Revelation, gives us a tremendous vision. He sees God upon His throne, high and lifted up, and in His hand He carries a scroll closely sealed with seven seals. The scroll contains the meaning of life – God's meaning for each life and every life.

But we are told there is a big problem. This scroll that is sealed with seven seals contains all the things we need to know – indeed all the things we must know if we would live and find meaning and joy in life. The problem is that no one can be found that is worthy to break the seals and to open up the contents of the scroll.

When I moved back to Rome in 1997, my daughter, Deborah, and I were trying to put together a ceiling fan and were having trouble understanding the directions. Debi, in fun, said; "You and I are both literate. In fact, each one of us happens to have a Master's degree from an accredited university. What is the problem?" We finally realized at least a part of the problem was that the people who wrote the instructions for putting the fan together had English as a second language. It was a cultural as well as a language problem.

Revelation is a difficult book to understand. In fact, as I read through chapter 4 with the throne and then 24 more thrones surrounding that throne, I just about gave up on understanding. Then I got to chapter five and the talk of seven seals kept me reading.

It was first century tradition to validate and secure books and scrolls with a wax seal or a clay seal imprinted with the special mark of the sender of the scroll. The recipient then, in order to read the scroll, had to break or remove the seal. In some cases more than one seal was placed upon the document.

The document in our lesson today was sealed with seven seals. As you know, The Bible uses the number seven to indicate perfection and completion. Most likely it was sealed with seven seals because it contained such a large amount of material that was written on the front and the back and was God's final disposition in the affairs of the world. It was so secret that none but God might dare to open it.

So this fifth chapter of Revelation begins with a profound question that echoes, not just throughout the Earth, but also throughout the whole created order. The Bible says, "...throughout Heaven, Earth, and under the Earth." "Under the Earth" means the realm of death and Hell.

And the texts tell us that John was devastated. He wept loudly as no one was found worthy to take hold of this scroll and to claim its seals as their rightful owner. Serious problem!

Serious indeed. Sadly, here is God's priceless scroll, telling us who we are, but no one in the whole of creation from Heaven to Hell is able to open the seals of the priceless scroll of profound value and meaning.

I remember, as a child, lying on the grass in our yard, looking up at the sky and watching the formation of the clouds and wondering about God and about what life was all about and about my relationship to God. Probably some of the reasons we have such an interest in tracing family history are the questions: "Who am I? What is the meaning of my life, my name, my past, my present, my future? How did it all come about? What is the meaning of life and the world? Why am I here? Where am I going?"

The *Lion King* movie released in 1994 tells the story of Simba the lion who was born to the king but ran away after his father died. Simba believed he was responsible for his father's death and set out to run from that guilt and also from his responsibilities. There was an important scene in the movie where he spoke with an image of his late father. His father said, "Simba, you have forgotten me." Simba, shocked and hurt, said, "No, Father. How could I?" And his father said, "You have forgotten who you are and so have forgotten me. Look inside yourself, Simba. You are more than what you have become." Simba needed to be reminded of who he was.

In our "God-phobic" world today, where people seem afraid to even utter God's name in public, the greatest causes of death among our youth are suicide and automobile accidents (most of which are alcohol-related). It seems that many of us have lost the meaning of life.

We all search for meaning. When John heard that the scroll contained the answers to these questions about life and meaning but it couldn't be opened and known, he broke down weeping as many before him and since him have wept in the face of the questions of the meaning of their lives and in the face of loss of meaning.

But in the midst of John's weeping, in verse 5, one of the elders said to John, "Do not weep, the problem is solved. Look, behold, the Lion of the tribe of Judah, the Root of David has prevailed to open the scroll and has come forward to loose the seven seals."

The lion is the most often named animal in the Bible, but only here in this passage in Revelation is the lion given such messianic meaning. He is the Lion King of Judah!

Following the description of the kingly Lion, John looked toward the throne to see the Lion King, and as he looked he beheld a lamb standing as though it has been slain. It bore the marks of death, yet it had triumphed over death. John looked toward the throne to see the Lion King and sees the slain Lamb. The Lamb was alive and on the throne! This Lion/Lamb, who was identified as Jesus Christ, now took the scroll.

The theological implications of John's dramatic vision for us here today cannot be overemphasized. It is the conviction of every New Testament writer that the whole of human history finds its meaning and its convergence point in the LION-LAMB who is Jesus Christ who alone is worthy to open the seals. Jesus is the critical center from which all parts make sense and toward which all parts converge.

Hebrews 1:1-2 tells us, "In many and various ways God spoke of old to our fathers by the prophets, but in these last days he has spoken to us by the Son, whom He appointed the heir of all things, and through whom He created the world."

So this scripture in Revelation 5 would have us know that it is the Lamb of God who has this powerful scroll. Not the devil. Not the emperor. Not the president. Not the Supreme Court. None of these make sense of the scroll of history. It is Jesus Christ who is worthy and who holds history in his hands. History in Revelation 5 here is indeed His Story! We are talking about an invisible world – a world beyond this world – a person <u>outside of history</u>.

As I told in another sermon, Charles died on December 3, and I thought that Christmas, "All I want is to hear a great choir and symphony sings *The Messiah* and "The Hallelujah Chorus." But the only churches presenting it would have meant I had to drive through Atlanta and some distance away. I was not up to that. Then on Friday night before Christmas I turned on television and the famous Robert Shaw Choral was on and *The Messiah* was being sung.

When they got to "The Hallelujah Chorus," I stood to my feet alone in our family room and, with as good a soprano as I've ever sung, sang with the famous chorale, "And He shall reign forever and ever. HALLELUJAH! HALLELUJAH!"

We think that when we sing "The Hallelujah Chorus," we have gotten to the end of this treasured piece of music. But "The Hallelujah Chorus" is not the final word. In *The Messiah*, there is a postscript. If God so loved the world that he came down to save us, why are so many people lost? Why is there so much sin and suffering still in the world?

Part 3 of *The Messiah* comes after "The Hallelujah Chorus" and gives us a thought-provoking answer. What could follow "The

Hallelujah Chorus?" The very words and music just automatically lift Christians to their feet in a standing ovation of praise: "…and He shall reign forever and ever!" What could possibly follow that? *The Messiah* does not end with "The Hallelujah Chorus."

Beyond the images of Bethlehem and Calvary, one more messianic image is needed. The Messiah as sovereign Lord (tough love) is allowing us to reap the end result of our sins in a fallen (full of sin) world. The incarnation where we attempt to tell how Christmas means that "Love loves us" did not usher in the end of history – only the beginning of the end. Much work remains to be done before creation is restored to God's original intent.

Part three of *The Messiah* opens with a quotation from Job. Job was that man who had a lot of tragedy in his life. Throughout his trials, he continued to say, "I know that my Redeemer lives." Job continued to believe in a world that thought that wealth and good health were signs of God's favor, and poverty and sickness were signs of sin. Job was to finally learn that good people also suffer.

Have you ever wondered why you continue to believe when your life seems to be tumbling down, when you pray for healing and seem to be getting worse instead of better, when people all around you are throwing in the towel, when there is a constant assault on the truth of the gospel in the media and academia in both overt and covert ways? C.S. Lewis said, "God whispers to us in our joys and pleasure, but he shouts to us in our defeats and sorrows."

And Handel's *The Messiah* is saying here through this scripture, "So should we continue to believe, knowing that God, the voice of God, is heard in a whisper in our pleasures and joys, but the voice of God is heard in shouts that drown out other voices in the sorrows and pains of life."

Paul explains the theological implication of Jesus' death and resurrection, "Death is swallowed up in victory!"

Looking at the world and seeing no hope, Handel saw this. And in the final part of his inspired music, after "The Hallelujah Chorus," using the verse from Revelation, Handel wrote, "...<u>then I saw a Lamb</u>."

The great Creator God became a human baby, unable to hold up His head without the help of one of His creatures. The Lion of Judah became the Lamb of God to take away the sin of the world. He became our sacrificial lamb. This great God, the Lion of Judah, who bore our stripes and dies our death and who alone is worthy. "Worthy is the lamb." Handel leaves us with this message: "Worthy is the lamb," followed by jubilant amens.

> *History has proved beyond a shadow of a doubt that nothing fashioned by the hand of man or woman will last.*

In our country today, in our materialistic culture, we are light years from the imagery of a slaughtered lamb, but Handel understood that history and civilization are not what they appear. Auditoriums, dynasties, civilizations – they all rise and fall. History has proved beyond a shadow of a doubt that nothing fashioned by the hand of man or woman will last.

No historical character is worthy to open the seal. We need something greater than history – something outside of history – beyond history – greater than history. The scripture tells us that "we need the Lamb slain BEFORE THE FOUNDATIONS OF THE WORLD."

John caught his vision, recorded here in the book of Revelation, of the Kingdom of God and the destruction of the power of evil. He saw the force of evil conquered by the "blood of the Lamb and the word of their testimony."

The Christians had to die, but they loved not life if they could win the victory. Overcoming evil is the history of Christianity. The coming of the Lamb was related to overcoming evil. This Lion of Judah, who was to become the Lamb who was wounded for our transgression and bruised for our iniquities and who alone is worthy.

It seems to me that Handel, in the last part of *The Messiah*, has caught the surprise and joy of this vision of John in Chapter 5 of Revelation. The mighty Lion King who became the humble Lamb, despised and rejected, broken on Mount Calvary, is now alive and rightly honored.

God is so sure of Himself and His love for us that He came in humility to find us. Augustine said, "Proud man would have died unless a lowly God had found him." Whatever may happen in life or in death, the One who is worthy and able to open the gates to eternal life has found us. With Christ as our Savior, we have nothing to fear. The Lamb has won the battle against death. We see Him, who was dead, alive at the throne of Heaven.

In Revelation 5:2, we read, "And I saw a strong angel proclaiming with a loud voice, 'Who is worthy to open the book and to loose the seals thereof?' And no one in Heaven, or in Earth, neither under the Earth, was able to open the book, neither to look thereon. And I wept much. And one of the elders said unto me, 'Weep not; weep not; behold the Lion of Judah hath prevailed to open the book and loose the seven seals!'"

Maxie Dunnam tells about visiting, with his wife, churches in what was then Czechoslovakia. For forty years every church in Czechoslovakia was severely restricted by the communist government. Christians could not evangelize. They could not post public notices or erect signs on church buildings. They could not ring church bells. Then in November 1989, a group of students confronted a group of young soldiers, and that catalyst brought the revolution against the communist government out in the open. Everybody took to the streets, and the old communist regime knew that it was over.

It was decided that on November 27th at noon, everybody in the country would walk out of homes, businesses, offices, factories, and fields. Everybody would simply walk out into the streets at noon.

Every bell in every church in Czechoslovakia would be rung at noon. When that day and time came, church bells that had been silent for 45 years began to ring. It was electric. Everybody knew that something new had come.

Dr. Vilem Schnieberger, one of the pastors, said that when they were finally allowed to put a sign in front of their church in Prague, they simply posted "The Lamb Has Won." What a truth! The Lamb has won! Amen.

About The Author

Ruth Baird Shaw holds a Master of Divinity degree from Candler School of Theology, Emory University. She also Graduated from Georgia State University with a bachelor's degree in Interdisciplinary Studies from the College of Arts and Sciences and was certified in Gerontology for work in the field of aging.

As an Elder in the United Methodist Church, North Georgia Conference, Mrs. Shaw served as pastor at Rico United Methodist Church in Palmetto, Grantville First United Methodist Church and East Point Avenue United Methodist Church in East Point, Georgia.

After retiring in 1998, Ruth served on the staff at Trinity United Methodist Church in Rome, Georgia, for 4 years. She served as an interim pastor at Lyerly United Methodist Church for five months, at Oostanaula United Methodist Church for 13 months and with Livingston United Methodist for 12 months.

In addition to *Fifty-Two Sundays*, Mrs. Shaw is the author of *The Chronicles of Ruth, Life with Wings* and three editions of *Recipes, Rhymes and Reflections*.

Ruth Baird Shaw is the widow of the Reverend Charles C. Shaw who was an Elder and served in the North Georgia Conference of the United Methodist Church from 1954 until his death on December 3, 1986. He served as a student pastor in the Kentucky Methodist Conference from 1950 to 1954.